The Law Commission

(LAW COM. No. 192)

FAMILY LAW

THE GROUND FOR DIVORCE

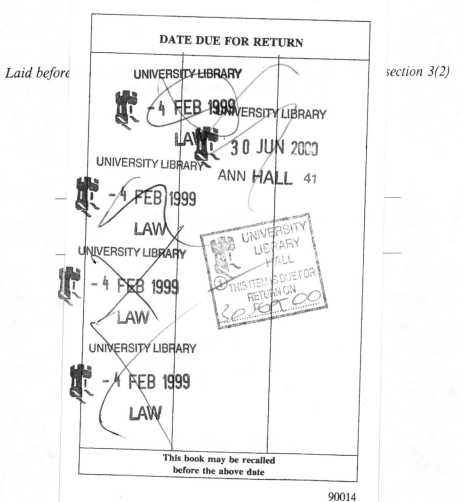

Laid before ... *section 3(2)*

The Law Commission was set up by section 1 of the Law Commissions Act 1965 for the purpose of promoting the reform of the law.

The Commissioners are—
The Honourable Mr Justice Peter Gibson, *Chairman*
Mr Trevor M. Aldridge
Mr Jack Beatson
Mr Richard Buxton, Q.C.
Professor Brenda Hoggett, Q.C.

The Secretary of the Law Commission is Mr Michael Collon and its offices are at Conquest House, 37–38 John Street, Theobalds Road, London WC1N 2BQ.

THE GROUND FOR DIVORCE

CONTENTS

THE LAW COMMISSION

Item 6 of the Fourth Programme: Family Law

THE GROUND FOR DIVORCE

To the Right Honourable the Lord Mackay of Clashfern,
Lord High Chancellor of Great Britain

PART I

INTRODUCTION

1.1 There is widespread concern about the current prevalence of divorce in this country and the consequences which this can have both for the couple concerned and for their children. There is also concern that the present divorce process may be making these worse. There have been many calls for reform of the law, and from many quarters.[1] In order to stimulate debate about the shape such a reform might take, we published in May 1988, Facing the Future—A Discussion Paper on the Ground for Divorce.[2] This examined in some detail the current law and practice, the criticisms which might be made of them, and the various options for reform. A shorter summary of the issues was prepared for general distribution.[3] These provoked a large response, from a wide variety of groups and individuals, including those organisations professionally involved with families undergoing marital breakdown, separation or divorce; religious bodies; and many with personal experience of the present system. A list of those who responded appears as Appendix B to this report and we are most grateful to them all.

1.2 At the same time, we conducted a study of divorce files in the Principal Registry of the Family Division and in 18 divorce county courts across the country, in order to discover a little more about the working of the system in practice. A brief account of this study appears as Appendix C, and we shall refer to its findings in several places in this report. We are most grateful to the staff of the courts concerned, and to the Registrars whose views we sought, for all the help they have given us.

1.3 The views of those with personal experience of the system are well represented, not only amongst respondents to Facing the Future, but also in academic research studies.[4] We also thought it important to canvass the views of a representative cross-section of members of the general public. From time to time there are surveys, both popular and academic, asking basic questions about attitudes to marriage and divorce;[5] but there has been no study specifically designed both to explain the present law of divorce and to present some of the complex and sensitive issues involved to people who may never have considered them in detail before. Accordingly, we commissioned Public Attitudes Surveys Ltd. to conduct a public opinion survey, along with a similar inquiry into the rules governing distribution on intestacy.[6] This, instead of simply listing the disadvantages of the present law and asking whether it should be changed, attempted to identify what people see as its good and bad features, to assess the acceptability of a variety of bases for divorce and to probe two possible reforms in more depth. In this way we were able to obtain quite a detailed picture of the values and attitudes of a cross-section of the adult population. A report of the survey appears as Appendix D.

1.4 Such surveys can only be part of a wider inquiry in which considerations of moral and legal principle, as well as the views of informed professionals, must play the

---

[1] E.g. from the Law Society's Family Law Sub-Committee, in *A Better Way Out*, (1979) and *A Better Way Out Reviewed*, (1982); in Parliament during debate on the Matrimonial and Family Proceedings Bill, *Hansard* (H.C.), 13 June 1984, vol. 61, col. 963; the "general consensus" of respondents' views reported in the Report (the Booth Report) of the Matrimonial Causes Procedure Committee (the Booth Committee) chaired by the Hon. Mrs. Justice Booth, (1985), para. 2.9; by researchers G. Davis and M. Murch, in *Grounds for Divorce*, (1988).
[2] (1988), Law Com. No. 170.
[3] Facing the Future? A Summary of the Issues arising from the Law Commission's Discussion Paper on the Ground for Divorce (1988).
[4] Principally, in this connection, the studies reported in Davis and Murch, *op. cit.*; also M. Murch, *Justice and Welfare in Divorce*, (1980); N. Hart, *When Marriage Ends: A Study in Status Passage*, (1976); J. Burgoyne and D. Clark, *Making a Go of It, A Study of Step-families in Sheffield*, 1984); A. Mitchell, *Children in the Middle*, (1985); Y. Walczak and S. Burns, *Divorce: The Child's Point of View*, (1984); G. Davis and M. Roberts, *Access to Agreement*, (1988); G. Davis, *Partisans and Mediators*, (1988).
[5] E.g. The British Public Attitudes Survey, in *British Social Attitudes, The 1987 Report*, (1987), pp. 122–123, Table 6.1; the National Opinion Poll Survey, conducted for the *Mail on Sunday*, 5 March 1989.
[6] Distribution on Intestacy (1989), Law Com. No. 187, Appendix C.

larger part. Our consultations have included discussions, both formal and informal, with representatives of many of the organisations and agencies active in this field. We are particularly grateful to the Standing Committee for Inter-Disciplinary Co-operation in Family Proceedings, for organising a conference at which most of those bodies were represented. This provided a broadly-based forum for discussion of the issues amongst informed people with a wide variety of perspectives, which we found especially helpful.

1.5 Our inquiries have made three things absolutely plain. First, of the existence of the problem there can be no doubt. The response to Facing the Future overwhelmingly endorsed the criticisms of the current law and practice which it contained. The present law is confusing and unjust. It now fulfils neither of its original objectives. These were, first, the support of marriages which have a chance of survival, and secondly, the decent burial with the minimum of embarrassment, humiliation and bitterness of those that are indubitably dead.[7]

1.6 Secondly, it is clear that those basic objectives of a "good" divorce law, as set out by our predecessors in 1966, still command widespread support, difficult though it may be to achieve them in practice. In 1990, however, any summary would include two further objectives: to encourage so far as possible the amicable resolution of practical issues relating to the couple's home, finances and children[8] and the proper discharge of their responsibilities to one another and their children; and, for many people the paramount objective, to minimise the harm that the children may suffer, both at the time and in the future, and to promote so far as possible the continued sharing of parental responsibility for them.[9]

1.7 Thirdly, there was overwhelming support for the view expressed in Facing the Future that irretrievable breakdown of the marriage should remain the fundamental basis of the ground for divorce.[10] This means, first, that divorce should continue to be restricted to those marriages which have clearly broken down and should not be available for those which are capable of being saved; and secondly, that any marriage which has broken down irretrievably should be capable of being dissolved. The criticism is not of the principle itself, but of the legal rules and processes by which the irretrievable breakdown of a marriage is at present established in the courts.

1.8 Our consultations have led us to the firm conclusion that there is one particular model for reform which is to be preferred. It has not only received the support of the great majority of those who responded to Facing the Future, but has also been shown by our public opinion survey to be acceptable to a considerable majority of the general population. This was the model described in Facing the Future as divorce as a "process over time" but here described as divorce after a period of consideration and reflection, colloquially a "cooling-off" period or breathing space. In the light of this conclusion, it was decided to depart from our previous practice in this area[11] and prepare a draft Bill to give effect to this proposal. We have therefore worked it out in a great deal more detail than would otherwise have been the case. We hope that our recommendations have thereby been improved: we hope also that it will help others to decide whether or not they should be implemented. They constitute in many ways a radical departure from the present law: one designed to retain what are seen as the strengths of the present system while meeting the most serious criticisms.

1.9 In Part II of this report we summarise the main advantages and disadvantages of the present law and practice. In Part III we discuss the various possible models for reform in the light of the response to consultation, concluding with a recommendation in favour of divorce after a period of consideration and reflection. In Part IV we consider the implications of that recommendation for other matrimonial remedies which depend upon the same grounds. In Part V we explain the details of the procedures proposed and in Part VI we make some incidental recommendations about financial provision and property adjustment orders. Part VII contains a summary of our recommendations and the draft Bill to give effect to our proposals appears, with explanatory notes, at Appendix A.

---

[7] Reform of the Grounds of Divorce—The Field of Choice (1966), Law Com. No. 6, para. 120(1).

[8] An objective laid down in the terms of reference of the Booth Committee who were asked to recommend procedural reforms which would, *inter alia*, mitigate the intensity of disputes and encourage settlements; see Booth Report, para. 1.1.

[9] Objectives which are fundamental to the reforms recently enacted in the Children Act 1989.

[10] Law Com. No. 170, para. 6.2

[11] Both in The Field of Choice (1966), Law Com. No. 6, and in The Financial Consequences of Divorce (1981), Law Com. No. 112.

PART II

THE CASE FOR REFORM

The present law and practice

2.1 Under the Matrimonial Causes Act 1973, the sole ground for divorce is that the marriage has broken down irretrievably.[1] However, a petitioner can only establish this by proving one or more of five "facts".[2] In summary, these are:

(a) that the respondent has committed adultery and (whether for this or any other reason[3]) the petitioner finds it intolerable to live with him;

(b) that the respondent has behaved in such a way that this petitioner cannot reasonably be expected to live with him;[4]

(c) that the respondent has deserted the petitioner for at least two years out of the previous two and a half;[5]

(d) that the parties have lived apart[6] for at least two years out of the previous two and a half[7] and the respondent consents to a divorce;

(e) that the parties have lived apart for at least five years out of the previous five and a half.[8]

2.2 In theory, the court must inquire as best it can into the facts alleged.[9] In practice, more than 99% of divorces are undefended.[10] All but a tiny number of undefended cases[11] are proved under the so-called "special procedure" where the petition and supporting affidavits are scrutinised by a Registrar and the decree is formally pronounced by the Judge in reliance on the Registrar's certificate. Our examination of court files in a wide selection of courts around the country revealed that the Registrar's scutiny may well be effective in picking up technical errors in procedure or presentation but is unlikely to reveal defects of substance, particularly in behaviour cases.[12] There are also regional and even local variations in the extent to which corroborative evidence is required. This is not to suggest that the old system of formal oral hearings of undefended cases was any more effective:[13] rather, that without an extensive and expensive court investigation branch it is in practice impossible adequately to test the facts if the respondent, for whatever reason, decides not to do so. The divorce itself is granted in two stages: first, a decree nisi pronounced by the Judge, and second, a decree absolute issued by the court at least six weeks later.[14]

2.3 In practice, roughly 71.4% of divorces are granted to wives and 73.3% of divorces are based either on adultery (fact (a)), or on behaviour (fact (b)).[15] The proportion based on behaviour has been rising steadily. The use of the five facts varies according to the

---

[1] Matrimonial Causes Act 1973 (MCA), s.1(1).

[2] MCA, s.1(2).

[3] *Cleary* v. *Cleary* [1974] 1 W.L.R. 73.

[4] The leading cases are *Livingstone-Stallard* v. *Livingstone-Stallard* [1974] Fam. 47; *O'Neill* v. *O'Neill* [1975] 1 W.L.R. 1118; and *Thurlow* v. *Thurlow* [1976] Fam. 32.

[5] MCA, s.2(5) provides that periods of cohabitation totalling less than six months are to be ignored provided that the total period apart is two years.

[6] MCA, s.2(6) provides that parties are living apart unless they are living with each other in the same household; it is possible to conduct two separate households under the same roof, *Mouncer* v. *Mouncer* [1972] 1 W.L.R. 321.

[7] MCA, s.2(5).

[8] *Ibid.*

[9] MCA, s.1(3).

[10] It is not possible to identify the exact proportion from published statistics; the *Judicial Statistics, Annual Report 1989*, (1990) Cm. 1154, Tables 5.5 and 5.6, show 635 defended divorces listed for trial during 1989, 394 disposed of, 280 after trial, and 285 decrees granted, out of a total of 151,309 decrees nisi that year.

[11] The number of undefended cases set down to be heard in open court by a judge is not collected centrally; there was probably only one in our study of 476 divorce and separation cases, see Appendix C, para. 33.

[12] Appendix C, paras. 26 *et seq.*

[13] Indeed, it is possible that an unhurried scrutiny of the documents, with power to call for further information if required, is more effective than a five-minute oral hearing during which the petitioner was asked a series of leading questions by counsel or solicitor and the result was a foregone conclusion; see E. Elston, J. Fuller and M. Murch, "Judicial Hearings of Undefended Divorce Petitions", (1975) 38 M.L.R. 609.

[14] MCA, ss.1(5), 9(2); Matrimonial Causes (Decree Absolute) Order 1972. There is power to reduce the period, but this will "very rarely" be necessary, *Practice Direction* [1977] 1 W.L.R. 759.

[15] O.P.C.S., *Marriage and Divorce Statistics 1988*, (1990), Table 4.6: Fact proven at divorce 1988. These figures relate to decrees absolute.

petitioner's sex, age, social class and whether or not there are dependent children.[16] Sometimes these variations reflect genuine differences in marital behaviour: it is, perhaps, unlikely to be a coincidence that 87% of behaviour decrees are granted to wives. But sometimes they reflect quite different considerations: adultery or intolerable behaviour are the only facts on which divorce proceedings may be started immediately the breakdown occurs.[17] Either may therefore be used, not because the behaviour is any worse than in other cases, or because it is the real reason for the divorce, but because the couple have agreed to end their marriage as quickly as possible, or because one of them wishes or needs to bring proceedings quickly in order to obtain rehousing, maintenance or income support, and to setttle the children's future. It appears that separation is least used by those who find it difficult to live apart because of housing or financial problems.[18] Even if the parties can afford to live apart, the increasing use of adultery and behaviour suggests that many find two years too long to wait.

2.4 Before turning to the criticisms of the present law, we should bear in mind that it also has strengths. Our public opinion survey revealed a large measure of public support for its principal features: thus 72% agreed that it was good that anyone who wants a divorce can get one sooner or later, although 71% found the present five year period too long; 83% agreed that it was good that couples who did not want to put the blame on one of them did not have to do so; and 84% agreed that it was good that one could begin proceedings immediately if the other had committed adultery or behaved intolerably.[19] Furthermore, divorce under both fault and no-fault grounds is obviously acceptable to a very high proportion of people. 67%, including 71% of divorced people, found divorce under the present law "acceptable".[20] At the very least, we can confidently repeat the assertion in Facing the Future that "the present law is a considerable improvement on the previous position"[21] which relied almost entirely upon proof of fault.[22]

2.5 It is not surprising the respondents to our survey saw strengths in some features of the present law and objections to others, or that they found a variety of different bases for divorce "acceptable", and in the end were fairly evenly divided over whether the law should be changed. We were anxious not to present them with simple questions with easy answers, but to tease out some of their underlying values and objectives. They clearly found this a challenging process and came to share some of the indecision which affects many thinking people in this difficult area. As the Archbishop of York has observed, "Over the last 12 to 15 years the Church of England has been going through agonies on the subject of divorce ... it is not a bad thing that the Church of England has been unable to come to any clear decision because there are no easy answers. To go on being in agony about this at least represents publicly that there is still a problem to be dealt with".[23]

2.6 Respondents to Facing the Future were in no doubt at all that there is a problem to be dealt with. Only three of them[24] considered that the present law was working satisfactorily. The overwhelming majority agreed with the criticisms made of the current system and supported the case for reform. In doing so, there were some who attached greater weight to the aim of buttressing the stability of marriage and family life and others who were more concerned that the law should minimise bitterness and

---

[16] J. Haskey, "Grounds for Divorce in England and Wales—A Social and Demographic Analysis", (1986) 18 J. Biosoc. Sci. 127; Davis and Murch, op. cit., pp. 78–80; see also Appendix C, paras. 4, 5.

[17] A petition cannot be based upon adultery if the couple have lived together for a total of more than six months since the petitioner learned of it, MCA, s.2(1); there is no equivalent in behaviour cases, but the longer the petitioner waits the more likely it is that he or she can reasonably be expected to go on living with the respondent, Katz v. Katz [1972] 1 W.L.R. 955; cf. Bradley v. Bradley [1973] 1 W.L.R. 1291, Court v. Court [1982] Fam. 105; cohabitation of less than six months is ignored in both cases, MCA, s.2(2) and (3).

[18] I.e. by petitioners in lower socio-economic groups and/or with young children; Haskey, op. cit.; Davis and Murch, op. cit., pp. 78–80; Appendix C, paras. 4, 5.

[19] Appendix D, Tables 15, 16.

[20] Appendix D, Tables 17, 18.

[21] Law Com. No. 170, para. 3.47.

[22] The grounds were adultery, cruelty, three years' desertion, five years' incurable unsoundness of mind, and rape, sodomy or bestiality by the husband; Matrimonial Causes Act 1965, s.1(1). Then as now, however, a substantial majority were undefended.

[23] His Grace, The Lord Archbishop of York, Dr. John Hapgood, DD, "Conciliation and Reconciliation", Address to the Annual General Meeting of the National Family Conciliation Council, 28 September 1989 (N.F.C.C., 1990), pp. 1–2.

[24] One Circuit Judge, one County Federation of Women's Institutes, and one group from another County Federation of Women's Institutes.

distress for the parties and their children. All were agreed that the law does neither satisfactorily at present.

Criticisms of the present law and practice

2.7 The criticisms of the present law, and in particular its failure to live up to its original objectives, were set out at length in Facing the Future.[25] There is no need for us to repeat them here, but we should like to draw attention to the features which seem to us most objectionable. These, not only in our view but also in that of our respondents, add up to a formidable case for reform.

(i) *It is confusing and misleading*

2.8 There is a considerable gap between theory and practice, which can only lead to confusion and lack of respect for the law. Indeed, some would call it downright dishonest. There are several aspects to this. First, the law tells couples that the only ground for divorce is irretrievable breakdown, which apparently does not involve fault. But next it provides that this can only be shown by one of five "facts", three of which apparently do involve fault. There are several recent examples of divorces being refused despite the fact that it was clear to all concerned that the marriage had indeed irretrievably broken down.[26] The hardship and pain involved for both parties can be very great.

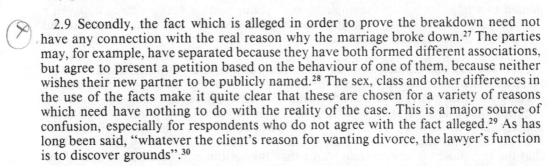

2.9 Secondly, the fact which is alleged in order to prove the breakdown need not have any connection with the real reason why the marriage broke down.[27] The parties may, for example, have separated because they have both formed different associations, but agree to present a petition based on the behaviour of one of them, because neither wishes their new partner to be publicly named.[28] The sex, class and other differences in the use of the facts make it quite clear that these are chosen for a variety of reasons which need have nothing to do with the reality of the case. This is a major source of confusion, especially for respondents who do not agree with the fact alleged.[29] As has long been said, "whatever the client's reason for wanting divorce, the lawyer's function is to discover grounds".[30]

2.10 The behaviour fact is particularly confusing. It is often referred to as "unreasonable behaviour", which suggests blameworthiness or outright cruelty on the part of the respondent; but this has been called a "linguistic trap",[31] because the behaviour itself need be neither unreasonable nor blameworthy: rather, its effect on the petitioner must be such that it is unreasonable to expect him or her to go on living with the respondent, a significantly different and more flexible concept which is obviously capable of varying from case to case and court to court.[32] Although the test is to be applied by an objective reasonable outsider, the character and personality of the petitioner are particularly relevant in deciding what conduct he or she should be expected to bear.[33]

2.11 Finally, and above all, the present law pretends that the court is conducting an inquiry into the facts of the matter,[34] when in the vast majority of cases it can do no such thing.[35] This is not the fault of the court, nor is it probably any more of a problem under the present law and procedure than it was under the old. It may be more difficult to evaluate the effect of the respondent's behaviour from the papers than from the petitioner's account in the witness box,[36] but it has always been difficult to get at the

---

[25] Law Com. No. 170, Part III.

[26] E.g. *Beasley* v. *Beasley*, reported in *The Daily Telegraph* on 16 April 1986; *Buffery* v. *Buffery* [1988] 2 F.L.R. 365; *Chilton* v. *Chilton*, reported in *The Daily Mail* on 18 January 1990.

[27] *Stevens* v. *Stevens* [1979] 1 W.L.R. 885.

[28] As generally required by MCA, s.49; see further Appendix C, paras. 40–42.

[29] Davis and Murch, *op. cit.*, esp. ch. 3.

[30] R. Chester and J. Streather, "Cruelty in English Divorce: Some Empirical Findings", (1972) 34 Jo. of Marriage and the Family, 706 at p. 712; see also Davis and Murch, *op. cit.*, ch. 5.

[31] *Bannister* v. *Bannister* (1980) 10 Fam. Law 240, per Ormrod L.J.

[32] See further Appendix C, paras. 44–49.

[33] E.g. *Astwood* v. *Astwood* (1981) 131 N.L.J. 990.

[34] MCA, s.1(3).

[35] See para. 2.2 above and Appendix C.

[36] The Booth Report, para. 2.17, observes that "In the great majority of cases the court is quite simply in no position to make findings of fact or, in a case based on behaviour, to evaluate the effect . . .".

truth in an undefended case. Moreover, the system still allows, even encourages, the parties to lie, or at least to exaggerate, in order to get what they want. The bogus adultery cases of the past may have all but disappeared, but their modern equivalents are the "flimsy" behaviour petition[37] or the pretence that the parties have been living apart for a full two years. In that "wider field which includes considerations of truth, the sacredness of oaths, and the integrity of professional practice",[38] the present law is just as objectionable as the old.

(ii) *It is discriminatory and unjust*

2.12 83% of respondents to our public opinion survey thought it a good feature of the present law that couples who do not want to put the blame on either of them do not have to do so,[39] but these couples have to have lived apart for at least two years. This can be extremely difficult to achieve without either substantial resources of one's own, or the co-operation of the other spouse at the outset, or an ouster order from the court. A secure council house tenancy, for example, cannot be re-allocated between them without a court order which is only obtainable on divorce or judicial separation.[40] The law does recognise that it is possible to live apart by conducting two separate households under the same roof.[41] In practice, this is impossible in most ordinary houses or flats, especially where there are children: it inevitably requires the couple to co-operate in a most unnatural and artificial lifestyle. It is unjust and discriminatory of the law to provide for a civilised "no-fault" ground for divorce which, in practice, is denied to a large section of the population. A young mother with children living in a council house is obliged to rely upon fault whether or not she wants to do so and irrespective of the damage it may do.

2.13 The fault-based facts can also be intrinsically unjust. "Justice" in this context has traditionally been taken to mean the accurate allocation of blameworthiness for the breakdown of the marriage. Desertion is the only fact which still attempts to do this: it requires that one party has brought about their separation without just cause or consent. Desertion, however, is hardly ever used, because its place has been taken by the two year separation fact. A finding of adultery or behaviour certainly need not mean that the respondent is any more to blame than the petitioner for the breakdown of the marriage. If one has committed adultery or behaved intolerably there is usually nothing to stop the other obtaining a divorce based upon it, even though that other may have committed far more adulteries or behaved much more intolerably himself or herself.[42] Nor does the behaviour fact always involve blame: it may well be unreasonable to expect a petitioner to live with a spouse who is mentally ill or disabled[43] or has totally incompatible values or lifestyle.[44] Even when the catalogue of complaints contained in the petition includes violence or other obviously blameworthy behaviour, this might look different if weighed against the behaviour of the other. In a defended case, the petitioner's own character and conduct may be relevant in determining the effect of the respondent's conduct upon her, but if his conduct is sufficient, it is irrelevant that she may have behaved equally badly in some other way. In an undefended case, of course, the matter will appear even more one-sided.

2.14 This inherent potential for injustice is compounded by the practical problems of defending or bringing a cross-petition of one's own. It is extremely difficult to resist or counter allegations of behaviour. Defending them requires time, money and emotional energy far beyond the resources of most respondents. Even if the parties are

---

[37] See *A Better Way Out, op. cit.*, para. 50; there is some support from the files examined in Appendix C, at paras. 46–49.

[38] *Putting Asunder, A Divorce Law for Contemporary Society*, the Report of a Group appointed by the Archbishop of Canterbury in 1964, (S.P.C.K., 1966), para. 45.

[39] Appendix D, Tables 15, 16.

[40] Unless it is a joint tenancy and one of them voluntarily surrenders it, but this brings the whole tenancy to an end, *London Borough of Greenwich* v. *McGrady* (1983) 81 L.G.R. 288.

[41] The test is the same as under the old law of desertion: it is not sufficient to have separate bedrooms; they must no longer share meals, washing, cleaning or other household tasks, see *Mouncer* v. *Mouncer* [1972] 1 W.L.R. 321.

[42] Although in *Ash* v. *Ash* [1972] Fam. 135, at p. 140, it was said that a violent petitioner can reasonably be expected to live with a violent respondent, it might be argued that neither could be expected to live with the other.

[43] *Katz* v. *Katz* [1972] 1 W.L.R. 955; *Thurlow* v. *Thurlow* [1976] Fam. 32.

[44] *Livingstone-Stallard* v. *Livingstone-Stallard* [1974] Fam. 74; *Astwood* v. *Astwood* (1981) 131 N.L.J. 990; *Balraj* v. *Balraj* (1981) 11 Fam. Law 110.

prepared to go through this, what would be the point? If the marriage is capable of being saved, a long-fought defended divorce, in which every incident or characteristic that might amount to behaviour is dragged up and examined in detail, is not going to do this.[45] It can only serve to make matters worse and to consume resources which are often desperately needed elsewhere, particularly if there are children. Legal aid will only be granted if the case cannot be disposed of as an undefended suit without detriment to the interests of either party.[46] As the basis on which the divorce is granted is usually irrelevant to ancillary issues, the parties' *legal* positions are unlikely to be affected whatever their personal views. Small wonder, then, that lawyers advise their clients not to defend and that their clients feel unjustly treated.[47]

(iii) *It distorts the parties' bargaining positions*

2.15 Not only can the law be unjust in itself, it can also lead to unfair distortions in the relative bargaining positions of the parties. When a marriage breaks down there are a great many practical questions to be decided: with whom are the children to live, how much are they going to see of the other parent, who is to have the house, and what are they all going to live on? Respondents to Facing the Future told us that the battles which used to be fought through the ground for divorce are now more likely to be fought through the so-called ancillary issues which in practice matter so much more to many people. The policy of the law is to encourage the parties to try and resolve these by agreement if they can, whether through negotiation between solicitors or with the help of a mediation or conciliation service.[48] Questions of the future care of children, distribution of family assets, and financial provision are all governed by their own legal criteria. It is not unjust for negotiations to be affected by the relative merits of the parties' cases on these matters. Yet negotiations may also be distorted by whichever of the parties is in a stronger position in relation to the divorce itself. The strength of that position will depend upon a combination of how anxious or reluctant that party is to be divorced and how easy or difficult he or she will find it to prove or disprove one of the five facts. That might not matter if these represented a coherent set of principles, reflecting the real reasons why the marriage broke down; but as we have already seen, they do not. The potentially arbitrary results can put one party at an unfair disadvantage.

(iv) *It provokes unnecessary hostility and bitterness*

2.16 A law which is arbitrary or unjust can exacerbate the feelings of bitterness, distress and humiliation so often experienced at the time of separation and divorce.[49] Even if the couple have agreed that their marriage cannot be saved, it must make matters between them worse if the system encourages one to make allegations against the other. The incidents relied on have to be set out in the petition. Sometimes they are exaggerated, one-sided or even untrue. Allegations of behaviour or adultery can provoke resentment and hostility in a respondent who is unable to put his own side of the story on the record. We are not so naive as to believe that bitterness and hostility could ever be banished from the divorce process. It is not concerned with cold commercial bargains but with the most intimate of human relations. The more we expect of marriage the greater the anger and grief when marriage ends. But there is every reason to believe that the present law adds needlessly to the human misery involved. Our respondents confirmed this.

(v) *It does nothing to save the marriage*

2.17 None of this is any help with the law's other objective, of supporting those marriages which have a chance of survival. The law cannot prevent people from separating or forming new relationships, although it may make it difficult for people to

---

[45] Booth Report, para. 2.6; see para. 3.43 below.

[46] *The Legal Aid Handbook 1990*, at p. 65–66 points out that "the policy of the Matrimonial Causes Act 1973 is to avoid defended suits in relation to the decree unless there are reasons why the suit should be defended in the interests of either party, and to ensure that normally the award of a decree will not compromise decisions over issues relating to the custody of, access to, and maintenance of, children, and the other ancillary matters". cf. *McCarney* v. *McCarney* [1986] 1 F.L.R. 312, per Lord Donaldson M.R. at p. 314.

[47] See particularly Davis and Murch, *op. cit.*, ch. 7.

[48] The terms of reference given to the Booth Committee were to recommend reforms which might be made (a) to mitigate the intensity of disputes; (b) to encourage settlements; and (c) to provide further for the welfare of the children of the family; Booth Report, para. 1.1.

[49] Davis and Murch, *op. cit.*, chs. 6 and 7, provide ample evidence of this.

get a divorce. The law can also make it difficult for estranged couples to become reconciled. The present law does make it difficult for some couples—in practice a very small proportion—to be divorced, but does so in an arbitrary way depending upon which facts may be proved. It also makes it extremely difficult for couples to become reconciled. A spouse who wishes to be divorced is obliged either to make allegations against the other or to live apart for a lengthy period. If the petitioner brings proceedings based on behaviour, possibly without prior warning, and sometimes while they are still living together,[50] the antagonism caused may destroy any lingering chance of saving the marriage. The alternative of two or five years' separation may encourage them to part in order to be able to obtain a divorce, when their difficulties might have been resolved if they had stayed together. From the very beginning, attention has to be focussed on how to prove the ground for divorce. The reality of what it will be like to live apart, to break up the common home, to finance two households where before there was only one, and to have or to lose that day-to-day responsibility for the children which was previously shared, at least to some extent: none of this has to be contemplated in any detail until the decree nisi is obtained. If it had, there might be some petitioners who would think again.

2.18 It is a mistake to think that, because so few divorces are defended, the rest are largely consensual. There are many, especially behaviour cases, in which the respondent indicates an intention to defend, but does not file a formal answer, or files an answer which is later withdrawn. Some of these are a reaction to the unfairness of the allegations made against them, but some reveal a genuine desire to preserve the marriage.[51] A defended suit is not going to do this, and if a case is, or becomes, undefended, there is little opportunity to explore the possibility of saving the marriage. An undefended decree can be obtained in a matter of weeks.[52] If both parties are contemplating divorce, the system gives them every incentive to obtain a "quickie" decree based on behaviour or separation, and to think out the practical consequences later.

(vi) *It can make things worse for the children*

2.19 The present system can also make things worse for the children. The children themselves would usually prefer their parents to stay together.[53] But the law cannot force parents to live amicably or prevent them from separating. It is not known whether children suffer more from their parents' separation or from living in a household in conflict where they may be blamed for the couple's inability to part.[54] It is probably impossible to generalise, as there are so many variables which may affect the outcome, including the age and personality of the particular child. But it is known that the children who suffer least from their parents' break-up are usually those who are able to retain a good relationship with them both. Children who suffer most are those whose parents remain in conflict.[55]

2.20 These issues have to be faced by the parents themselves, as they agonise over what to do for the best. However regrettably, there is nothing the law can do to ensure that they stay together, even supposing that this would indeed be better for their children. On the other hand, the present law can, for all the reasons given earlier, make the conflict worse. It encourages couples to find fault with one another and disputes

---

[50] More than a quarter of the behaviour petitioners in our study were still living at the same address when the petition was filed; see Appendix C, para. 23.

[51] Davis and Murch, *op. cit.*, ch. 7.

[52] Appendix C, paras. 8–12; see also O.P.C.S., *Marriage and Divorce Statistics 1988*, (1990), Table 4.8. Interval between petition and divorce, fact proven, 1988; longer intervals are associated with using fault-based facts and having children under 16.

[53] A. Mitchell, *Children in the Middle*, (1985); Y. Walczak and S. Burns, *Divorce: the Child's Point of View*, (1984); G. McCredie and A. Horrox, *Voices in the Dark: Children and Divorce*, (1985).

[54] That there are adverse effects upon some children from some divorces cannot be doubted; see, e.g., J.S. Wallerstein and J.B. Kelly, *Surviving the Breakup*, (1980); however, the claims of J.S. Wallerstein and S. Blakeslee in *Second Chances*, (1989), as to the high risk of such effects, have to be treated with some caution; see reviews by J.B. Kelly and R. Emery, [1989] Fam. Law 489; and J. Elliot, G. Ochiltree, M. Richards, C. Sinclair and F. Tasker, [1990] Fam. Law 309. One difficulty is distinguishing the effects of divorce itself from the poverty and consequent disadvantages which so often result; see M. Maclean and R.E.J. Wadsworth, "The Interests of Children after Parental Divorce: A Long-Term Perspective", (1988) 2 Int. J. of Law and the Family 155.

[55] M.P.M. Richards and M. Dyson, *Separation, Divorce and the Development of Children: a review*, (D.H.S.S., 1982); S. Maidment, *Child Custody and Divorce*, (1984).

8

about children seem to be more common in divorces based on intolerable behaviour than in others.[56] The alternative is a long period of separation during which children can suffer from the uncertainty before things can be finally sorted out or from the artificiality of their parents living in separate households under the same roof.[57] This is scarcely an effective way of encouraging the parents to work out different ways of continuing to discharge their shared parental responsibilities. It is often said that couples undergoing marital breakdown are too wrapped up in their own problems to understand their children's needs.[58] There are also couples who, while recognising that their own relationship is at an end, are anxious to do their best for their children.[59] The present system does little to help them to do so.

Conclusion

2.21 These defects alone would amount to a formidable case for reform. The response to Facing the Future very largely endorsed its conclusion that "Above all, the present law fails to recognise that divorce is not a final product but part of a massive transition for the parties and their children".[60] It is all too easy to think of divorcing couples in simple stereotypes. In fact they come in many different shapes and sizes. But for most, if not all, the breakdown of their relationship is a painful process, and for some it can be devastating. It affects each party in different ways: one may be far ahead of the other in withdrawing from the relationship before the other even realises that there is a problem.[61] The anger, guilt, bitterness and regret so often felt have little to do with the law, which can seem an irrelevant game to be played by the lawyers. But the law does nothing to give the parties an opportunity to come to terms with what is happening in their lives, to reflect in as calm and sensible a way as possible upon the future, and to re-negotiate their relationship. Both emotionally and financially it is better for them and their children if they can do this by agreement rather than by fighting in the courts. There are always going to be some fights and the courts are there to resolve them. But the courts should be kept to their proper sphere of adjudicating upon practical disputes, ensuring that appropriate steps are properly taken, and enforcing the orders made. They should not be pretending to adjudicate upon matters they cannot decide or in disputes which need never arise.

---

[56] J. Eekelaar and E. Clive, *Custody after Divorce*, (1977), para. 13.3.
[57] See note 6 above.
[58] A. Mitchell, *op. cit.*, pp. 101 and 113; J.S. Wallerstein and J.B. Kelly, *op. cit.*, pp. 41–42.
[59] G. Davis and M. Roberts, *Access to Agreement*, (1988), p. 27.
[60] Law Com. No. 170, para. 3.50.
[61] D. Vaughan, *Uncoupling—Turning Points in Intimate Relationships*, (1987).

PART III

MODELS FOR REFORM

The aims of the law

3.1 In reviewing possible models for reform we have in mind the following broad objectives for the law which we believe to be generally agreed:[1]

(i) It should try to support those marriages which are capable of being saved.

(ii) It should enable those which cannot be saved to be dissolved with the minimum of avoidable distress, bitterness and hostility.

(iii) It should encourage, so far as possible, the amicable resolution of practical issues relating to the couple's home, finances and children and the proper discharge of their responsibilities to one another and to their children.

(iv) It should seek to minimise the harm that the children of the family may suffer, both at the time and in the future, and to promote so far as possible the continued sharing of parental responsibility for them.

3.2 These aims are similar to those expressed in The Field of Choice[2] but with important differences in emphasis. There is now a much greater understanding of the needs of children whose parents divorce. It is important for their sake that the law should seek to minimise bitterness and hostility and to promote amicable settlements. There is also a sound public interest in doing so. It does no good to anyone if resources are wasted away in costly legal battles. The family's claims on the public purse may also increase, if parents are not obliged at the outset of their marital difficulties to consider how their financial responsibilities, principally towards their children but also to one another, should be met.

3.3 There is also a sound public interest in helping to preserve those marriages which can be saved. It is generally accepted that the law neither can nor should force people to live together or keep alive the empty shell of a marriage which is undoubtedly dead.[3] There are also some marriages which cannot or should not be saved. It is important, both for their sake and for the sake of their children, that people whose marriages have failed are not burdened with an even greater sense of guilt or personal failure. But it is legitimate to try to avoid the damage done by decisions taken in haste and without full consideration of the consequences. As our predecessors put it, "a divorce law . . . can and should ensure that divorce is not so easy that the parties are under no inducement to make a success of their marriage and, in particular, to overcome temporary difficulties".[4]

3.4 The aim of supporting those marriages which can be saved can be distinguished from the aim of upholding the institution of marriage itself.[5] For some of our respondents, as for our predecessors, it was important that divorce law should send the right messages, to the married and the marrying, about the seriousness and permanence of the commitment involved.[6] We agree. Despite a rapid recent growth in cohabitation outside marriage, marriage remains an extremely popular institution. Couples see it as offering, not only an "important signifier" of their commitment to one another, but also a home of their own, financial and emotional security, and an "accepted context" for having children.[7] Marriage involves mutual legal obligations of support and sharing which other relationships do not. The law should certainly do its utmost to recognise and enforce these. It must also be realistic and practical. If people who are unhappily married are denied a means of reordering their lives in a sensible fashion, many of them

---

[1] Para. 1.6 above.

[2] (1966), Law Com. No. 6, paras. 15 and 120(1).

[3] Law Com. No. 6, para. 15.

[4] *Ibid.*, para. 16.

[5] Cf. Law Com. No. 6, para. 15 and para. 120(1).

[6] This view is eloquently put by one of our respondents, Helen Oppenheimer, a member of the group appointed by the Archbishop of Canterbury which produced the Report, *Putting Asunder, A Divorce Law for Contemporary Society*, (1966), in her recent book *Marriage*, (1990), ch. 8, and by the National Campaign for the Family and National Family Trust in *A Secure Basis for Divorce Law Reform*, (1988).

[7] P. Mansfield and J. Collard, *The Beginning of the Rest of Your Life? A Portrait of Newly-Wed Marriage*, (1988), p. 229; see also J. Burgoyne and D. Clark, *Making a Go of It, A Study of Step-families in Sheffield*, (1984), esp. ch. 1.

will simply walk away. Others may be deterred from marrying in the first place, but will live together instead.[8] Support for the institution of marriage cannot be achieved by turning it into an institution which no-one any longer wishes to enter. But the recognition that a marriage has broken down does not mean that the obligations resulting from it should be ignored.

The options in Facing the Future

3.5 In Facing the Future[9] and its summary, we canvassed six possible bases for the ground for divorce: return to a wholly fault-based system; a full inquiry into whether or not the marital relationship had indeed broken down; mutual consent; immediate unilateral demand; separation for a specified period; and divorce after a period of reflection and consideration of the arrangements, referred to as a "process over time". We concluded that the first four of these were, for various reasons, impracticable or unacceptable. Consultation has confirmed that conclusion. It may, however, be helpful to expand a little upon the reasons before turning to those models which now seem to constitute the acceptable "field of choice".

The rejected options

(i) Return to fault

3.6 None of our respondents argued for a return to a system based wholly on the matrimonial offence. However, this was implicit in some of the arguments put forward in support of its retention as part of a "mixed" system. It was said both to provide a moral framework for marriage and to act as a restraint on the parties' behaviour.[10] These are important objectives. Nevertheless, it is clear that they cannot be achieved through a return to a wholly fault-based divorce law. First, divorce law is only capable of assessing fault in the crudest possible way. The law is, of course, used to deciding whether or not a crime has been committed. It is much less well-suited to engaging in the complex and sensitive factual and moral judgments which would be necessary accurately to reflect the relative blameworthiness of the parties to a marriage. The history of fault-based divorce was one of ever-increasing complexity as the law vainly tried to solve this problem.[11] In the end it became clear that it could not do so without relying to an unacceptable and even more unprincipled extent upon the value judgments of the particular judge trying the case.[12] The complexities of family life are no longer capable of being reduced to simple certainties.

3.7 Secondly, and perhaps more importantly, restricting divorce to matrimonial fault is an illogical and ineffective means of trying to achieve acceptable standards of marital behaviour, because the sanction cannot work. Logically, of course, where both parties are equally guilty, it denies them *both* a divorce, but the law recognised some time ago that that was absurd. If only one is "guilty", but divorce is what he wants, then it is scarcely acting as a restraint on behaviour or providing a sound moral framework to give him just that. Allowing the innocent party to punish the guilty by refusing the divorce is unlikely in today's society to change that behaviour. If divorce is *not* what the guilty party wants, then the important sanction is not so much the public marking of his or her guilt but the breakdown of the marriage itself. The fact that adultery or violence or other bad behaviour may lead to an unwanted break up of the marriage is the real deterrent—and long may it remain so.

3.8 Respondents to our public opinion survey were presented with a number of possible bases for divorce and asked whether or not these were acceptable.[13] The object was to introduce them to a range of possibilities and to see what might be ruled out.

---

[8] The marriage rate among those eligible to marry has fallen in recent years, in part it is thought because of an increase in cohabitation outside marriage; and see J. Haskey and K. Kiernan, "Cohabitation in Great Britain, characteristics and estimated numbers of cohabiting partners", (1989) 58 Population Trends 23.

[9] Law Com. No. 170, Part V.

[10] E.g. G. Brown, *Finding Fault in Divorce*, p. 14.

[11] See e.g. R. Phillips, *Putting Asunder, A History of Divorce in Western Society*, (1988); also standard textbooks on Divorce or Family Law before 1969.

[12] *Ibid.*, p. 563. Subjectivity is a common phenomenon in assessing guilt; as Davis and Murch, *op. cit.* at p. 49, wryly observe, "where the woman had embarked on another relationship, there was a tendency for her to accept *all* responsibility for the subsequent breakdown of her marriage. This was a perception which husbands, in similar circumstances, found easier to resist"; outsiders assessing the same marriage may also find it difficult to leave their own preconceptions about marriage and family life behind.

[13] Appendix D, Tables 17, 18.

They were not at this stage asked whether they would approve of any of these as the *sole* ground for divorce. In this context, 84% found divorce for fault acceptable, alongside even higher figures for certain non-fault grounds. Further, 83% agreed that the present law is good because couples who do not want to put the blame on either of them do not have to do so.[14] While these findings certainly give some support to the continuation of the present "mixed" system, they cannot be read as a call for a return to a law based wholly on fault.

3.9 There is, however, no serious call for the law to return to a wholly fault-based system. Such a system is now virtually unknown in Western society.[15] Quite apart from the objections above, it would deny divorce to couples who both want it but who have not behaved badly or who do not wish to cast blame on one another. It would also keep in being many marriages which on any view have been dead for years. It is incompatible with the principle that irretrievable breakdown of the marriage should remain the basis for divorce, a principle which now appears to command almost universal support in this country.

(ii) *Inquest*

3.10 Irretrievable breakdown of the marriage became the ground for divorce in our law largely because of the arguments of principle put forward in *Putting Asunder*,[16] the report of a group appointed by the Archbishop of Canterbury. The group also proposed that divorce should only be granted after a full judicial inquiry into the history of the marriage and the possibility of saving it. This proposal was rejected in the 1969 reforms, largely because it was thought to be impracticable and unhelpful. Facing the Future suggested that this rejection should be confirmed, as the point made in 1966 that breakdown *of itself* is not a justiciable issue has been widely recognised.[17]

3.11 Most of those respondents who commented upon this issue agreed that a judicial inquest into the past was not the best way of identifying those marriages which could be saved. It would tend to be even more destructive of the relationship; it would encourage the parties to exaggerate their problems in order to convince the inquisitor; it would therefore increase hostility and bitterness between them. It must be doubted whether requiring all divorcing couples to disclose the most intimate details of their married life serves any useful purpose. Nor would it be easy to define uniform standards by which the necessary multitude of inquisitors could determine whether or not the relationship was at an end. This would have to be governed, either by subjective and inevitably inconsistent criteria, or by rough and ready "rules of thumb". In practice, where both parties wanted the divorce, it could easily become the sort of charade that the old-style undefended divorce used to be;[18] where they did not, the battle might become even more destructive than a defended behaviour case under the present law. The Church of England's Board for Social Responsibility, in their response, considered that the main strength of the inquest concept lay in helping the couple to talk about their own experiences and needs, in an appropriate family court setting with the support of trained conciliators. As they recognised, much the same approach could also be adopted during the "process over time". For the principle of using the divorce process to explore the possibilities and consequences for the parties and their children, there is indeed much to be said; but there must be better ways than a judicial inquest over the past for the system to support those marriages that could and should if possible be saved.

(iii) *Immediate unilateral demand*

3.12 In Facing the Future, we concluded that immediate divorce on unilateral demand would be unacceptable; it would provide no safeguard against precipitate divorce and no opportunity to resolve the practical consequences before the divorce was granted.[19] Those respondents who commented at all agreed, although one respondent with considerable knowledge of the present system[20] observed that in

---

[14] *Ibid.*, Tables 15, 16.
[15] R. Phillips, *op. cit.*, ch. 13.
[16] (1966), *op. cit.*
[17] Law Com. No. 170, para. 5.6.
[18] As the Archbishop of York, *op. cit.*, p. 2., has observed, "If a law is not easy to operate, my experience is that the lawyers will find a way to make it easy to operate".
[19] Law Com. No. 170, paras. 5.10, 5.21.
[20] The management team and staff of the divorce section of a busy county court in a large provincial city.

practice it already exists. As we have already seen,[21] the system is not capable of preventing the adultery and behaviour facts being used in this way. It is noteworthy that immediate application for divorce by unilateral demand was the one basis rejected as unacceptable by 57% of the respondents to our public opinion survey, although as many as a third thought it acceptable.[22]

(iv) *Mutual consent*

3.13 By contrast, immediate application for divorce by consent was considered acceptable by 90% of respondents in the public opinion survey.[23] However, the argument advanced in Facing the Future was that, for obvious reasons, mutual consent cannot be the *sole* ground for divorce.[24] Of those respondents who commented on this option, only one favoured it as the sole ground for divorce. The others agreed that there would have to be other ways of establishing breakdown, to cater for those denied consent by a bitter or unreasonable spouse, and for those whose spouses could not be traced. The difficulty then is that giving or withholding consent can become a powerful weapon in the bargaining between the parties about other matters, such as the home, money, or children. The strength of that weapon would depend, as it does at present, upon what the alternatives were to be. A few respondents were also convinced that such a system might facilitate hasty and ill-considered divorce and ignore the need to adjust to its social and emotional consequences.

3.14 Providing a separate "ground" based on consent should, however, be distinguished from providing for the system to recognise that divorce can sometimes be a joint decision, responsibly agreed upon between the parties, who may also be encouraged or helped to agree on all the other matters which flow from it. This was the approach adopted by the Booth Committee.[25] There was also substantial support for it in our own consultations and it should be an important element in any reform of the law.

The new Field of Choice

3.15 The three possible models for reform which therefore emerged from our consultations were:

   (i) retention of a "mixed" system along the present lines, perhaps with some modification;

   (ii) divorce after a fixed minimum period of separation; and

   (iii) divorce after a fixed minimum period for reflection and consideration of the arrangements, referred to in Facing the Future as divorce by a process over time.

(i) *A mixed system*

3.16 Our public opinion survey indicated that divorce for fault remains acceptable to 84% of the population, alongside other non-fault bases for divorce.[26] However, only 13 respondents to Facing the Future argued for the retention of fault in ground for divorce. In this there was a marked difference between the responses which we received and those received by the Scottish Law Commission, in their separate review of the law in Scotland.[27] The Scottish Law Commission therefore concluded that adultery and behaviour should be retained, as alternatives to the two separation "facts"; these should be reduced to one year (where the respondent consents) and two years (where he or she does not) respectively; desertion could be deleted.

3.17 The Scottish Law Commission shared our concern at the over-emphasis on fault within the current system, and at the bitterness and hostility which can result. In their view, reducing the separation periods would solve most of the problems.[28] In Scotland this may well be so. In 1988, the number of divorces granted for two years'

---

[21] Para. 2.2 above.
[22] Appendix D, Tables 17, 18.
[23] *Ibid.*
[24] Law Com. No. 170, paras. 4.12 and 5.17.
[25] Booth Report, para. 3.2.
[26] Appendix D, Tables 17, 18.
[27] Report on Reform of the Ground for Divorce (1989), Scot. Law Com. No. 116.
[28] *Ibid.*, para. 2.12.

separation slightly exceeded the total number granted for adultery and behaviour.[29] There are probably procedural reasons for this: a simplified procedure is not available in Scotland, as it is here, for all undefended divorces, but only for some separation cases.[30] Although the requirement of formal corroboration has been abolished, it is still necessary to have evidence from someone other than a party to the marriage, except in those same separation cases.[31] Both factors will have increased the attractions of relying on separation, especially for those who want a "civilised" divorce. As the Scottish Law Commission point out, "this is an area where the legal and procedural differences in the two countries could well be important".[32] In England and Wales, however, more than 73% of divorces are based on adultery or behaviour and it is very unlikely that this would change if the separation periods were reduced. Once a client has decided on divorce, he or she wishes to proceed as quickly as possible and legal advisers have become accustomed to using a system which allows them to do so.

3.18 More importantly, our respondents recognised that retaining the present apparently fault-based facts would meet hardly any of the serious criticisms of the present system. Indeed, it would perpetuate the major defects. It encourages the destructive raking up of the past. It often produces considerable feelings of injustice in respondents. It exacerbates bitterness and hostility. It stands in the way of calm and sensible negotiation about what is to happen in the future, in particular for the children. It provides a quick and easy route to divorce which makes no provision for a cooling-off period. For all these reasons, the overwhelming majority of respondents to Facing the Future rejected the present system and supported more fundamental reform. We share their views.

3.19 This is not to say that fault should be completely removed from the system. It may still play a part if it is relevant to a particular issue to be decided between the parties. The arrangements made for the children will be affected if one of the parties has behaved in a way which reflects adversely upon his or her capabilities as a parent. The adjustment of the parties' property and finances generally depends upon their respective needs and resources, the needs of their children, and the fair sharing of the assets accumulated between them. But if one has behaved so much more badly than the other that it would be inequitable to ignore this, it will be taken into account.[33] We do not suggest that this should be a frequent occurrence, for we agree with our predecessors' views that the courts "cannot reasonably be expected to apportion responsibility in any save exceptional cases".[34] But the principle is now well-settled and was confirmed by Parliament after prolonged consultation and debate only six years ago.[35] It has the merit of enabling the court to consider the conduct of *both* parties, in a way which the present ground for divorce does not. In this context, it may have a part to play which is genuinely relevant to the matters at issue, and could well supply a practical reinforcement of the underlying moral principles involved, which using it as an artificial test of breakdown does not.

(ii) *Separation*

3.20 Divorce after a fixed minimum period of living apart was put forward in Facing the Future as one of the two most realistic options for reform.[36] It had been advocated by the Family Law Sub-Committee of the Law Society in their 1979 paper *A Better Way Out*. It is also the law in both Australia and New Zealand, countries with considerable legal and cultural similarities to England and Wales and comparable rates of marriage

---

[29] *Hansard* (H.C.), 14 June 1990, Written Answers, col. 347.

[30] The Act of Sederunt (Rules of Court Amendment No. 6) (Simplified Divorce Procedure) 1982, S.I. 1982/1679 (S.181) applies to separation cases where there are no children under 16, no application for financial provision, no other proceedings, and neither party is mentally disordered.

[31] Civil Evidence (Scotland) Act 1988, ss.1(1) and 8(3), (4); Evidence in Divorce Actions (Scotland) Order 1989, S.I. 1989/582 (S.67).

[32] Scot. Law Com. No. 116, para. 3.7.

[33] MCA, s.25(2)(g); e.g. *Kyte* v. *Kyte* [1988] Fam. 145.

[34] Law Com. No. 112, para. 37.

[35] Matrimonial and Family Proceedings Act 1984, Part II, largely based on the Law Commission's Report on The Financial Consequences of Divorce (1981), Law Com. No. 112.

[36] Law Com. No. 170, para. 6.3.

breakdown and divorce.[37] The advantages identified on consultation were as follows. It avoids the problems associated with the retention of fault. It provides solid evidence of a breakdown in the marital relationship. It restrains hasty or rash petitioning and ensures that the parties have experienced what life apart will be like. It also provides an opportunity to reflect upon the children's best interests and to explore the possibility of reconciliation. The social and emotional processes of separation and "letting go" can take place separately from the legal process. By the time that the legal process begins, the practical issues and even their solutions should have become apparent in most cases, so that the likelihood of costly legal battles should be diminished.

3.21 As this was one of the two proposals which we thought most realistic as replacements for the present law, we asked respondents to our public opinion survey to consider it in more detail. In particular, we asked whether they would approve of a fixed period of separation as the sole ground for divorce. It emerged that 52% would approve, while 28% would not.[38] It was less popular amongst younger, single or divorced people, and it was they who mostly preferred a shorter period of separation, such as six months. But approval for this model was considerably less than for the third model, of divorce after a period of consideration and reflection.[39]

3.22 Most of the respondents to Facing the Future who commented on the separation option specifically rejected it. These included the Law Society and all the other lawyers' organisations who responded to us; the Church of England Board for Social Responsibility and the Mothers' Union; and the main voluntary organisations helping divorced and separated parents. A major problem with separation as a ground for divorce is that it discriminates against lower income families, especially women with dependent children, who for purely financial reasons cannot arrange to live apart without either the co-operation of the other spouse or an order from the court. This is already a criticism of the present law[40] and would be much worse if separation were to become the sole ground for divorce. As was pointed out in Facing the Future, the result might well be an increase in ouster applications under the Matrimonial Homes Act 1983, in which the conduct of the parties remains an important factor.[41]

3.23 Respondents also agreed that the possibility of living in two separate households under the same roof[42] is scarcely practicable or desirable in many homes. In practice it requires the co-operation of both spouses. It produces a highly artificial situation; both the National Children's Bureau and the National Council for One-Parent Families thought that it would increase hostility and cause further distress to children. Some respondents also drew attention to the increased risk of perjury which would stem from insisting upon a period of separation before bringing proceedings. In practice, as the Law Society pointed out, there is no way of verifying the parties' statement that they have been living apart for the requisite period.

3.24 In reality, therefore, this model would be unlikely to provide much of an obstacle to those determined and agreed upon a speedy divorce. But it would undoubtedly make divorce very much more difficult for those who are able to rely upon adultery or behaviour at present. Some of these are, of course, disguised consensual divorces. Others are almost "put-up jobs" acquiesced in but not consented to by the respondent. But also amongst them, perhaps in a majority,[43] are the most needy and deserving of the present petitioners, including the victims of prolonged marital violence or persistent infidelity, and parents who wish to protect their children from serious abuse.

3.25 The separation option would therefore only be practicable if it were combined,

---

[37] The divorce rate in New Zealand in 1986 was (provisionally) 11.88 per thousand existing marriages, while in England and Wales it was 12.9; Judicial Statistics 1986, Part A, Section 1, Table 1 (New Zealand); O.P.C.S., *Marriage and Divorce Statistics 1988*, (1990), Table 2.1. The rate in England and Wales was 12.7 in 1987 and 12.8 in 1988.

[38] Appendix D, Tables 19A and 19B; 20% were undecided.

[39] See para. 3.34 below.

[40] See para. 2.12 above.

[41] Law Com. No. 170, para. 5.13.

[42] See para. 2.1, n. 6, above.

[43] Violence was mentioned in 64% of behaviour petitions examined in our court record study; Appendix C, para. 47.

as indeed it is in Australia and New Zealand, with the power to deal with all the ancillary matters, which at present are normally dealt with only after the decree nisi, during the period of separation. Otherwise, the hardship and uncertainty suffered by some petitioners and their children would be a great deal worse than they already are. If this is so, the difference between this option and the next becomes very small.

(iii) *Consideration and Reflection*

3.26 The final model discussed in Facing the Future[44] treated the grant of a divorce, not as a separate event, but as part of a process of facing up to and resolving its practical, social and emotional consequences over a period of time. A divorce would be granted only after a fixed period, not necessarily of separation, but for consideration, both of the alternatives and of the practical consequences involved. This model shares many of the advantages of divorce after a fixed period of separation. It avoids the injustices and other problems associated with the retention of fault. The lapse of a substantial period of time provides solid evidence of a permanent breakdown in the marital relationship. It restrains hasty or rash applications and ensures that the couple have given some consideration to what the future will hold before finally committing themselves to a divorce. It provides an opportunity to reflect upon the children's best interests and to explore the possibility of reconciliation.

3.27 It also avoids two of the major pitfalls associated with insisting on a period of separation. First, the period of consideration could be initiated by a formal statement, which would be officially recorded, that one or both of the parties believed that the marital relationship had broken down. There would then be no scope for pretending that it had begun when in fact it had not. Secondly, the court could have power to deal with the practical questions, the arrangements to be made for the children, the home, and financial support, as well as protection from violence and other forms of molestation, at any time during the period, rather than after it had elapsed. This would avoid the discrimination against the more needy and deserving petitioners involved in requiring them to separate. In practice, of course, few couples would remain together throughout the period but those who wished to do so in the hope of saving their marriage would not be prevented. Only at the end of the period could an application for a divorce be made.

3.28 This option was also overwhelmingly endorsed by the respondents to Facing the Future. These included all the lawyers' organisations in this country who responded to us: the Association of County Court and District Registrars, the staff of Birmingham County Court, the Family Law Bar Association, the Law Society, the Solicitors' Family Law Association, the Institute of Legal Executives, the Children's Legal Centre, and the Christian Lawyers' Action Group. The Law Society, in particular, now preferred this proposal to its earlier recommendations for divorce after a period of separation, for the underlying principles were the same. Support also came from the main professional groups concerned with helping families going through the problems of marital breakdown and separation, specifically Relate Marriage Guidance, the National Family Conciliation Council, the Family Meditators' Association, and the Association of Chief Officers of Probation (who head the divorce court welfare service); the two principal self-help groups for divorced and separated parents, Gingerbread and the National Council for One-Parent Families; and the major children's charities, Barnardo's, The Children's Society and the National Children's Bureau. The Church of England Board for Social Responsibility thought the concept attractive and worthy of further consideration and there was support from a number of other religious bodies, including the Mother's Union, the National Board for Catholic Women and the Board of Deputies of British Jews. We were also told that it would receive support from members of other religious faiths whose traditional approach to divorce has been rather different from that of English law.

3.29 Several features particularly commended themselves to respondents. One was the recognition that divorce is not a single event but a social, psychological and only incidentally a legal process, which takes place over a period of time. Relate Marriage Guidance considered that acknowledging the time people need to adapt emotionally, socially and psychologically to their new circumstances could have far reaching—and

---

[44] Law Com. No. 170, paras. 5.22–5.52.

beneficial—effects, not only for the parties and their children, but also for any new families formed through re-marriage. It is thought that one reason why so many re-marriages fail is the unresolved legal and emotional legacy of the first.[45]

3.30 Another advantage emphasised was the encouragement given to focus upon the practical consequences of separation and divorce and to work these out *before* rather than after the divorce itself. Several respondents, including Relate, the Law Society, and the Association of Chief Officers of Probation, believed that the encouragement to look to the future instead of attacking the past would foster constructive rather than destructive attitudes towards the practical issues. The removal of the need to allege fault should reduce the temptation to adopt hostile and adversarial positions in the parties' discussions. This was seen as an incentive for the parties to recognise and meet their responsibilities towards the family, and therefore as a protection for the children and the financially weaker party. The financial position of the weaker spouse would also be improved by the power to make orders during this period. The period itself would assist in negotiations by providing a clear beginning and end to the process.

3.31 The potential for the increased use of conciliation and mediation, in order to resolve practical issues in a more constructive atmosphere, was also favoured, not only by professionals who are currently engaged in conciliation or mediation, including the Association of Chief Officers of Probation, the National Family Conciliation Council, and the Family Mediators' Association, but also by the legal profession and many others. One advantage seen was that the parties could set their own pace for the proceedings, giving time for a person who was less ready to cope emotionally, rather than progress at a pace dictated by one of them. The more constructive environment which this proposal would bring to the provision of counselling services was also welcomed by many respondents, including Relate Marriage Guidance.

3.32 Several features were thought likely to increase rather than decrease the chances of reconciliation. First was the removal of the need to separate or allege fault, with all the accompanying stigma and bitterness. Second was the encouragement to work out the practical consequences of a divorce before committing themselves to it. Third was the period of time itself, which would prevent hasty divorces and discourage people from rushing into remarriage. One respondent thought that it might even be sufficiently onerous to act as a deterrent to divorce itself.

3.33 Finally, it was thought that all these features would foster more constructive and co-operative attitudes towards the children's future and reduce the damage which they can suffer from prolonged uncertainty and hostility.

3.34 This model therefore received very substantial support from a wide variety of quarters. There is also good reason to believe from our public opinion survey that it would be acceptable to the general public. 87% of respondents to our public opinion survey thought a model along these lines might be "acceptable", but as we have already explained,[46] that was alongside other models. More importantly, it was approved as the sole ground for divorce by 67% and disapproved by 15%,[47] an "acceptability" rate well above that for separation as the sole ground for divorce. If the law is to be reformed, as respondents to Facing the Future clearly thought that it should, then this is evidently the model to be preferred.

3.35 However, there was understandable concern among some of our respondents about the details of how it would work in practice. We shall discuss those details further in Part V; but we should point out here the central features which were implicit, or in some cases explicit, in the support which it received. First, a substantial period of time should be required to elapse, in order to demonstrate quite clearly that the marriage has irretrievably broken down. There can be no better proof of this than that one or both parties to the marriage have stated their belief that their marital relationship has broken down and that either or both of them persist in that belief after the lapse of a considerable period. This must be longer than the present interval between petition and

---

[45] This point was also made by the National Campaign for the Family, *op. cit.*, p. 9.
[46] Appendix D, Tables 17, 18; see para. 3.21 above.
[47] *Ibid.*, Tables 20A and 20B.

decree, which is six months or less in a substantial proportion of cases.[48] It must also give the parties a realistic time-scale within which, in the great majority of cases, the practical questions about the children, the home and the finances can be properly resolved. It must avoid rushing them towards a resolution of those issues, so that they can go at their own pace and draw back if they wish. It must discourage hasty and ill-thought-out applications. In our view, an overall period of one year would be required to achieve all these objectives. We shall return to this point in more detail in Part V.[49]

3.36 Secondly, there should be an orderly but unhurried procedural timetable during the period, for the exchange of information and proposals, the negotiation of those matters which can be resolved by agreement, and the adjudication of those which cannot, together with the possibility of making orders to have effect during the period, and of extending it where matters have not been properly resolved.

3.37 Many respondents also attached particular importance to the provision of adequate counselling and conciliation services during this time. The National Campaign for the Family,[50] for example, argued that there should be professionally monitored counselling and conciliation services available in all localities, with trained staff and a firm funding base. As we explain in more detail later,[51] counselling and conciliation are two very different things: counselling may either help a couple who wish to try to save their marriage or give support to one or both of them, or to a child, who is suffering particular trauma or distress from the breakdown of a marriage which cannot be saved. Conciliation or mediation provide a neutral figure who helps both parties to negotiate an agreed solution to the issues concerning their children, and sometimes their property and finances, which will have to be resolved if the divorce proceeds. It was considered important that both such services should be available for all couples (and their children) who want them and that opportunties to make use of them should be built into the procedure itself.

3.38 We share our respondents' views of the importance of both counselling and conciliation services. Indeed, we think this just as great whether or not the law of divorce is to be changed. Similarly, we would consider our proposals a great improvement upon the present law, whether or not more resources were to be made available for these services; but there is no doubt that, just as our proposals would provide a much more constructive and less damaging context for both counselling and conciliation to be successful, so would our proposals greatly benefit from increased provision for them. We say this because we believe that it is by the provision of these services, to the people who want and need them, that the most harmful emotional, social and psychological effects of marital breakdown and divorce can best be avoided or mitigated. The law and legal processes cannot do this, although they can, and at present do, make matters worse. The law's processes are principally designed to adjudicate disputes and to oblige people to meet their financial and legal liabilities. This is an important element in the model which we propose.

3.39 There were of course some respondents who specifically rejected this model. It is necessary, therefore, both to explain their objections and if possible to attempt to meet them.

3.40 Some objections centred round the removal of fault from the ground for divorce. Two different types of advantage are claimed for retaining fault. The first is that it provides a moral base for conduct within marriage. The main difficulty with this is that, logically, it can only be done by returning to a system based wholly on fault. The present mixed system of fault and no-fault "grounds" is, as the authors of *Putting Asunder* recognised in 1966,[52] incapable of supplying a coherent and consistent moral base. As we have already pointed out,[53] there is no serious call for a return to a wholly fault-based system. Furthermore, granting or withholding the divorce itself is an inappropriate and ineffective sanction against marital misbehaviour; the real and

---

[48] See further in Appendix C, paras. 8–12, and O.P.C.S., *Marriage and Divorce Statistics 1988*, (1990), Table 4.8.

[49] See paras. 5.25–5.28.

[50] *Op. cit.*, p. 10.

[51] Paras. 5.19 *et seq.*

[52] *Op. cit.*, para. 69.

[53] Paras. 3.6 and 3.7 above.

effective sanction is the unwanted breakdown of the marriage. Conduct still has a part to play in determining the practical consequences of that breakdown.

3.41 Secondly, it is argued that the retention of fault provides a public affirmation of "guilt" and "innocence" within the marriage which enables the innocent party to feel vindicated in his or her decision to end it. This is an important psychological point. However, one of the difficulties with the whole concept of divorce for fault is that it assumes that fault is the only possible justification for divorce. People who hold this belief, whether for religious or other reasons, may well need to feel that they are morally justified in what they have done. Unfortunately for them, experience has shown the law cannot accurately allocate moral blameworthiness, for there are always two sides to every marital history and different people assess these in different ways; nor do the great majority of divorcing couples want it to do so. They may wish that something could have been done to stop the other spouse behaving as he or she did, or even for the other to be publicly branded in some way, but they shrink from the detailed examination of their marital lives which would necessarily be involved in making a proper assessment in every case.[54] The human as well as the financial costs in making the attempt would be enormous. If that is so, then the sometimes (although obviously not invariably) inaccurate allocation which takes place at present is itself morally wrong, quite apart from the other problems it can cause.

3.42 Another objection was that this model amounts to divorce by unilateral demand, albeit not immediately. This is the inevitable consequence of any system based on irretrievable breakdown of the marriage, including the present one. The present law expressly provides for unilateral divorce after five years' separation, and 71% of respondents to our public opinion survey thought this period too long.[55] In practice, it also provides for divorce by unilateral demand a great deal more quickly, because of the practical and legal problems of defending a petition based on behaviour or, sometimes, adultery.

3.43 It is also the case that this model does not supply an opportunity for one spouse to contest the other's allegation that the marriage has broken down. There are many divorces where one party believes that the marriage can be saved. Sometimes both may do so. Contests in court, however, cannot be the way to do this. As the Booth Committee observed, "The court itself discourages defended divorce not only because of the futility of trying a contention by one party that the marriage has not broken down despite the other party's conviction that it has, but also because of the emotional and financial demands that it makes upon the parties themselves and the possible harmful consequences for the children of the family".[56] A reasonably long period of delay, where each party has every opportunity to reflect upon the position and explore the alternatives, coupled with the availability of counselling services if need be, and the removal of the necessity to make damaging allegations against one another, stand a better chance of helping those marriages which can and should be preserved.

3.44 However, it is one thing to accept that the marriage has irretrievably broken down once one party has become convinced, after a considerable period of delay, that it has done so. It is another thing to conclude that that person should "be able to switch resources to a new family"[57] irrespective of the hardship caused to the first. Under the present law, it is possible to resist a divorce, although only if based on five years' separation, on the ground that the divorce will cause the respondent grave financial or other hardship. In the vast majority of marriages, of course, it is the break-up and separation which cause the hardship, rather than the divorce as such. However, it would be both possible and logical to combine this model with such a hardship bar, if this were considered appropriate. We shall therefore return to this point in Part V.[58]

3.45 On the other hand, there were some respondents who objected that this model would in fact make divorce more difficult, particularly for couples who are agreed upon

---

[54] Davis and Murch, op. cit., p. 49, found very few cases where both parties agreed that one of them (i.e. the same one in each case) was responsible for the breakdown.
[55] Appendix D, Tables 15, 16.
[56] Booth Report, para. 2.16.
[57] Oppenheimer, op. cit., p. 74.
[58] See paras. 5.72–5.77 below.

divorce and for petitioners who need a speedy decree for other reasons. Both groups would, however, be catered for by the availability of ancillary remedies at the outset, so that all they have to wait for is the decree itself, with its consequent permission to remarry. While we appreciate that there are young and childless couples who realise early in their marriage that they have made a mistake, it does not seem unduly intrusive to require a period of delay before granting what is, in effect, a licence to remarry.[59]

Easier or harder?

3.46 This debate indicates quite clearly how impossible it is to characterise any particular divorce system as "too easy" or "too difficult". "Easy" may mean short or painless, whereas "hard" may mean long or painful. For some, the model we are recommending might provide "easier" divorce, in that they would not have to separate for years before proceeding; for others, for example most of those who now rely on adultery or behaviour, it would be "harder" because they would have to wait for longer than they do at present. For some, it might be "easier", because they would no longer, justly or unjustly, be branded the wrongdoer; for others, it might be harder, because they would have to disclose their financial circumstances and confront their responsibilities towards their families before they could obtain a decree.

3.47 The emotional pain which many people feel at the breakdown of their marriages is not necessarily linked in any way to the ease or difficulty of the legal process. Divorce is almost always painful for their children, but if there is to be a divorce at all, the system should certainly try to make it as easy for them as it can. This was the unanimous view of all those organisations whose principal concern is the welfare of children. They supported the model we recommend as a considerable improvement from the child's point of view, not only upon the present law but on any alternative model which be proposed.

Conclusion

3.48 For all these reasons, we therefore *recommend*:

(i) that irretrievable breakdown of the marriage should remain the sole ground for divorce; and

(ii) that such breakdown should be established by the expiry of a minimum period of one year for consideration of the practical consequences which would result from a divorce and reflection upon whether the breakdown in the marital relationship is irreparable.

---

[59] See also paras. 5.62–5.65 below.

PART IV

EFFECT OF OTHER MATRIMONIAL REMEDIES

4.1 In Part V we shall discuss the details of our recommendations for obtaining a divorce, that is an order bringing the marriage to an end. There are, however, two other matrimonial remedies which depend in part upon the same grounds. These are decrees of judicial separation, granted by the divorce courts, and orders for financial provision, made by magistrates' domestic courts. We must therefore consider the impact of our recommendations on the ground for divorce upon these other two remedies.

Judicial separation

Background

4.2 A decree of judicial separation is the successor to the old ecclesiastical courts' decree of divorce *a mensa et thoro*, which was the only release from marriage available from the courts until 1857.[1] It releases husband and wife from the duty to live together but effects no change of status. Thus neither is free to remarry and the survivor will be the widow or widower of the deceased, which will often be important for pension purposes. However, if either spouse dies intestate, the estate devolves as if the other spouse were already dead.[2] On making a decree of judicial separation, the court has power to make the same orders relating to the children and for financial provision and property adjustment as it has on divorce.[3]

4.3 Under section 17(1) of the Matrimonial Causes Act 1973, the court has power to grant a decree of judicial separation upon proof of one of the five facts which is required to establish irretrievable breakdown for the purpose of obtaining a divorce.[4] Thus the method of proof of breakdown for the purpose of obtaining a decree of divorce is itself the ground for obtaining a decree of judicial separation. There is a single decree, rather than a decree nisi which is later made absolute, as there is in divorce.

4.4 A decree of judicial separation may be obtained within the first year of marriage, whereas a petition for divorce cannot be presented until a year has elapsed from the date of the marriage.[5] This absolute ban replaced an earlier ban on petitioning within three years of the marriage, unless certain exceptional circumstances could be shown.[6]

4.5 Although proof of one of the five facts for the purpose of a decree of judicial separation may later be used as proof of irretrievable breakdown so as to obtain a divorce, the whole divorce procedure must be gone through from the beginning, and the court must have evidence from the petitioner.[7] There is thus no automatic procedure for conversion and a consequent duplication of legal and other costs.

4.6 If our recommendation that the five facts be abolished for the purpose of obtaining a divorce is accepted, it would obviously be anomalous to retain them for the purpose of judicial separation. The question therefore arises whether judicial separation should be retained as a separate remedy at all and, if so, how it might be reformed to parallel our recommended reforms in divorce.

4.7 Judicial separation has been the subject of two research studies[8] which focussed on the reasons for its use. At the time of this research, a divorce petition could not be

---

[1] Dissolution of marriage by judicial decree was first introduced by the Matrimonial Causes Act 1857. Before then, couples could be divorced by private Act of Parliament, of which there were approximately 325 in all; see R. Phillips, *op. cit.*, pp. 227–241; S. Anderson, "Legislative Divorce—Law for the Aristocracy?", in G.R. Rubin and D. Sugarman (eds.), *Law, Economy and Society, Essays in the History of English Law, 1750–1914*, (1984); S. Wolfram "Divorce in England 1700–1857", (1984) 5 Ox. J.L.S. 155.

[2] MCA, s.18(2).

[3] MCA, ss.21–24A.

[4] Para. 2.1 above.

[5] MCA, s.3.

[6] Matrimonial and Family Proceedings Act 1984, s.1, amending MCA, s.3, as recommended by the Law Commission in its Report on Time Restrictions on Presentation of Divorce and Nullity Petitions (1982), Law Com. No. 116.

[7] See MCA, s.4(1), (2).

[8] P.A. Garlick, "Judicial Separation: A Research Study", (1983) 46 M.L.R. 719 and S. Maidment, *Judicial Separation—A Research Study*, (1982).

presented within three years of the marriage, except in cases of exceptional depravity in the respondent or exceptional hardship for the petitioner.[9] Many petitions for judicial separation were presented within the first three years of marriage and were subsequently converted into divorces. Other reasons for petitioning, however, included religious or conscientious objections to divorce; leaving the door open to reconciliation, as of course this decree does not finally dissolve the marriage; and preservation of pension rights. One solicitor referred to it as the "older person's remedy".

4.8 After the three year bar was reduced to one year in 1984, the number of petitions fell quite sharply, but now appears to have levelled off somewhat; in 1989, there were 2,741 petitions and 1,678 decrees, in contrast to the 7,430 and 4,852 respectively in 1983.[10] Thus, compared with divorce, where there were 184,610 petitions and 150,477 decrees absolute in 1989, this remedy is relatively little used and more than a third of petitions do not proceed to a decree.

4.9 Taking these figures together with the fact that one of the research studies found that a very high proportion of parties later proceeded to divorce,[11] it might be argued that it is not necessary to retain the remedy at all. This was the view taken in Australia when their divorce law was reformed by the Family Law Act 1975. More recently, the Scottish Law Commission have provisionally recommended its absolution as a preliminary to the codification of Scottish family law.[12] Earlier reviews in this country, while recommending its retention, have tended to regard it as an unsatisfactory limbo between marriage and divorce.[13]

4.10 However, the few respondents to Facing the Future who commented on judicial separation all thought that it ought to be preserved, for those couples who had not been married for one year or who had religious, conscientious or other objections to divorce. The Law Society's Family Law Committee reached the same conclusion in 1979.[14] While we understand that most religions which are opposed to divorce also draw a distinction between civil and religious divorce, to abolish this remedy would mean there was no choice. Couples who neither wanted nor needed to divorce in order to re-arrange their lives would be obliged to do so, sometimes against conscience, purely in order the obtain the type of ancillary relief not available in the magistrates' courts or under section 27 of the Matrimonial Causes Act.[15] This cannot be right. It would increase the hardship caused to older spouses, especially wives, whose husbands were unable to compensate them for the loss of pension rights or other benefits flowing from marriage or widowhood. A choice must be available, even if only a small proportion of couples choose this remedy.

4.11 We therefore *recommend* that judicial separation remain available as an alternative to divorce.

The ground

4.12 Some alternative therefore must be found to the five "facts" which are at present grounds for judicial separation. All the criticisms of those facts,[16] particularly those which are fault-based, must apply equally to judicial separation; their continued existence could only serve to undermine the recommended reform of the law of divorce; nor are they conducive to reconciliation, which is stated to be one of the attractions of judicial separation, compared with divorce, for some people.[17]

---

[9] See para. 4.4, above.

[10] *Judicial Statistics, Annual Report 1989*, (1990) Cm. 1154, Tables 5.1, 5.2 and 5.3.

[11] Maidment, *op. cit.*, para. 3.6.

[12] Scottish Law Commission, Discussion Paper No. 85, *Family Law: Pre-consolidation Reforms* (1990), paras. 7.1–7.8.

[13] Report of the Royal Commission on Divorce and Matrimonial Causes (the Gorell Report) (1912), Cd. 6478; Report of the Royal Commission on Marriage and Divorce (the Morton Report) (1956), Cmd. 9678.

[14] *A Better Way Out*, paras. 194 and 195.

[15] Magistrates' domestic courts may award lump sums of up to £1,000 at a time and periodical payments of any amount; the higher courts may award unlimited lump sums, and secured or unsecured periodical payments, under MCA, s.27. Orders for the adjustment or sale of property, under MCA, ss.24 and 24A, however, and orders for the transfer of tenancies under the Matrimonial Homes Act 1983, s.7 and Sched. 1, can only be made on divorce, nullity or judicial separation.

[16] Paras. 2.7 *et seq.* above.

[17] Maidment, Garlick, *op. cit.*

4.13 It may be argued that, as judicial separation is not concerned with the dissolution of the marriage, it would be inappropriate to base such decrees on irretrievable breakdown. The reality, however, is that in the vast majority of cases the marital relationship is at an end. As the Commission stated in 1969 "... [separation] ends the obligation to live together and almost invariably denotes the death of the marriage".[18] In practice, when dealing with the ancillary consequences of a decree, it appears that the courts do treat judicial separation as if it represented a final breakdown.[19] In reality, therefore, adopting the same ground for judicial separation as that for divorce would not act as a deterrent to reconciliation: reconciliations certainly take place after divorce petitions have been filed and even between decree nisi and absolute. It is more likely that retention and use of fault-based grounds would deter reconciliation than would adoption of the breakdown ground. Alternatively, it could be argued that there is no need for any ground at all, as the main object is to achieve a re-ordering of the couple's affairs. However, as this re-ordering involves the possibly compulsory adjustment of the parties' property rights, there is value in requiring a clear indication that their relationship is at an end. It would be a radical step, going far beyond the scope of this exercise, to introduce what would be, in effect, a power to re-arrange a couple's property from time to time.

4.14 We therefore *recommend* that irretrievable breakdown of the marriage become the ground for judicial separation, as it is for divorce.

Procedure and proof of breakdown

4.15 If irretrievable breakdown becomes the ground, it should be proved in the same way as for a divorce, that is by requiring a period of time for consideration and reflection. The consequences of marital breakdown are manifold and potentially just as serious, irrespective of whether a divorce or separation is granted. The parties should therefore be encouraged to consider them in just the same way. Given that petitions or decrees of judicial separation often lead to divorce within a relatively short period of time, and that the types of orders which may be obtained in relation to the children, finance or property are identical, it seems that parties and their children would benefit from time to reflect and encouragement to focus upon the practical arrangements to be made. One of the respondents who commented on this remedy, the Law Society suggested assimilation of the procedures for judicial separation with those for divorce.

4.16 We therefore *recommend* that the procedure for obtaining a judicial separation be the same as for divorce, and subject to the same period of consideration and reflection, namely one year. As at present, it should remain possible for the period to begin within the first year of marriage and for the order to be made immediately the period has elapsed.

4.17 In recommending the same overall period, we are conscious of the need to avoid a situation whereby it would be possible to obtain a divorce more quickly and simply, without due regard to the consequences, by a back-door route of separation, followed by conversion to divorce.

Integration of divorce and separation procedures

4.18 There is a further advantage in assimilating the grounds and procedures for obtaining a divorce or judicial separation. The process may be initiated in the same way for both, by a formal statement that the marital relationship has broken down. But the choice of which remedy to seek may be made at a much later stage. Thus a spouse or a couple who made an initial statement would not thereby be committed to the finality of divorce, or to a procedure which can have a "roller-coaster" effect, developing its own momentum irrespective of the parties' wishes. Further, if during the process of considering the arrangements it appeared to them preferable to seek a separation rather than a divorce, they could do so: for example, because it became apparent that the wife would be seriously disadvantaged by the loss of pension rights for which the husband could not compensate her, or because both recognised that all they wanted was the

---

[18] Family Law: Financial Provision in Matrimonial Proceedings (1969), Law Com. No. 25, para. 65.
[19] Maidment, *op. cit.*, p. 77. However, the requirement to consider a "clean break", contained in MCA, s.25A, does not apply in judicial separation cases.

separation and re-arrangement of their affairs, rather than a permanent change of status.

4.19 We therefore *recommend* that the procedures for divorce and separation be integrated into a single system. To preserve the present position, however, no divorce could be granted until a total of two years after the marriage, that is the current one year bar, together with the one year period for consideration and reflection. In consequence, the detailed description of the procedure, in Part V, should apply equally to separation. We also recommend a procedure for converting a separation order into a divorce, which is dealt with at paragraphs 5.86 and 5.87 below.

Financial Provision in Magistrates' Courts
Background

4.20 Magistrates' courts have power under section 2 of the Domestic Proceedings and Magistrates' Courts Act 1978[20] to make unsecured periodical payments orders and lump sum orders for a party to the marriage or a child of the family provided that one of the grounds set out in section 1 has been made out.[21] These grounds are:

(a) that the respondent has failed to provide reasonable maintenance for the applicant;

(b) that the respondent has failed to provide, or to make a proper contribution towards, reasonable maintenance for any child of the family;

(c) that the respondent has behaved in such a way that the applicant cannot reasonably be expected to live with the respondent; and

(d) that the respondent has deserted the applicant.

4.21 Facing the Future did not invite comments on whether the grounds for financial provision in magistrates' courts should be brought into line with any proposed changes to the ground for divorce. However, it was put to us[22] that, as the current grounds mirror the facts which can be used to establish irretrievable breakdown for divorce, the grounds should continue to do so in future.

4.22 One of the broad objectives of the Law Commission's recommendations, which resulted in the Domestic Proceedings and Magistrates' Courts Act 1978, was indeed "to bring the family law administered by the magistrates' courts, so far as can appropriately be done, into line with the law administered by the divorce court".[23] This was not, however, the primary reason for the inclusion of the behaviour and desertion grounds. Behaviour was included to cover the case of a wife who is anxious to leave her husband because of his conduct, but knows that if she does so he would cease to maintain her. The Commission wished to avoid a situation whereby a woman was compelled to continue to live with a husband who was treating her badly for fear that she would be left destitute.[24] Similarly, desertion was included so as to enable a deserted wife whose husband was providing her with reasonable maintenance to obtain an order immediately, without having to wait for him to stop doing so. It was thought that this would enable her to obtain some security against his future failure to maintain her.[25] An additional advantage of including behaviour and desertion was stated to be the preservation of evidence which could later be used in divorce proceedings. This would, of course, no longer be relevant in the context of our recommendations.

4.23 In practice, it is unlikely that either of these grounds is able to provide the degree of security which the Commission envisaged. A woman who is in fear of her husband is unlikely to take the risk of applying for maintenance before she leaves him. Once they are separated, he will either continue to maintain her voluntarily, in which case she should be able to obtain either an agreed order under section 6 of the Act, or eventually a confirmation of voluntary payments order under section 7; or he will cease

---

[20] (DPMCA).

[21] Orders can also be made by consent under s.6 and after a period of voluntary payments while the parties are living apart by agreement under s.7.

[22] By C.T. Latham, O.B.E., a Stipendiary Magistrate for Greater Manchester with great experience in this area of the law.

[23] Report on Matrimonial Proceedings in Magistrates' Courts (1976), Law Com. No. 77, p. 155.

[24] Matrimonial Proceedings in Magistrates' Courts (1973), Working Paper No. 53, para. 39.

[25] Law Com. No. 77, paras. 2.7, 2.9, 2.10.

to do so, in which case she can allege failure to maintain under section 1(a). If there is indeed a need to obtain an order to gain security in advance of such a failure, it is illogical to distinguish between desertion and other reasons for separating. In any event, the availability of income support cannot be ignored in the context of a woman who fears that she may be left destitute. Whatever arrangements may eventually be negotiated or ordered, this is a far more reliable immediate safety net than any court-based procedure could ever be.

4.24 It is not known how many marriages in respect of which financial orders are made by magistrates later proceed to divorce. Undoubtedly quite a number do so. It seems undesirable that cases which might later proceed to the divorce court should have started off by one of the parties alleging fault. This could undermine the objectives of the proposed reforms for divorce. When the divorce court comes to deal with children and financial matters during the period for consideration and reflection, it is unlikely that a husband will forget that his wife has already made a number of allegations in court about his behaviour. This could also serve to undermine the effectiveness of any attempts at conciliation or mediation.

4.25 A further factor which should not be ignored is that an application to a magistrates' court leaves the door open to reconciliation. However unlikely this may be in many cases, it is even more desirable than it is in divorce to seek so far as possible to minimise the bitterness and conflict between them, so as to preserve the possibility of an amicable and peaceful resumption of cohabitation.

4.26 Finally, it is worth bearing in mind the findings of earlier research that the magistrates' jurisidiction is predominantly the resort of the poor.[26] This may now have changed, particularly since the introduction of agreed orders under section 6 of the 1978 Act, but the law should seek to avoid giving the impression of "one law for the rich and another for the poor" which has for so long been a criticism of our matrimonial procedures.

Conclusion

4.27 In our view, the power to make an order on the ground of failure to provide reasonable maintenance, together with the power to make an agreed order,[27] and the power to make an order where the parties have been living apart for three months and one party has been voluntarily paying maintenance to the other or for a child of the family,[28] would cover all the practical requirements of those who are likely to use this jurisdiction. Any short intervening period where maintenance is either not being paid, or is below subsistence level, will be covered by income support or family credit. There is separate legal machinery available to the Department of Social Security to recover income support from a liable relative.[29] It is therefore unlikely that any person would be left destitute as a result of a reform in the grounds for obtaining a financial provision order in the magistrates' court.

4.28 We therefore *recommend* the abolition of the separate grounds of behaviour and desertion, and accordingly that section 1(c) and section 1(d) of the Domestic Proceedings and Magistrates' Courts Act 1978 should be repealed. Further, the power in section 7, to make an order where the parties have been living apart for three months and one has been voluntarily maintaining the other or any child of the family, should no longer be limited to cases where neither has deserted the other but cover all types of separation.[30] The deletion of desertion from sections 1 and 7 would incidentally result in an enormous simplification of family law, for desertion is one of the most complex and technical concepts which it contains.[31]

---

[26] Report of the Committees on One-Parent Families (the Finer Report) (1974), Cmnd. 5629, para. 4.383; the principal evidence was in O.R. McGregor, L. Blom-Cooper and C. Gibson, *Separated Spouses, A Study of the Matrimonial Jurisdiction of Magistrates' Courts*, (1970).

[27] DPMCA, s.6.

[28] DPMCA, s.7; if the amount paid voluntarily is inadequate, the court can treat the case as an application for an order under section 2, s.7(4).

[29] Social Security Act 1986, ss.24, 26; ss.24A and 24B, inserted by the Social Security Act 1990, s.8.

[30] The applicant's conduct can still be taken into account, in deciding whether or not to make an order, by virtue of ss.3(2)(g) and 7(5).

[31] See, e.g. *Rayden and Jackson on Divorce*, 15th Edn. (1988), which devotes 55 pages to desertion, but only 14 to behaviour.

PART V

THE PROCEDURES IN DETAIL

5.1 In considering the detailed procedures of the "process over time", we have been heavily influenced by the general approach and particular recommendations of the Booth Committee on Procedure in Matrimonial Causes.[1] In the Committee's view, "procedural reform should be directed towards helping a couple whose marriage is in crisis to come to terms with the issues and to make informed decisions as to the future ... [The] primary decision-making responsibility should rest with the spouses themselves and ... they should be given all necessary help in deciding for themselves what should happen to their children, their property and their marriage".[2] In this way, the Committee hoped that much contentious litigation would be avoided, for the sake of the parties and their children alike. The Committee were, of course, constrained by the limitations of the present law, which is in many ways inimical to their basic objectives of mitigating the intensity of disputes and promoting the welfare of children. We are able to adopt a more fundamental approach, but we share the Committee's objectives and are extremely grateful for the contribution which they have made to our own proposals.

Terminology

Petition and Petitioner

5.2 The Booth Committee[3] observed that the current form of petition introduces an accusatorial tone to the proceedings at the outset and uses archaic wording reminiscent of its ecclesiastical origins. It also has strong associations with the concepts of matrimonial offence, collusion and condonation. The use of petitioner and respondent in the title adds to the impression of proceedings between an innocent and a guilty party. It may even colour the approach to ancillary relief, by suggesting that one is more deserving than the other. The Committee suggested that a change in terminology, to avoid the use of the terms "petition" and "petitioner", would reflect the fundamental change from the concept of the matrimonial offence to the concept of irretrievable breakdown, which is taken one stage further in our present recommendations. This would help to remove the misconception that one of the objects of divorce proceedings is to apportion blame.

5.3 We agree with all of these observations and consequently *recommend* that a divorce or separation be sought, rather than "prayed" for, by application rather than petition. Wherever possible parties should be referred to as "husband" and "wife", with use of applicant and respondent only where it is essential to distinguish which of the spouses is seeking relief. We *recommend* that where it is necessary to use a title this should be "In the matter of the marriage of" with the full names of the spouses following. As in Australia, cases should be reported as, for example, *Smith and Smith* instead of *Smith versus Smith*.

Decree

5.4 Although the Booth Committee were unable to question the appropriateness of the use of "decree" to dissolve a marriage, we consider that a divorce "order" would be more consistent with the use of an application instead of a petition. Decree follows from the fact that dissolution is prayed for in a petition and is no less a legacy of the ecclesiastical courts than is "petition". We *recommend* accordingly.

Judicial separation

5.5 We see no reason why the terminology for separation should not follow that of divorce and *recommend* accordingly.

5.6 It is also necessary to consider the use of the term "judicial". Although the order

---

[1] Booth Report (1985); Consultation Paper (1983). The Law Commission had recommended such a review in its Report on The Financial Consequences of Divorce (1981), Law Com. No. 112, paras. 13–15, in part because it was thought that adversarial procedures contributed to the feelings of bitterness and injustice engendered by the courts' financial orders.

[2] Para. 3.2.

[3] Para. 4.3.

will still be made in a court, it would be helpful to avoid any implication that this by itself will be a matter for judicial decision. We therefore *recommend* that "separation order" be substituted.

Neutral separation or divorce order

5.7 We also *recommend*, as did the Booth Committee,[4] that an order should be in a neutral form, simply stating that the marriage of named spouses has been dissolved, or that the named spouses are separated.

Initiation of the period of consideration and reflection

5.8 Initiation of this period should be regarded as a serious step and we therefore *recommend* that it should involve the making and lodging of a formal statement.

The statement of marital breakdown

5.9 We *recommend* that the statement take the form of a document stating that the maker, or makers, believe that the marital relationship has broken down. This form of wording places a greater personal responsibility on initiators by requiring them to express a view about the state of their relationship rather than merely recite a statutory ground which may bear no resemblance to what they are thinking or feeling. They should not, however, be required at this stage to state that the breakdown is irreparable. One of the purposes of the period itself is to test this out and the parties should not be encouraged to reach a final conclusion at the outset.

Joint and sole statements

5.10 We also *recommend* that it should be possible for the parties to make such a statement jointly. This reflects the recommendations of the Booth Committee,[5] who were anxious to move away from the adversarial and pejorative connotations of the law's present insistence that there be one "petitioner" and one "respondent". This is difficult to avoid if fault-based facts are retained, but if they are not it should present no problem. Where both spouses are agreed that their relationship has broken down, their joint acknowledgement of this should help considerably towards the amicable resolution of the practical matters involved and to avoid unnecessary bitterness between them. It will also reflect the widespread view revealed in our public opinion survey[6] that couples should be able to dissolve their marriages by agreement.

5.11 If the spouses are not agreed, then one should make the statement which would then be sent to the other. Once the period has been initiated in this way, however, it should be open to either spouse to apply for a separation or divorce at the end of it.[7] This again would avoid the adversarial connotations of one spouse proceeding *against* the other and allow both to participate as equals in the processes of negotiation and consideration of the eventual arrangements. Considerable injustice might otherwise be done to the spouse who did not make the initial statement, but who came to terms with the other's decision and co-operated fully in making the necessary arrangements, only to find that the other withdrew at the last moment. It would also emphasise to the sole initiator the importance of the step being taken, in that matters would no longer be wholly within his or her control. This is a considerable source of grievance in the present law, which allows so much power to the spouse who happens to be petitioner. Both parties would be in exactly the same position and entitled to the same remedies and also to the same protection.[8]

In or out of court?

5.12 One reason for preferring a formal period of consideration and reflection, rather than a period of separation, is that the date when it begins can be recorded by a public authority, with no room for the parties either to lie or to dispute it.[9] The statement should therefore be made to and lodged at some public office. There is much to be said

---

[4] Para. 4.107.

[5] Para. 4.10.

[6] Appendix D, Tables 17, 18.

[7] See para. 5.71 below.

[8] In particular, the power to seek an extension of the period in certain circumstances, or to invoke the hardship bar; see paras. 5.56–5.61 and 5.72–5.77 below.

[9] See para. 3.27 above.

for setting up a specialist office for this purpose. It would remove this initial and revocable step from the adversarial, coercive and potentially stigmatising associations of the courts. It would avoid any impression that a formal application for a court order was being made at this stage. Above all, it would provide an opportunity to develop associated information, counselling and conciliation services, which it appears are much better provided away from the formal court structure.[10]

5.13 We have concluded, however, that it would be impracticable to remove even this stage of the procedure from the courts, for several reasons. First, it is important that all the protective remedies which are available at present should continue to be available to those who need them. Many marital breakdowns are quite amicable, but many are not, and some are accompanied by violence or other forms of molestation against which the protection of the courts is required. It may be necessary to decide who is to remain in the matrimonial home during the period. Some financial provision may be needed by either spouse or the children. Secondly, one of the objects of the period is to enable the parties to make proper arrangements for their own future and that of their children. These will usually take the form of court orders, although often by consent. The courts must therefore have power to make such orders during the period, and it follows that they must also have power, in the last resort, to compel the observance of procedural steps, such as attendance at court or filing the necessary documents. As we later recommend,[11] there must also come a point during the period when the court is required to consider the case and give directions for its future conduct. It would be impracticable and time-consuming for the papers to begin in one place and then be transferred at some unpredictable stage to another. Finally, there are several other purposes for which the initiation of the period must be regarded as if it were "proceedings" even though no formal application for relief has yet been made. Principal amongst them is the duty to stay the case if it ought to proceed in another jurisdiction.[12]

5.14 We therefore *recommend* that statements of marital breakdown be made to and lodged at a court.

Formalities

5.15 The precise formalities to be observed in the making and lodging of statements of marital breakdown are matters for subordinate rather than primary legislation. Nevertheless, we consider it important that these are framed with two main objects in mind: first to emphasise the seriousness of the step being taken; and secondly to ensure so far as possible that both spouses understand the nature, purpose and requirements of the period upon which they are embarking, and are fully acquainted with the various types of professional help which may be required and how to obtain it.

5.16 Furthermore, although many people will be legally represented at this stage, the procedure should be designed to cater just as satisfactorily for those who are not. Even under the present procedure, this is a not insignificant proportion.[13] In particular, there are couples who are able to agree upon their own arrangements and who may prefer not to take what may be seen as the hostile step of instructing a lawyer who, of necessity, may act for only one of them. Also, although we have recommended that statements be lodged at a court,[14] they should, so far as possible, be differentiated from the bringing of ordinary civil proceedings by one person against another.

5.17 Accordingly, to meet the first objective in paragraph 5.15 above, we *recommend* that statements of marital breakdown be made on a prescribed form and sworn (or affirmed) in the usual manner before a Commissioner for Oaths or court official. The prescribed form should be so drafted as to emphasise the seriousness of the step being taken and to outline its legal consequences. These are, first, that it sets in motion a

---

[10] University of Newcastle upon Tyne, Conciliation Project Unit, *Report to the Lord Chancellor on the Costs and Effectiveness of Conciliation in England and Wales* (the Newcastle Report), (1989), ch. 20.

[11] Para. 5.50 below.

[12] Domicile and Matrimonial Proceedings Act 1973, s.5(6) and Sched.1.

[13] Our court record study indicated that more than 15% of petitioners may neither be legally represented nor in receipt of legal advice and assistance under the green form scheme; this may, however, be an over-estimate; see Appendix C, paras. 19, 20.

[14] Paras. 5.12–5.14, above.

period during which steps will be taken to consider the arrangements to be made should the breakdown prove irreparable; and secondly, that at the end of the period either party may, should he or she then be of the view that the breakdown is irreparable, apply for a divorce or separation order to be issued. Only in exceptional circumstances can the period be extended or a hardship bar imposed.

5.18 However, making the statement should not be seen merely as the formal initiation of a predominantly legal process. There is as yet no formal application, either for divorce or separation, or for any ancillary relief, before the court.[15] If the period is to be put to good and effective use, it is important that both parties are made aware of the various sources of help available to them and their children during this difficult time. They need to know the differences between marriage guidance, counselling and reconciliation, conciliation and mediation, and divorce counselling.[16] They need to know what services for all of these purposes are available locally and how they may be contacted. In many ways, it would be ideal if statements were to be made in person during an interview with a senior official who could give such explanations in person. It would, however, be quite impracticable to require this in every case. For one thing, it would be impossible to insist on the attendance of both parties in all cases. Further, there are some couples whose marriages have clearly broken down and who have no need of such information or services. There are also circumstances in which they are quite inappropriate.[17] It would be equally inappropriate for such an official to proffer advice or counselling of any sort or to conduct an inquiry into the reasons for the breakdown in the relationship. To do so would be to reintroduce the inquiry into the past which is the major objection to the present law and to confuse the distinct functions of the various professions and services involved. There would also be the risk of deterring the very people who are most in need of the protection of the law.

5.19. However, the court at which the statement is lodged should certainly be under an obligation to provide such information and to assist those people who wish to do so to make contact with the relevant services. We therefore *recommend* that a comprehensive information pack be supplied by the court to both parties when the initial statement is lodged. This should explain:
  (i) the purpose of the period of consideration and reflection, the procedures during it, and the options available at the end of it;
  (ii) the legal effects of divorce and separation;
  (iii) the powers and duties of the court in relation to children, financial provision and property adjustment; and in particular;
  (iv) the nature and purposes of counselling, reconciliation, conciliation or mediation and the services for each which may be available in the area. At this stage, it is important that these services are, and are shown to be, quite independent of the court and legal processes, not only to avoid any suggestion of compulsion,[18] but also because research suggests that they are more effective if this is so.[19] Even so, the information pack should make it clear that the court office is prepared to make the initial contact for those who request this.

5.20 The parties' legal advisers should also be regarded as under an obligation, in addition to their ordinary duty to explain their clients' legal position, to inform them of other services and to make referrals where appropriate. There is a precedent for this in section 6(1) of the Matrimonial Causes Act 1973, under which the petitioner's adviser is required to file a certificate with the petition, stating whether or not he has discussed reconciliation with his client or given his client the names of any people qualified to help.[20] One problem with this provision is that it applies only to a solicitor who is acting for the petitioner for the purpose of the petition. This is a relatively small proportion of petitions, as legal aid is not available for this purpose.[21] If this duty were to encompass all solicitors acting or advising either party at any stage in the proceedings, it would have a much greater impact, particularly in proceedings relating to children or ancillary

---

[15] The former will only be made at least eleven months later, see para. 5.27 below. The latter will be made whenever the parties wish to do so, see para. 5.53 below.

[16] See paras. 5.29 *et seq.* below.

[17] See para. 5.33 below.

[18] See para. 5.33 below.

[19] Newcastle Report, *op. cit.*

[20] Matrimonial Causes Rules 1977, r.12(3) and Appendix 1, Form 3.

[21] See Appendix C, paras. 19, 20.

relief. Secondly, at present the duty is limited to reconciliation, which may be impossible or inappropriate in many cases. Even so, our court record study revealed a perhaps surprisingly high proportion of solicitors who had either discussed reconciliation or referred their clients to other agencies.[22] This may be because of the broader interpretation of reconciliation, to include conciliation, encouraged by Practice Direction in 1971.[23] If the duty were to encompass counselling, reconciliation and conciliation, it would not only require solicitors to understand them but also make such referrals appropriate in a much higher proportion of cases. We consider that, as with section 6(1) of the 1973 Act, the most efficacious way of imposing such a duty is for the Lord Chancellor to make rules requiring solicitors acting for either party, at *any* stage in the proceedings, to certify whether or not they have informed their clients of the nature and purposes of counselling, reconciliation, or conciliation or mediation and the services available in their area, or referred them to people qualified to offer such services. We *recommend* accordingly.

Accompanying documents

5.21 We also *recommend* that the statement relating to marital breakdown be accompanied by detailed statements, as proposed by the Booth Committee,[24] giving particulars of the children, home, other property and income resources of the parties, together with proposals for the future in respect of all these matters. Such statements are already required in respect of the children of the family,[25] and it is anticipated that they will be improved and extended once the Children Act 1989 is implemented, in October 1991. They are not, however, required in respect of the couple's property and finances, where there is often difficulty and delay in obtaining the necessary disclosure.

5.22 Whenever a statement of marital breakdown is made jointly, the statement of information and proposals should if possible be made jointly, although if necessary, separate statements relating to some or all matters should be made. Respondents to Facing the Future were enthusiastic about the use of joint statements as a way of manifesting the parties' joint responsibility, especially for their children. However, where only one party makes the statement, the other party should be sent, not only a copy of the statement of marital breakdown, but all the accompanying documents, together with the information pack supplied by the court. He or she should then have the opportunity of commenting on the other's statements and submitting his or her own at this stage. As with the present statements of arrangements for children, these should not be seen as formal pleadings or evidence, but rather as an exchange of information which may later form the basis of an agreement or order. The preparation and completion of such forms should encourage couples to start thinking seriously about the future and emphasize exactly what will be involved if the separation or divorce is to proceed.

5.23 Lodging such statements at the time of the initial statement of marital breakdown is important for several reasons. The degree of disclosure required will deter some who might be tempted to begin the process without considering what provision they may have to make for the other spouse and, more importantly, for the children. It should diminish the risk of precipitate action or the use of the statement as a "warning shot", without any real intention of considering or making arrangements for the future. It is unlikely that spouses would go to those lengths simply as a form of insurance in case their marriage ran into difficulties. It would reverse the present order of events, in which the petition and formal application come before the detailed disclosure of the present circumstances and proposals for the future, particularly in relation to the parties' property and finances.

5.24 We *recommend* that the precise details relating to form and manner of making the statement of marital breakdown and lodging them with the court; the content and distribution of information packs; service of documents; and the obligations to be imposed upon the parties' legal advisers should be the subject of rules to be made by the Lord Chancellor.

---

[22] *Ibid.*, paras. 21, 22; Davis and Murch, *op. cit.*, report similar findings at pp. 56–57.

[23] *Practice Note (Divorce: Conciliation)* [1971] 1 W.L.R. 223.

[24] Booth Report, paras. 4.31, 4.39, and Appendix 4, Form 4.

[25] In connection with the court's duty under MCA, s.41, to consider the arrangements made for them, whether or not there is any dispute before the court; see Matrimonial Causes Rules 1977, r.8(2) and Appendix 1, Form 4.

The period of consideration and reflection

Objectives

5.25 As we explained earlier,[26] the period is primarily designed to provide convincing proof that the breakdown in the marital relationship is indeed irreparable. It should also give the parties a realistic time within which to resolve the practical questions and to decide whether or not they wish to be reconciled. Unlike the current system, the parties will have to consider the consequences of a separation or divorce order before it actually happens. This will entail the often painful exercise of deciding whether or not their home should be sold, with whom the children are to live, how much contact the other parent is to have with the children, and how their furniture and other possessions should be divided. This will be in addition to learning to adjust emotionally, socially and psychologically to the dramatic change of circumstances in their lives. In some cases, the period may become a more potent encouragement to remain together than the present system, which provides an almost automatic passport to divorce, with every encouragement to dwell on the past and ignore the future.

5.26 It should therefore be distinguished from a purely passive period, during which parties merely wait out the legally required time without any clear objectives and without any real attempt to focus upon the dramatic changes which will occur if and when divorce does actually happen. Where the marriage has obviously and irreparably broken down before the period begins, consideration of the practical consequences will be a much more constructive use of the inevitable delay before a divorce can be obtained. Where there remains any doubt at the outset, a more active preparation for life apart will provide far more cogent evidence that the parties have no future together—why else would the person or persons concerned wish to put themselves through such an experience? When faced with the problems of dealing with the practical consequences some couples may come to realize that they need to re-consider their position and, perhaps with the help of counselling, find some way of re-negotiating their relationship so that they and their children can have a future together.

Length

5.27 There was overwhelming agreement amongst respondents to Facing the Future that these objectives could not be achieved in less than nine months. The great majority favoured a period of nine or twelve months, with only a few suggesting longer. It was pointed out that a twelve month period would make divorce a significantly more lengthy process for a substantial number of people. Respondents to our public opinion survey chose periods ranging from six months to over two years, with the highest number (35%) choosing one year.[27] We *recommend* an overall period of twelve months. This should give sufficient time to enable all but the most difficult and complex matters to be decided and to establish that the breakdown is indeed irreparable. It should also allow sufficient time for the benefits of conciliation or mediation to be explored. We also *recommend* that the actual application for a separation or divorce order should not be made until at least eleven months of the period have elapsed. However, there would be no compulsion to apply for an order upon expiration of this time. Parties could take longer if they wished, as an order should not be made unless it is actually applied for. Once applied for, it would not be granted for a further month,[28] making a minimum total of one year overall.

5.28 A few respondents to Facing the Future suggested that the period should be longer if there were children.[29] Most, however, did not support this. A child's sense of time is quite different from an adult's and considerable harm can be done by prolonged uncertainty. Harm may also be done by the additional bitterness which can be caused by having to wait longer on their account. The general view, both on this and on previous occasions,[30] has been that to make divorce inevitably more difficult for those who have children will not benefit the children themselves and could make matters worse. Thus, "it would amount to a denial that childless marriage is real marriage

---

[26] Para. 3.35 above.

[27] Appendix D, Table 20A.

[28] Para. 5.79 below.

[29] Among them the National Campaign for the Family, *op. cit.*, who suggested periods of 15 and 24 months respectively, with the possibility of reduction if the parties had participated in counselling.

[30] E.g. Time Restrictions on Presentation of Divorce and Nullity Petitions (1982), Law Com. No. 116, paras. 2.34–2.35; also Working Paper No. 76 (1980), paras. 84–87.

... Unhappy motives would be introduced for having, or not having, children; and a child once there could become a focus of bitterness for the parent who wanted to be free".[31] We *recommend*, therefore, that the period should not automatically be longer where there are children. The parties and the court will, however, have to consider what arrangements should be made for them and, if it is desirable to prolong the period in their interests, this should be done.[32]

Counselling, conciliation and mediation

5.29 We have already referred[33] to the range of professional services which may be required by couples and individuals who are facing the often painful processes of marital breakdown, separation or divorce. The umbrella term "counselling" is used in Australia and New Zealand to encompass a variety of different types of help. All share the characteristic of keeping an open mind about the eventual outcome, while helping the couple or individuals involved to gain a greater understanding of their situation and to reach their own decisions about the future. The focus and method, however, can differ sharply, as can the organisational context in which the service is offered.[34]

5.30 Broadly speaking, there are three different types of activity which may be involved:
  (i) Marital counselling is offered, either to a couple or to an individual spouse, with a view to helping the couple to strengthen or maintain their marital relationship. If they are estranged or separated, the aim is to reconcile or reunite them. Historically, attempts at reconciliation were part of the role of "police court missionaries" who became the probation and divorce court welfare service of today. Generally speaking, however, such services are offered by voluntary organisations, principally Relate Marriage Guidance. Relate counsellors are carefully selected and trained, but do not hold any particular professional qualification and offer their services voluntarily;
  (ii) Divorce counselling and other forms of therapy aim to assist individuals, couples, and their children, to come to terms with the fact that their relationship is breaking down, to reduce the sense of personal failure, anger and grief, to disengage from and negotiate a new relationship with the former spouse and with the children, and eventually to move on to new relationships with confidence, avoiding the mistakes of the past. In other words, it seeks to minimise the harm done to either partner and to their children by the breakdown of their marriage. Once again, this is generally offered by voluntary organisations such as Relate, although some probation services offer divorce experience courses, and specialist therapy may be available privately or in some parts of the health service;
  (iii) Conciliation or mediation[35] is a way of resolving disputes without resort to traditional adjudication. The aim is to help the couple to reach their own agreements about the future, to improve communication between them, and to help them to co-operate in bringing up their children. Conciliation in this country developed first in the context of resolving disputes about children, often through the efforts of registrars and divorce court welfare officers at the court where a custody or access dispute was to be tried, but also through independent conciliation services, most of which are now affiliated to the National Family Conciliation Council. Conciliators generally hold professional qualifications in social work, undergo specialist training in family conciliation, and are paid for their services. The costs and benefits of various conciliation services have recently been the subject of a major research study conducted by the University of Newcastle.[36] This has revealed that conciliation is indeed effective, both in

---

[31] Helen Oppenheimer, *op. cit.*, p. 73.
[32] See paras. 5.57, 5.58 below.
[33] Paras. 3.37, 3.38 above.
[34] There is now a voluminous literature on this subject. Principal sources include the Newcastle Report, *op. cit.*; the Finer Report, paras. 4.288–4.314; *Marriage Matters. A Consultative Document by the Working Party on Marriage Guidance set up by the Home Office in consultation with the D.H.S.S.*, (1979); J. Brannen and J. Collard, *Marriages in Trouble: the process of seeking help*, (1982); National Marriage Guidance Council, *Relating to Marriage*, (1984); L. Parkinson, *Conciliation in Separation and Divorce: Finding Common Ground*, (1986); R. Dingwall and J. Eekelaar, *Divorce Mediation and the Legal Process*, (1988); G. Davis, *Partisans and Mediators*, (1988); T. Fisher (ed.), *Family Conciliation within the United Kingdom*, (1990), and numerous less formal publications from the various organisations involved, principally Relate Marriage Guidance, the National Family Conciliation Council, and The Family Mediators' Association.
[35] For this purpose we consider that the terms are inter-changeable.
[36] Newcastle Report, *op. cit.*

reducing the areas of conflict and in increasing the parents' well-being and satisfaction with the arrangements made. In general, these benefits are greater when the service is provided away from the courts. The problems with conciliation conducted by or at the court, valuable and effective though it can often be, include the inevitable pressure to reach a settlement quickly, the inevitable authority of the registrar or court welfare officer conducting it, which may unconsciously or consciously dictate the outcome, and the risks of confusing the welfare officer's different roles of reporting to the court and assisting the couple to reach agreement. However, this is a fast-moving field in which developments are taking place all the time. For example, the independent sector is beginning to develop methods of comprehensive mediation, covering property and finance as well as child-related issues.[37]

5.31 Many of our respondents attached particular importance to the provision of adequate counselling and conciliation services during the period of consideration and reflection. One object in determining the length of the period is to give every opportunity to couples and individuals to avail themselves of such services as are available. With the exception of the efforts made by the courts themselves to encourage couples to reach amicable settlements, all these services are at present offered independently of the courts, usually by non-statutory organisations. It is not for us to make recommendations as to their future organisation and funding, which is currently under consideration in the light of the Newcastle Report. We nevertheless see them as an important element in developing a new and more constructive approach to the problems of divorce and marital breakdown in the interests, not only of the adults and children directly involved, but also of society as a whole.

5.32 Our concern is with the inter-relationship between these services and the legal processes involved in divorce or separation. In this respect, it is necessary to distinguish between counselling and conciliation services, although both are in themselves equally important.

Voluntary or mandatory?

5.33 Some of our respondents argued that counselling aimed at saving the marriage should be a compulsory part of the divorce process, but most were opposed to this. The matter has been considered on many previous occasions, most notably by the Denning Committee on Procedure in Matrimonial Causes in 1947,[38] by the Royal Commission on Marriage and Divorce in 1956,[39] by the Law Commission in The Field of Choice in 1966,[40] and by the Finer Committee on One-Parent Families in 1974.[41] They all concluded that mandatory reconciliation attempts within the court process were unlikely to succeed. We do not take the view that no reconciliation is possible once a person has taken the momentous step of consulting a solicitor and making a statement of marital breakdown: the evidence suggests that, even under the present law, couples become reconciled between petition and decree, and even between decree nisi and decree absolute.[42] Removing the need to separate or to make hostile allegations against one another should increase the prospect of reconciling those who can be reconciled; but we do not believe that the courts should require them, on pain of punitive sanctions, to make the attempt. There are several reasons for this. First, there are the views of the organisations at present involved in providing these services. They would of course like there to be a properly funded network of services readily available to all who wish to use them. But such counselling is a two-way process which can only be offered to volunteers, not conscripts. The hostility and bitterness induced by conscription is unlikely to lead to a real and lasting resolution. Secondly, and perhaps more importantly, there are some marriages which it would be wrong in principle to attempt to save. A wife who is regularly subjected to violence or abuse from her husband needs rescuing from her marriage, not pressure to return to it. A system of mandatory reconciliation could not be justified without some attempt to distinguish

---

[37] The Family Mediators' Association has been set up to provide this, at present on a fee-paying basis, through co-mediation by a lawyer and a social work professional. Methods of providing a similar service for couples with low or moderate means are currently being explored by the National Family Conciliation Council in consultation with the other professional bodies concerned.

[38] Final Report of the Committee on Procedure in Matrimonial Causes (1947), Cmd. 7024, paras. 3–29.

[39] Morton Report, paras. 327–341.

[40] Law Com. No. 6, paras. 29–32.

[41] Finer Report, paras. 4.288–4.314.

[42] G. Davis and M. Murch, *op. cit.*, ch. 4; see also Appendix C, paras. 13–15.

between marriages, which would only reintroduce the very inquiry into past misbehaviour which it is the object of these proposals to avoid. Thirdly, it would be impossible to justify the enormous public expenditure which would be involved in requiring such attempts in every case, without a better prospect of success than can be demonstrated at present. Finally, it was felt by some respondents that *conciliation* might, paradoxically, be more likely to result in reconciling some couples, by encouraging them to find a way through their difficulties relating to future arrangements while they were still amenable to discussion.

5.34 A more difficult question, therefore, is whether conciliation or mediation should be mandatory, if not in all cases at least in those which the court identifies as suitable for it. Once again, however, the majority of our respondents thought it should not. The professionals practising in the field said that mandatory conciliation or mediation was unlikely to be successful and indeed might be counter-productive. The Newcastle research indicated that the greatest benefits came from independent conciliation which was clearly distinguished from the coercive setting of the court.[43] It is also clear that, whatever its benefits in some cases, there are many issues or relationships in which it is quite unsuitable. If so, the aim must be to ensure that adequate services are available to those who wish to use them, and to secure efficient information and referral machinery, rather than coercive sanctions to achieve this. There are also dangers in relying too heavily upon conciliation or mediation instead of more traditional methods of negotiation and adjudication. These include exploitation of the weaker partner by the stronger, which requires considerable skill and professionalism for the conciliator to counteract while remaining true to the neutral role required; considerable potential for delay, which is damaging both to the children and often to the interests of one of the adults involved; and the temptation for the court to postpone deciding some very difficult and painful cases which ought to be decided quickly. It is important that, whatever encouragement is given by the system to alternative methods of dispute resolution, the courts are not deterred from performing their function of determining issues which require to be determined. Where time permits, alternative methods can be explored so as to enable the parties to try and reach their own agreements away from the pressures of the court door. Where, however, an immediate decision is needed in the interests of either party or of their children, the courts should be prepared to give it.

5.35 We therefore *recommend* that undertaking either relationship counselling, whether reconciliation or divorce motivated, or conciliation or mediation should be purely voluntary.

5.36 We further *recommend* that opportunities and encouragement to resolve matters amicably should be built into the system where appropriate. The first opportunity will be when the statement of marital breakdown is made;[44] the second will be at the preliminary and subsequent assessments by the court;[45] and the third will be whenever any contested issue arises for decision. Throughout, it can be encouraged by placing obligations upon the parties' legal advisers as to the provision of information and discussing the possibilities of both reconciliation and conciliation.[46]

5.37 Furthermore, although participation in conciliation or mediation should be voluntary, we *recommend* that the court should have two additional powers to encourage it. Neither of these powers should be seen as placing any pressure on the parties to participate. They are designed to ensure that the parties are better-informed and to facilitate participation if they wish. They are also designed to some extent to regulate what happens informally at present. Our recommendations are, of course, limited to those issues which arise in the context of divorce and separation.[47] They cover all the ancillary remedies, both short and longer term, which may be sought in the context of a statement of marital breakdown, whether before or after a divorce or separation order is made. They also include the power to postpone divorce or

---

[43] *Op. cit.*, chs. 11 to 19, summarised at paras. 20.6–20.10.
[44] Paras. 5.18–5.20 above.
[45] Para. 5.50 below.
[46] Para. 5.20 above.
[47] A definition of "proceedings connected with the breakdown of the marriage" for this and other purposes is given in clause 21(2) and (3) of the draft Divorce and Separation Bill which appears, with explanatory notes, in Appendix A.

separation[48] or to impose a hardship bar.[49] There would appear, however, to be no reason in principle why similar powers, with the safeguards we recommend, should not be available in all family proceedings.[50]

Referral for an explanation of conciliation or mediation

5.38 It is likely that in a number of cases one spouse, or perhaps both spouses, will not appreciate the nature and effectiveness of conciliation or mediation, or even if aware have a totally closed mind on the subject. Many people are confused about the distinctions between counselling, reconciliation and conciliation and are instictively resistent to reconciliation. We therefore *recommend* that the court should have power, whether on application or of its own motion, to give a direction that the spouses meet a specified conciliator or mediator, in order to discuss the nature and potential benefits of conciliation or mediation in their case. An application for such a direction might be made by either party at any time after the statement of marital breakdown. Except in relation to children, however, the court would only be able to act of its own motion if seized of the case, either because a formal application is made for the exercise of any of its powers, or because it has begun to conduct its preliminary assessment.[51] The object of such a meeting would be to enable the parties to reach a better informed decision as to whether or not they wished to embark upon conciliation or mediation and to offer them an opportunity of participating should they agree to do so. We also *recommend* that the conciliator or mediator specified should be under a duty to report back to the court within a given time limit on whether or not the parties have kept the appointment and whether or not they have agreed to take up an offer of conciliation and mediation. We understand that this is how the new referral procedure in Scotland[52] operates and that the first indications are that it is working well.

Adjournment for participation

5.39 We further *recommend* that, where the parties are in dispute about any issue arising in the context of divorce or separation,[53] the court should have power, whether on application or of its own motion,[54] to adjourn the hearing of that issue, for the purpose of enabling them to participate in conciliation or mediation, or generally with a view to the amicable resolution of the dispute. In deciding to do this, the court should take the interests of any children into account (whether, for example, they will be more helped by the amicable resolution or harmed by the delay). It should, of course, be open to the parties not to participate and if either of them feels unable to do so this should not affect the handling of the case thereafter. It is also important to avoid this being used as a method of procrastination and manipulation. We therefore *recommend* that any such adjournment should be for a fixed period, and that one or both parties should be required to report back to the court on the outcome. However, this power to adjourn a particular issue should be distinguished from the quite separate power to extend the period of consideration and reflection in certain limited circumstances, which is discussed below.[55]

Privilege

Reconciliation

5.40 It now appears well settled that privilege attaches to communications made between spouses with a view to reconciliation.[56] This is an extension of the privilege attaching to "without prejudice" negotiations, the reason for which is that it is in the public interest for disputes to be settled and litigation avoided. The rationale behind extending it to reconciliation was that in matrimonial disputes the State is also an interested party, being more interested in reconciliation than in divorce.[57] The privilege

---

[48] See paras. 5.56–5.61 below.

[49] See paras. 5.72–5.77 below.

[50] A convenient definition appears in the Children Act 1989, s.8(3) and (4).

[51] See paras. 5.50–5.52 below.

[52] Act of Sederunt (Amendment of Sheriff Court Ordinary Cause, Summary Cause, and Small Claim, Rules) 1990, S.I. 1990/661 (S.81); Act of Sederunt (Rules of the Court of Session Amendment No. 1) (Miscellaneous) 1990, S.I. 1990/705 (S.86).

[53] See para. 5.37 above.

[54] Once again, the court would have to be seized of the case in the manner described in para. 5.38 above.

[55] In paras. 5.56 to 5.61 below.

[56] *McTaggart* v. *McTaggart* [1949] P. 94; *Mole* v. *Mole* [1951] P. 21; *Theodoropoulas* v. *Theodoropoulas* [1964] p. 311.

[57] *Mole* v. *Mole*, per Bucknill L.J. at p. 23.

is that of the spouses and not of the third party through whom, or in the presence of whom, communications are made. Such third parties may include probation officers, clergy, marriage guidance counsellors, and private individuals not falling into any of the above categories who assist voluntarily. The privilege thus attaches to the process rather than to the professional standing of the third party. The effect is that evidence of statements and offers of settlement made during negotiations is inadmissible in subsequent litigation unless the spouses jointly agree to waive the privilege. The third party involved cannot veto the spouses' waiver and could thereafter be called to give evidence in any subsequent proceedings.

5.41 The Royal Commission on Marriage and Divorce recommended that a privilege be conferred upon marriage guidance counsellors themselves, but not upon court welfare officers because of their principal role of investigating and reporting to the court.[58] The Law Reform Committee, however, rejected this suggestion as neither practicable nor justifiable in principle. They did not, however, recommend any change in the privilege enjoyed by the parties, which had been developed by some very experienced judges and was working well in practice.[59]

5.42 We agree with these conclusions. Accordingly we *recommend* that communications relating to reconciliation should continue, as at present, to be privileged at common law.

Conciliation and Mediation

5.43 Unlike reconciliation, the law relating to any privilege which might attach to communications during conciliation or mediation processes is not yet settled. Given the rationale behind the development of "without prejudice" privilege, it is likely that the same privilege would be extended to conciliation and mediation, as the same public policy considerations must surely apply to them. However, this has not yet been the subject of any reported case and professionals working in these areas have, quite rightly, expressed concern that this matter has not yet been settled.

5.44 In practice all professionals regard communications as privileged[60] and in respect of in-court conciliation it is clear that the court so regards it.[61] Both the Booth Committee[62] and the Newcastle Report[63] emphasised the desirability of "without prejudice" privilege extending to conciliation. As the Booth Committee pointed out, conciliation requires that there should be a full and free exchange between the parties and this is unlikely to occur if there is a possibility of matters disclosed in conciliation being referred to in subsequent proceedings. We consider that, although it is likely that privilege would attach were the matter to be tested, it is desirable, given the increasing role of conciliation and mediation in divorce, that the matter should be placed beyond doubt. This will also provide an opportunity to clarify its nature and extent. We therefore *recommend* that a statutory privilege should be conferred upon statements made during the course of conciliation or mediation processes. Once again, our recommendation has to be limited to conciliation or mediation in disputes which are or may become connected with divorce or separation; but there appears no reason in principle why they should not be applied to all disputes which are or may become the subject of family proceedings.

Extent of the privilege

5.45 We further *recommend* that, consistently with the privilege for "without prejudice" negotiations and reconciliation attempts upon which it is based, the privilege should attach to the parties rather than to the conciliator or mediator. It follows that statements made could be admitted with the consent of both parties. This

---

[58] Morton Report, paras. 358–359.

[59] Law Reform Committee, Sixteenth Report (Privilege in Civil Proceedings) (1967), Cmnd. 3472, paras. 36–40.

[60] National Family Conciliation Council, Code of Practice, para. 4B(ii); Family Mediators' Association, Code of Practice, para. B4.

[61] *Practice Direction (Family Division: Conciliation Procedure)* [1982] 1 W.L.R. 1420; this is one reason why it should be clearly distinguished from the investigative role of the welfare officer preparing a report for the court which cannot be privileged.

[62] Booth Report, para. 4.60.

[63] Newcastle Report, paras. 2.32–2.33, 5.78–5.84, 20.44.

would accommodate the practice of some types of mediation,[64] in which there is both an "open" and a "closed" statement; the open statement relates to the facts set out and agreed between the parties and the closed statement relates to their proposals for the future, which are only placed before a court after final agreement is reached. This is made clear to, and agreed by, the parties before mediation begins.

5.46 Professional conciliators and mediators also make it clear to their clients from the outset that they feel free to report any statements which could impinge upon the welfare of a child to the relevant authorities. In this connection, however, it is easy to confuse the concepts of confidentiality and evidential privilege.[65] Like other professionals, conciliators and mediators believe that their duty to protect a child who may be at risk transcends their duty of confidentiality to the client. However, any report which they make, in confidence, to the authorities will itself be covered by public interest immunity.[66] It does not, therefore, follow that they should be obliged to testify in court to any admissions which may have been made. Were the matter to be tested before a court, the court might regard the welfare of the child as overriding all other considerations and require the mediator to testify irrespective of the wishes of the spouses. It is equally possible that a court might decide that the public policy considerations which led both to the extension of "without prejudice" privilege to this area, and to the public interest immunity, should prevail.

5.47 The Booth Committee[67] concluded that they would wish to see absolute privilege attaching to conciliation, whereas the Newcastle Report concluded that there should be an exception for "allegations of child abuse".[68]

5.48 It seems to us that the basic concern is that essential information which could help to protect a child from harm should be passed to the relevant authorities. We are in complete agreement with this objective, but see it as quite distinct from whether the conciliator who passes on the information should have to give evidence in any proceedings which follow, irrespective of the wishes of the spouses. It is a matter of judgment whether the welfare of the child would be better protected by compelling the conciliator to give evidence in such proceedings or by the greater frankness which an absolute privilege would encourage during the conciliation or mediation process. In practice, once the information is passed to the authorities, an investigation will take place and it is upon that rather than the initial referral that any subsequent proceedings will be based. We consider that, on balance, the welfare of any children would be better protected by an absolute privilege, given that the codes of practice of the relevant professionals include a provision to the effect that confidence will not be maintained in respect of matters relating to protection of children, such as allegations of abuse. We therefore *recommend* that statements made during the course of any conciliation or mediation process which indicate a risk of harm to a child should be privileged but not confidential. This recommendation follows the approach in other jurisdictions.[69]

Legal Professional Privilege

5.49 Legal professional privilege enables a client to maintain privilege in respect of two types of communication—those between a person and his lawyer made for the purpose of obtaining and giving legal advice and those between him or his lawyer and third parties, the dominant purpose of which was preparation for contemplated or pending litigation. This type of privilege is therefore not relevant to any of the situations discussed above. Even where one is dealing with mediation which involves the presence of a lawyer-mediator, the relationship is in the nature of a conciliator, and not that of a legal adviser. Our recommendations that communications during conciliation or mediation should be privileged should not in any way derogate from the common law relating to legal professional privilege or the privilege relating to reconciliation.

---

[64] Family Mediators' Association, Code of Practice, para. B4.
[65] Newcastle Report, para. 5.78.
[66] *D.* v. *N.S.P.C.C.* [1978] A.C. 171.
[67] Booth Report, para. 4.60.
[68] Newcastle Report, para. 20–44; presumably they meant admissions.
[69] Family Law Act (Australia) 1975, s.18; Family Proceedings Act (New Zealand) 1980, s.18.

Preliminary assessment by the court

5.50 It is important that couples are free to meet their responsibilities towards their families by making their own arrangements in their own time and their own way, if required with professional help. However it is equally important that they be encouraged to get on with making those arrangements and not to defer decisions which need to and can be made. We therefore *recommend* that, no later than twelve weeks from the date when the statement of marital breakdown is made, the court shoud hold a preliminary assessment, in order to monitor progress on the arrangements being made and dispose of those matters which can conveniently be dealt with by then. This would be roughly equivalent to the "initial hearing" recommended by the Booth Committee,[70] but taking place rather later in the procedure. This is in order to avoid rushing the parties into precipitate decision-making or inducing the feeling that a separation or divorce is inevitable in every case.

5.51 The broad functions of the court on this occasion should be to review progress in making the arrangements for the future and to make any orders relating to the children, financial provision and property adjustment, or exercise any of its other powers, including its power to postpone the divorce or separation in certain cases,[71] as may be appropriate in the circumstances. In addition, it should have the following specific duties:

(i) to perform the duty to protect the interests of the children of the family which is currently contained in section 41 of the Matrimonial Causes Act 1973; as substituted by the Children Act 1989,[72] this requires the court to consider whether there are any children to whom this section applies,[73] and if there are, to consider whether (in the light of the arrangements made or proposed for their upbringing and welfare) it should exercise any of its powers under the Children Act with respect to any of them; the powers in question may be to make orders relating to the child's residence or upbringing, or to call for a welfare officer's report, or to refer the case for investigation by the local social services authority;[74]

(ii) to identify issues which are in dispute between the parties and to consider how they might most amicably be resolved, including how best to encourage participation in conciliation or mediation procedures;

(iii) to give directions for the conduct of proceedings relating to those long term issues[75] which have not yet been resolved;

(iv) to consider what orders relating to financial provision or property adjustment have already been agreed between the parties;

(v) to consider whether or not to exercise its power to extend the period in order to protect a spouse who is incapacitated or prejudiced by a delay in service;[76] and

(vi) to consider whether, and on what grounds, an application is likely to be made to invoke the hardship bar, in order to avoid having to delay the case at a later stage.[77]

It is unlikely that the court will be in a position to complete all these tasks at this stage in all cases. In this event the court should have power to adjourn and re-convene the assessment within a specified time, and from time to time thereafter, until all matters have been finalised, the proceedings have been withdrawn or have lapsed, or a divorce order has been made. A separation order should not necessarily conclude the court's task, as it may well be converted into a divorce.

---

[70] Booth Report, paras. 3.5–3.9 and 4.53–4.90.

[71] See paras. 5.56–5.61 below.

[72] Sched. 12, para. 31.

[73] Those under 16 at the date of the court's consideration or whom the court directs should be included, MCA, s.41(3).

[74] In exceptional circumstances where this is desirable in the child's interests, the court also has power to delay the grant of a decree absolute, under s.41(2); for the equivalent power under our proposals, see para. 5.58(i) below.

[75] I.e. under the Children Act 1989, or for financial provision or property adjustment under the 1973 Act, or for a transfer of tenancy under the Matrimonial Homes Act 1983, or relating to the postponement of divorce or separation or the imposition of a hardship bar.

[76] See paras. 5.58(iii) and (iv) and 5.61 below; the court should be specifically required to consider these because the party concerned may not be able to protect himself.

[77] See paras. 5.72–5.77 below.

5.52 The procedure to be followed and the place and manner in which the preliminary assessment is to be conducted should be the subject either of rules made by the Lord Chancellor or of rules of court and provision enabling these to be made has been included in the draft Bill. Ideally, both parties should attend, with or without their legal advisers as appropriate. We appreciate, however, that the Booth Committee did not recommend a hearing in every case, and there may be some which are so straightforward that this would be a waste of everyone's time and energies. It is better that this be left to the discretion of the court; but the parties should always be informed of the date, time and place, and given an opportunity to attend or submit further information on current progress. We anticipate that rules governing procedure relating to the preliminary assessment and subsequent assessments would dovetail with procedures relating to formal applications relating to children and finance. As with all the essentially procedural time limits prescribed in the legislation, we *recommend* that the Lord Chancellor should have power, by order approved by each House of Parliament, to vary the period of twelve weeks within which the assessment must begin, should this prove impracticable or undesirable in the light of experience.

Orders during the period

5.53 The functions of the court during the preliminary assessment would in no way preclude, nor derogate from, the right of any spouse to make a formal application to the court for an order under the Children Act 1989, or for financial provision or property adjustment orders under the Matrimonial Causes Act 1973, or for a transfer of tenancy under the Matrimonial Homes Act 1983. Such applications should be possible at any time after a statement of marital breakdown has been made and be subject to the usual procedures for formal applications. However, it is also useful for the court to have power to make orders of its own motion in respect of these matters, particularly in combination with giving encouragement to the parties to avoid resort to adversarial proceedings wherever this is practicable or desirable. This power is clearly spelled out in relation to children,[78] but not in respect of financial provision and property adjustment orders under the 1973 Act,[79] where we *recommend* that it should arise once there are any proceedings connected with the breakdown of the marriage, including the preliminary assessment.[80] This will enable the parties to present the court with the basis of an agreed order at the preliminary assessment, or any subsequent assessment, without having had to make a formal application in advance. The court would, of course, have to have sufficient information to enable it to approve such an agreement, such as is provided for at present in respect of applications for consent orders under section 33A of the Matrimonial Causes Act 1973.

5.54 A necessary corollary of requiring consideration of future arrangements before the separation or divorce is that the court should have power to make final orders relating to financial provision for children and spouses, together with property adjustment orders, at any time during the period of consideration and reflection, rather than deferring them, as at present, at least until after the decree nisi. We therefore *recommend* that the court should have power to make orders, and that such orders may take effect, during the period. At present, although these may be made at any time after decree nisi they cannot take effect until after decree absolute.[81] This can in practice severely hamper the couple's attempts to resolve their affairs, particularly where they are still both living in the matrimonial home, often in an atmosphere of hostility and uncertainty which can be very damaging to the children. It is usually unrealistic to decide any issue relating to the children without also deciding the issue relating to the home. However, the need to resolve as many questions as possible before the couple are divorced must be balanced against the problems which will arise if the divorce or separation order is not made. Consequently, we *recommend* that property adjustment orders should only take effect before separation or divorce where the court is satisfied that there are special circumstances making it appropriate for them to do so. We further *recommend* that, if the parties become reconciled, it should be possible upon joint

---

[78] Children Act 1989, s.10(1)(b), relating to orders under the private law; orders placing a child in care or under supervision can only be made on application.

[79] MCA, ss.23 and 24.

[80] Equivalent provision should be made for transfer of tenancy orders under the Matrimonial Homes Act 1983.

[81] MCA, ss.23(5) and 24(3).

application by the parties to set aside a lump sum or property adjustment order.[82] If the order has already taken effect, this should only be possible if it will not prejudice the interests of children or third parties. If the couple do not make such an application, however, the order should stand even if they do not proceed to obtain a separation or divorce.

5.55 As we have already made clear,[83] the court must also be able to exercise its powers under the Matrimonial Homes Act 1983, to regulate the parties' rights of occupation in the home and even to exclude one of them from it, and to protect the parties and their children from molestation, whether under its inherent powers or under the Domestic Violence and Matrimonial Proceedings Act 1976 or any other legislation, during the period of consideration and reflection. Accordingly, we *recommend* that any new divorce and separation legislation should provide for the exercise of the inherent jurisdiction and that the procedural rules provide for orders under other legislation to be made as part of the separation or divorce process.

Extending the period

5.56 A number of respondents[84] argued that the divorced should not be granted until all the arrangements for the children, finance and property had actually been made. In their view this would protect the children and the economically weaker spouse and encourage couples to use the period to negotiate and resolve practical issues. This proposal has its attractions, particularly when the economically more powerful spouse is seeking a divorce which the weaker one does not want. However, the major objection to requiring this in every case is that it would play into the hands of an unreasonable, spiteful or malicious spouse, who could delay the resolution of issues for a long time in the knowledge that this would prevent the divorce.[85] In doing so, it could deny the protection of divorce to the weaker spouse and the children, and create a formidable bargaining chip for the more powerful or determined party.

5.57 Facing the Future[86] suggested a middle course. For the children, this would be equivalent to the protection given by section 41 of the Matrimonial Causes Act 1973, as recently amended by the Children Act 1989.[87] The court may postpone the grant of a decree absolute if it requires more time to consider what to do about the children's future *and* there are exceptional circumstances making it desirable in *their* interests to postpone the decree. As to the financial arrangements, it would be similar to the present safeguard in section 10(2) of the Matrimonial Causes Act.[88] This allows the respondent to a decree based on two or five years' separation to apply for the decree absolute to be postponed until either proper financial provision has been made or the court has decided that no provision need be made. Any new system must obviously try to balance the injustice which would be caused by allowing an unreasonable, irresponsible or vindictive spouse to delay matters indefinitely, against the injustice of allowing a spouse to escape from the marriage without making any serious attempt to consider how to discharge his or her responsibilities towards the children and the other spouse. We consider that this is best done by building on the models of section 41 and section 10 of the 1973 Act described above. The court should have a discretion to postpone the grant of the divorce or separation, but only where this is desirable in order to safeguard the interests of those who would be prejudiced if the divorce were allowed to go ahead before proper arrangements were made. We would not expect such a power to be frequently used, for in the great majority of cases the arrangements can be made quite independently of the grant of the divorce itself, and it will rarely be in the interests of anyone to prolong the uncertainty involved. The principal aim would be to provide some sanction against wilful non-disclosure or non-cooperation in the ordinary procedures for resolving these matters. To this end, we believe it essential that the grounds are limited and specific, but that the court should have power to act either of its own motion or upon application by either party.

---

[82] There is already power to discharge periodical payments orders, under MCA, s.31, and to order repayment, under s.33.

[83] Para. 5.13 above.

[84] Including the Law Society.

[85] See G. Davis, "Grounds for Divorce and The Law Commission Discussion Paper" [1989] Fam. Law 182.

[86] Law Com. No. 170, paras. 5.40–5.42.

[87] Sched. 12, para. 31.

[88] s.10(2)–(4).

5.58 Accordingly, we *recommend* that the court should have power, of its own motion or on application, to postpone the divorce or separation on any of the following grounds:

(i) where the court considers it likely that it will exercise any of its powers under the Children Act 1989, in respect of any child of the family, but is not yet in a position to do so (for example, because it does not have sufficient information, or the parties have not taken the necessary steps to place the court in a position to do so) and postponement of the separation or divorce is desirable in the interests of the child;[89]

(ii) where such financial arrangements, whether for spouse or child, as the court would consider proper in the particular case have not been made, it appears impracticable to make them before the divorce or separation order would ordinarily be made, and (subject to what is said in paragraph 5.60 below) postponement is desirable in order to allow time for such arrangements to be made;

(iii) where one party lacks legal capacity to act on his or her own behalf and postponement is desirable in order for steps to be taken to protect his or her interests (for example, by appointing a guardian *ad litem*);

(iv) where, if the period is initiated by one spouse alone or a sole application for separation or divorce is made, there has been delay in serving the other spouse with relevant documents, and postponement is desirable in order to prevent that other spouse from suffering any prejudice as a result; or

(v) where it is desirable, in the exceptional circumstances explained in paragraph 5.76 below, for a divorce to be postponed in order that an application for the imposition of a hardship bar can be properly determined.

5.59 In all cases we *recommend* that the court should specify the length of postponement; where postponement is ordered before the application for a divorce or separation order, by specifying the earliest date upon which the application may be made; where it is ordered after an application by specifying when the order is to be made. Further, if the court is requiring postponement for a particular purpose, the date could be defined by reference to the taking of specified steps or satisfying the court on specified matters. The court should have power to revoke or modify an order of postponement, upon application by either or both of the parties. Where, for example, arrangements are made, or such necessary steps as might be required by the court have been taken, within a shorter period of time than had been anticipated, the court should have power to allow the divorce to proceed. It should only be able to extend the period yet again if one of the grounds is made out.

5.60 We recognise that ability to apply for postponement could be a powerful weapon in the hands of an obstructive or vindictive party. To avoid misuse, therefore, we *recommend* that, where one party applies for postponement on the basis that proper financial arrangements have not been made, the court should direct its mind specifically to whether there are any circumstances making it appropriate for the arrangements to be made before the divorce or separation takes place, the conduct of the parties in relation to the making of those arrangements, and any prejudice that either party or the children may suffer if the divorce or separation is delayed. One party should not be allowed to take advantage of his or her own deliberate failure to make or contribute to the making of financial arrangements to the prejudice of the other party or children. Where postponement is applied for on the ground that arrangements have not been made for the children, then the court should be able to order postponement where it would be in the interests of the children to do so. In practice, cases where postponing the divorce or separation will of itself benefit the children are bound to be exceptional, but the court should always be free to do what is best for them. This should enable the court to distinguish between cases where there are genuine reasons to postpone the divorce or separation and cases where one party is attempting to use the power to postpone for vindictive or self-serving reasons.

---

[89] This is slightly wider than the MCA, s.41 as amended by the Children Act 1989, Sched. 12, para. 31, which is restricted to "exceptional circumstances"; we do not consider that this will make any material difference in practice, see para. 5.60 below.

5.61 In the cases of lack of legal capacity or delay in service, the object of postponement is principally to ensure that the party concerned is not prejudiced by having a shorter time for consideration and reflection than would normally be the case. Accordingly, we *recommend* that postponement on those grounds be possible at any time after the statement of marital breakdown has been made and the court should be specifically required to consider it at the preliminary assessment. However, in the case of arrangements relating to children and finance we believe it important that parties be given some time to consider the arrangements at their own pace without the threat of the period being extended. Such external constraints from a very early stage could result in more vulnerable parties being put under undue pressure to enter into arrangements which would not necessarily be in their interests. We therefore *recommend* that the earliest time when the court can order postponement in these cases should be when at least six months of the period of consideration and reflection have elapsed. If satisfactory arrangements have not begun to emerge by this stage, then some additional pressure may occasionally be justified but the court should not be obliged to consider it in every case. As with other such periods, the Lord Chancellor should have power to alter the six month provision, by order approved by each House of Parliament.

Abridging the period

5.62 A number of respondents thought that the court should have power to expedite a decree of divorce. Translated into terminology of the proposed new system this would in effect mean abridgement of the period. The possible grounds suggested were numerous and included the fact that the couple had no children, had reached agreement on all arrangements or had been separated for some time before making the statement of marital breakdown. It could be thought unduly paternalistic and even punitive to oblige responsible couples, who had in fact made satisfactory arrangements for all their affairs, to wait for a further year before obtaining their divorce.

5.63 The main objection to a power to abridge is that it is inconsistent with the principal aim of the one year period, which is to establish beyond doubt that the breakdown in the marital relationship is irreparable. It is an important object of these proposals to enable irretrievable breakdown of the marriage to be clearly and incontrovertibly demonstrated by a simple test which leaves no scope for argument or pressure between the parties and potentially subjective or inconsistent exercises of discretion in the courts.

5.64 The problem then is that all the various reasons put forward for allowing breakdown to be established within a shorter period are likely to perpetuate the problems of the present law. We have already stated our objections of principle and practice to making divorce more difficult for those who have children.[90] It might also be thought that a young mother who had been persistently beaten by her husband was a more meritorious case for an early divorce. Yet to provide for such cases would be open to all the same objections as the present fault-based facts.[91] Similarly, to provide for couples who had been separated for some time before the statement of marital breakdown had been made would not only discriminate in favour of those who could afford to do so, but, more importantly, would encourage some to deceive the court in order to gain a "quickie" divorce. To provide for those who had made all their arrangements might well put undue pressure upon the weaker party to reach agreements which were not in his or her interests. The fact that the parties are already agreed upon their arrangements is no guarantee that they have not rushed into these without proper consideration and it is certainly possible that they are also rushing into the divorce. Accordingly, we *recommend* that there should be no power to abridge the period of consideration and reflection.

5.65 We recognise that this will mean that some couples will have to wait rather longer than they do at present for a divorce. However, we do not believe that this will result in any real hardship, in view of our recommendation that the court should have

---

[90] Para. 5.28 above.
[91] Experience of the former discretionary power to allow a spouse to petition within three years of the marriage in cases of "exceptional depravity" by the respondent or "exceptional hardship" for the petitioner was not encouraging; there was good support for its abolition in 1984; see Time Restrictions in Presentation of Divorce and Nullity Petitions (1982), Law Com. No. 116, paras. 2.4–2.8; Working Paper No. 76 (1980), para. 54.

power to make orders relating to finance and property before the divorce and also to grant injunctions against violence or other molestation ancillary to the making of the statement of marital breakdown.[92] It is these remedies, rather than the divorce itself, which gives such protection as the law can give against violence and harassment by former spouses. All that will be denied is the right to re-marry. It will be recalled that some of our respondents thought it a positive advantage of the scheme we are recommending that it would prevent people from re-marrying too quickly after their previous marriage had broken down.[93] We appreciate that in some cases one of the spouses wishes to re-marry before a child is born of a new relationship. However, if the parents do eventually marry, the child will be legitimated and will suffer no legal discrimination as a result. If they do not, it may well be better for the child that they realised their mistake in time and were not put under any additional pressure to marry in haste or against their better judgement.

Reconciliation

Suspension of the period during an attempted reconciliation

5.66 The period itself is designed to facilitate attempts at reconciliation but some couples may feel that they would like more time. We therefore *recommend* that the running of either period[94] should automatically be suspended where the parties jointly notify the court they wish to attempt a reconciliation. There should be no compulsion to do this, and many may not feel the need to do so, given that one of the objectives of the period is to allow sufficient time for reconciliation to be explored without in any way prejudicing either party. It should therefore be open to either party to start the period running again by notifying the court to that effect.

5.67 In order to ensure that matters do not drag on indefinitely, and also to avoid the risk of the parties being tempted to allow that part of the period which had already run its course to be preserved as an insurance policy for the future, we *recommend* that where no such notification is received within 18 months of the date when the suspension began, then the period which had elapsed before suspension should lapse. This would, of course, be without prejudice to the right of either party to make a subsequent statement of marital breakdown in order to begin the procedure afresh. As with other such periods, the Lord Chancellor should have power to alter the limit of 18 months, by order approved by each House of Parliament.

Withdrawal

5.68 Where reconciliation is successful, it should be possible for the parties jointly to withdraw the statement of marital breakdown, so as to stop the period running straightaway. This would have, of course, to be a joint decision: for the reasons given earlier,[95] it would be most unfair if the spouse who initiated the process were able to play fast and loose with the other, by withdrawing the statement unilaterally even though there was no prospect of reconciliation between them.

Application for a divorce or separation order

5.69 We *recommend* that an order should not be made unless an application has been made by one or both spouses and that application has not been withdrawn. In order to give the parties ample time to consider whether or not they do wish to divorce or separate, it should only be possible to make an application for a divorce or separation order after at least eleven months of the period have elapsed.[96] This will enable irretrievable breakdown of the marriage to be demonstrated both objectively, by the passage of a considerable period of time, and subjectively, by the continued determination of one or both parties to arrange for a life apart. They may, of course, wish to wait for longer than this before applying; this would be a matter for either or both of them.

5.70 We *recommend* that the application should incorporate a declaration that the maker or makers believe that the breakdown in their marital relationship is irreparable

---

[92] Paras. 5.54, 5.55 above.
[93] Para. 3.29.
[94] Including any postponement ordered under the powers discussed in paragraphs 5.56 to 5.61 above.
[95] Para. 5.11 above.
[96] Para. 5.27 above.

and in consequence ask for either a separation or divorce order. We envisage that the same form of application will be used for both separation and divorce and will merely require the party or parties to choose between them.

5.71 As we have previously explained,[97] we *recommend* that either or both of the parties should be able to make the application, irrespective of who made the statement of marital breakdown. It is important for the law to treat each party equally, to get away from the idea of a "petitioner" and a "respondent", and to accept that it takes two to make or mend a marriage. If, having gone through the considerable period of consideration and reflection, and all the procedures attendant on it, either of the parties takes the view that the marriage is at an end, he or she should be able to apply for the order. Sometimes they will both have made the statement and will both join in the application. This may become a common practice, reflecting not only the apparently widespread acceptance of divorce by consent,[98] but also the best prospect of amicable co-operation in the future discharge of their mutual responsibilities, particularly towards their children. Sometimes, there will be a joint statement, but only one feels ready to make the application: it will then be for the other either to acquiesce or to apply if appropriate for the period to be extended.[99] Sometimes, there will be a single statement but by the end of the period the other has sufficiently come to terms with what has happened to feel able to join in the application. Sometimes, the one who made the statement will be the one who makes the application. Occasionally, it will be the other way round, when the one who makes the application is the one who did not make the statement. In some ways this is akin to the present position, where the respondent may apply for the decree nisi to be made absolute if the petitioner does not do so.[100] The spouse who made the original statement would, however, be able to choose between acquiescing in the application or applying where appropriate for the period to be extended. If they make a joint application, they may of course withdraw it jointly. But if only one wishes to withdraw, it should be treated as a sole application by the other. (Otherwise that person might not be able to put in a new application before the time for doing so had expired.) It would then be possible for the party who withdrew to seek to invoke the hardship bar discussed below, for example because she had been deceived as to the true financial position.

Grave financial or other hardship

5.72 Section 5 of the Matrimonial Causes Act provides a safeguard for respondents to petitions based on five years' separation, in that the court can refuse a decree if this would result in grave financial or other hardship to the respondent and it would in all the circumstances be wrong to dissolve the marriage. This was designed to meet the small number of cases in which the divorce itself will cause more hardship than the marital breakdown has already done.[101] Generally, it is the separation, and the problems of running two households rather than one, which causes financial hardship, often to both of the parties.[102] In practice, the only significant hardship which may flow from the divorce itself is the potential loss of an occupational widow's pension for which the husband is unable to provide sufficient compensation by way of periodical payments, lump sum or property adjustment.[103] The bar is therefore rarely invoked and even more rarely successful. It is possible to think of other grave hardships which might flow from the divorce, where for example divorce will result in severe stigma in the community where the respondent lives, with possible exclusion from religious and social life, and perhaps no prospect of remarriage within that community, but as yet no divorce has been refused on this basis.[104]

---

[97] Para. 5.11 above.

[98] See para. 3.11 above.

[99] Paras. 5.56–5.61 above.

[100] Matrimonial Causes Rules 1977, r.66(2).

[101] The Field of Choice (1966), Law Com. No. 6, para. 41.

[102] *Mathias* v. *Mathias* [1972] Fam. 287; *Talbot* v. *Talbot* (1971) 115 S.J.870.

[103] Cf. *Julian* v. *Julian* (1972) 116 S.J.763 and *Johnson* v. *Johnson* (1981) 12 Fam. Law 116, the only two reported cases in which the bar was imposed, with *Le Marchant* v. *Le Marchant* [1977] 1 W.L.R. 559 and *Reiterbund* v. *Reiterbund* [1975] Fam. 99.

[104] See *Banik* v. *Banik* [1973] 1 W.L.R. 860; *Rukat* v. *Rukat* [1975] Fam. 63; *Balraj* v. *Balraj* (1981) 11 Fam. Law 110; in *Lee* v. *Lee* (1973) 117 S.J.616, a decree was refused because the wife needed accomodation for her disabled son, but after a change in the circumstances, it was granted on appeal, (1975) 5 Fam. Law 48.

5.73 In Facing the Future[105] we pointed out that the rationale of this provision was to safeguard the position of the innocent spouse who did not wish to be divorced. In a no-fault system there is clearly a case for extending the protection of a hardship bar to all who wish to invoke it. There is still a substantial economic imbalance between the spouses in most marriages which have lasted for more than a few years, especially if there are children. The fact that the bar is rarely invoked does not mean that it is ineffective. In combination with the present five year delay in such cases, it may well have an effect upon the couple's bargaining positions whichever of the five facts is eventually relied upon. Furthermore, no means has yet been discoveed of dividing occupational pensions on divorce so as to mitigate the potential hardship involved.[106] To remove the bar would therefore be to remove what may be a substantial protection for the economically weaker spouse.

5.74 Against this, of course, it must be acknowledged, as does the present bar, that there are some spouses who do not deserve such protection, however great the hardship will be.[107] Considerations of fault, or at least of relative hardship to the other spouse of denying the divorce, would have to be taken into account. There is the further difficulty that to retain such a bar would raise the possibility, however remote, of a contentious hearing in every case. If successful, it would leave intact the empty shell of a marriage which on all objective criteria was undoubtedly dead.

5.75 Despite these disadvantages, those respondents to Facing the Future who discussed this issue were all in favour of retaining the bar. It provides an important protection for a small group of people who may still face serious hardship which the law is unable at present to redress in other ways. If it retains substantially the same form as the present bar, it is unlikely to be invoked, and even less likely to succeed, in any but a tiny minority of cases. On balance, therefore, we *recommend* that it should be possible to resist the grant of a divorce, on the ground that the dissolution of the marriage would result in grave financial or other grave hardship to the person concerned, and that it would be wrong, in all the circumstances, for the marriage to be dissolved.[108]

5.76 Given that the hardship bar can only apply to divorce rather than separation, it follows that an application to invoke such a bar can only be made once an application for a divorce order has been made. The court will then normally have only the one month period of transition to consider the merits of such an application before the divorce order is issued.[109] However, this should not usually cause insuperable difficulties, as it is almost inconceivable that the financial position of the parties as it is likely to be after divorce would not already have become clear to the court. The person wishing to invoke the bar should have made his or her position apparent in all the exchanges taking place during the period of consideration and reflection. We have already recommended[110] that, in appropriate cases, the court should give consideration at the preliminary assessment to whether or not the bar is likely to be raised. It should at that stage be possible to require a spouse to state whether he or she intends to invoke it should an application for divorce be made, and if so on what grounds. Occasionally, however, it may be impossible to resolve matters within the month between application and divorce. The court must therefore have power to delay the divorce for this purpose. It is vital, however, that this be strictly limited, so that it cannot be used as a tactical weapon in every case. Accordingly, we *recommend* that the court should have power to postpone the divorce but only where it is probable that the hardship part of the grounds can be established, there are exceptional circumstances making it impracticable to decide the application within the month, and postponement is desirable in order to enable it to be properly determined. Any delay in notifying the other party of an intention to invoke the bar, or any matters relevant to it, should be taken into account in deciding this. Thus, for example, it may only just have become apparent that the applicant will suffer hardship, because the other spouse has only just disclosed details

---

[105] Law Com. No. 170, paras. 5.37–5.39.

[106] In 1985, the Lord Chancellor's Department published a Discussion Paper on *Occupational Pension Rights on Divorce*, but there have been no official devlopments involving this very difficult problem since then.

[107] E.g. *Brickell* v. *Brickell* [1974] Fam. 31.

[108] As we have already pointed out in para. 3.44 above, however, this is a self-contained recommendation, the merits of which can be considered separately from the merits of the scheme as a whole.

[109] See para. 5.79 below.

[110] Para. 5.51 above.

of his pension scheme. On the other hand, the applicant may now be seeking to rely on matters which she could easily have raised much earlier. In the one case delay might well be desirable, in the other not. Only if it is probable that the applicant will succeed in establishing hardship should it be possible to delay in order for the full circumstances to be properly explored.

5.77 It would also be unjust were a bar imposed by the court on the ground of hardship to remain in force indefinitely, despite any change in the financial position of the parties. We therefore *recommend* that the court have power to revoke an order imposing a bar, upon application by either or both parties, where it is satisfied that the grounds for continuing the bar no longer exist. Revocation might be appropriate, for example, where the party who applied for the bar wished to re-marry or where the other party found the financial resources to compensate for any loss of pension rights. We further *recommend* that, provided all the other conditions have been met, the court should then have power to make an order for divorce either after the usual one month period of transition or earlier if appropriate. It would not at that stage make sense to require a further period of consideration.

Making the divorce or separation order

5.78 Once an application for a divorce order has been made, the order should be issued automatically by the court, provided that the following conditions are fulfilled:

(i) An application for divorce in the required form, containing the recommended declaration, has been made by one or both spouses before the time for doing so has expired.[111]

(ii) The required period of consideration and reflection had elapsed (taking into account any suspension for attempted reconciliation and any postponement ordered by the court) before the application was made.

(iii) The period was initiated in the required manner, by a statement by one or both spouses, of their belief that the marital relationship had broken down and that statement had not been jointly withdrawn by the parties.

(iv) The required period of transition (taking into account any suspension for attempted reconciliation and any postponement ordered by the court) has elapsed since the application,[112] the application has not been withdrawn (by them both if it is a joint application),[113] and no hardship bar has been imposed.

(v) There has been no stay under the Domicile and Matrimonial Proceedings Act 1973.[114]

5.79 It is obviously necessary to provide some interval between the application and the divorce, in order to give a last-minute chance to apply for extension of the period or to invoke the hardship bar. We therefore *recommend* that a period of one month should elapse between the application and the issue of the order, making a total minimum period of twelve months in all. The precise division of the overall period of one year, into eleven months and one month, may prove inconvenient in the light of experience. We therefore *recommend* that the Lord Chancellor should have power to alter this balance between them, but not the overall total of one year, by order subject to the approval of both Houses of Parliament.

5.80 With the exception of the hardship bar, the same conditions should apply to separation orders. We have already recommended that the ground for a separation order should be the same as for a divorce, namely that the marriage has irretrievably broken down.[115] It follows that, in the perhaps unlikely event that one spouse applies for divorce and the other for separation, the court must grant the divorce unless the hardship bar applies. This provides the only logical reason for refusing to dissolve a marriage which both are agreed has irretrievably broken down.

5.81 A number of respondents voiced strong objection to the requirement proposed

---

[111] See para. 5.85 below.
[112] See para. 5.79 below.
[113] See para. 5.71 above.
[114] Which relates to cases which ought to proceed in another jurisdiction.
[115] Para. 4.14.

46

in Facing the Future[116] that the parties should have ceased to cohabit by the end of the period. Their concern was that such a requirement would discriminate against those who have nowhere else to go, and might lead to contrivances such as one spouse moving out of the matrimonial home temporarily to coincide with the end of the transition period. These appear justified. Therefore we *recommend* that the parties should not have to satisfy a non-cohabitation requirement at the end of the period.

Position where the parties have not been married for one year

5.82 Although Facing the Future did not discuss the ban on petitioning for divorce within the first year of marriage, contained in section 3 of the Matrimonial Causes Act, a number of respondents raised this issue. About half these favoured retention, whilst the others favoured a longer ban to discourage precipitate divorce. In view of the fact that the present rule was introduced, after extensive consultation and Parliamentary debate, only six years ago,[117] we do not recommend any change. However we have already recommended[118] that it should remain possible to apply for a separation order within the first year of marriage.

5.83 We therefore *recommend* that the effect of the combination of the one year ban and the required period of eleven months' consideration and reflection would be as follows. The parties could make a statement of marital breakdown within the first year of marriage and apply for a separation order eleven months thereafter, but it would not be possible to apply for a divorce unless at the time of application they had been married for one year and eleven months. If either or both did apply for a divorce within this time the court would not have power to issue the order.

5.84. In effect, therefore, no divorce could be granted until at least two years after the marriage. This may mean that some recently married couples would have to wait rather longer than under the present system before obtaining a divorce. However, for the reasons explained earlier in relation to possible abridgement of the twelve month period,[119] we do not think that it would cause any real hardship. It would also help to prevent couples rushing into re-marriage too soon without having had time to think about why their previous marriage was so short-lived. This might help to prevent a subsequent marriage from breaking down.

Lapse of proceedings

5.85 A number of respondents agreed with the suggestion in Facing the Future that proceedings should lapse if no application for either a separation or divorce order was made within a specified time.[120] We believe it is important that proceedings are not allowed to drag on interminably causing uncertainty for the spouses and their children. It is also important that one party is not allowed to preserve the period of consideration and reflection indefinitely, just in case he or she may wish to proceed quickly to divorce at some time in the future. We therefore *recommend* that it should only be possible to apply for a divorce or separation order within six months of the end of the period of consideration and reflection, as extended by any period of suspension or any postponement. Where, for example, there have been no suspension or postponements the case would lapse if no application for an order is made within seventeen months of the statement of marital breakdown; where there has been a three months suspension, the case would lapse if no application is made within twenty months of the statement. This provision would be in addition to that recommended earlier,[121] for lapse of the period afer suspension for reconciliation. As with other periods of this nature, the Lord Chancellor should have power to alter the six month time limit by order approved by each House of Parliament.

Conversion of separation to divorce

5.86 Under section 4 of the Matrimonial Causes Act 1973, a petition for divorce may be filed after a decree of judicial separation; the court may treat the decree as sufficient proof of any fact by reference to which it was granted. However the court cannot grant a

---

[116] Law Com. No. 170, para. 5.50.
[117] Matrimonial and Family Proceedings Act 1984, s.1; Law Com. No. 116.
[118] Para. 4.16.
[119] Paras. 5.63–5.64.
[120] Law Com. No. 170, para. 5.52(xii).
[121] Para. 5.67 above.

decree of divorce without receiving evidence from the petitioner. Thus at present there is no automatic procedure for converting a decree of separation into one of divorce. The system requires the filing and service of two petitions, the first of which cites one of the five facts as the ground, and the second of which cites the fact that the marriage has irretrievably broken down as the ground, this being proved by one of the previously established five facts.

5.87 This system has been criticised[122] for being wasteful, causing duplication of work and additional costs. At present, this is difficult to avoid, given that in theory the grounds for separation and divorce are not the same. Under our recommendations, however, the ground for both orders would be identical, as would the period of consideration and reflection. We see no reason to require another statement of marital breakdown to be made, nor a further twelve month period to run, before a divorce can be granted. We therefore *recommend* that either spouse should be able to apply to convert a separation order into a divorce order at any time after the separation order is made, provided that the parties have been married for at least one year and eleven months. The court should automatically convert the separation order one month after the application, unless there is a postponement or the hardship bar is successfully invoked.

---

[122] Maidment, *op. cit.*, pp. 77–78.

PART VI

FINANCIAL PROVISION AND PROPERTY ADJUSTMENT ORDERS
FURTHER RECOMMENDATIONS

Interim periodical payments orders

6.1 Under the Matrimonial Causes Act 1973[1] the court has power to order maintenance for either spouse "pending determination of the suit". Given that we have recommended that the court have power to order final periodical payments during the period of consideration and reflection,[2] maintenance pending suit will become irrelevant. However where the court is not in a position to make a final periodical payments order, for example because of lack of adequate information about the spouses' resources, then we *recommend* that the court have power to make an interim periodical payments order. The court should have the same power in relation to the children of the family.

Variation of settlement of property orders

6.2 Property adjustment orders are intended to be a once and for all settlement of the couple's affairs.[3] Given that we have recommended that, if special circumstances warrant this, it should be possible for such orders to take effect before the divorce or separation, we *recommend* that the court should seek, so far as possible, to deal with all adjustments of property comprehensively on one occasion.

6.3 However, even under the present law there is concern that the courts have only very limited powers to vary property adjustment orders and this could cause even greater problems if our recommendations are implemented. Currently, transfer of property orders cannot be varied at all, and settlement of property orders can only be varied if they were made on or after a decree of judicial separation and this decree is either rescinded or superseded by a divorce.[4] This means that the court can do nothing about a settlement made on divorce; for example, it cannot revoke a settlement order and substitute a compensating property transfer or lump sum order. This has undoubtedly caused hardship and injustice. Experience has shown that settlement of property orders are usually made at a time in the lives of spouses and their children when it is extremely difficult to predict events which may occur and needs which may arise some ten to fifteen years ahead. This has been particularly so with the "Mesher" type order, where the house is settled upon the parties in fixed shares, but not to be sold until, for example, the youngest child reaches a certain age or the mother re-marries.[5] Such an order cannot be varied even though the shares were fixed on the assumption that, for example, one party would continue to pay mortgage instalments or make periodical payments, which in fact he or she has not done.[6]

6.4 Experience of "the chickens coming home to roost"[7] with such orders has led to their condemnation in the Court of Appeal as "likely to produce harsh and unsatisfactory results".[8] Nevertheless, there are still cases in which some form of settlement or resettlement is the most appropriate order. We consider that more flexibility should be given to the court, not in order to alter the underlying principle upon which the overall settlement was based, but to give better effect to that principle in the light of subsequent developments. We therefore *recommend* that the court should have power to vary property settlement orders, including variation of marriage settlement orders, which were made in contemplation of, at, or after, the making of a separation or divorce order, at any time thereafter.

---

[1] s.22.

[2] Para. 5.54 above.

[3] Financial Provision in Matrimonial Proceedings (1969), Law Com. No. 25, para. 87; *Carson* v. *Carson* [1983] 1 W.L.R. 285; *Norman* v. *Norman* [1983] 1 W.L.R. 295.

[4] MCA, s.31(2)(e) and (4).

[5] *Mesher* v. *Mesher and Hall* (1973) (Note) [1980] 1 All E.R. 126, CA; *Hanlon* v. *Hanlon* [1978] 1 W.L.R. 592, CA; *Carson* v. *Carson* [1983] 1 W.L.R. 285; *Harvey* v. *Harvey* [1982] Fam. 83; *Harman* v. *Glencross* [1985] Fam. 49; *Mortimer* v. *Mortimer-Griffin* [1986] 2 F.L.R. 315, CA.

[6] E.g. *Carson* v. *Carson* [1983] 1 W.L.R. 285.

[7] *Ibid.*, per Omrod L.J. at p. 291.

[8] *Mortimer* v. *Mortimer-Griffin* [1986] 2 F.L.R. 315, per Parker L.J. at p. 319.

6.5 In order that the parties know at the outset where they stand, however, we *recommend* that the court should only have such a power to vary if the original order contains a clause enabling it to do so, either in general or in limited respects. In our view, it would not be practicable to limit this power in any other way. The circumstances of cases are infinitely various and the settlement order in question will often be only one part of a complex picture which may, or may not, include lump sum payments, periodical payments for either spouse or the children, or the outright transfer of other property. The courts can be expected to exercise a variation power reasonably and in accordance with the spirit of the overall settlement. It would, however, be helpful for everyone to know at the outset whether or not the settlement order would be capable of variation in the future. The possibility of variation might then be taken into account in structuring the original settlement. If there were no such clause in the relevant court order, therefore, the court should not have power to vary, even to the limited extent that it now has power to do so.

6.6 We also *recommend* that the extent to which the court may vary should include not only variation of the terms of the settlement, for example by bringing forward or postponing sale, but also extinguishing the settlement. The court should have power at the same time to order a transfer of property or lump sum in substitution for the interests extinguished by the variation, irrespective of whether the court has previously made a transfer or lump sum order. This power to order a subsequent transfer or lump sum should be seen in the context of the exercise of a special variation power and not as a way round the generally accepted principle that property transfer orders are final, once and for all orders.

6.7 The above recommendations would produce an inconsistency with the Children Act 1989 which similarly does not permit the variation of settlement orders made for the benefit of children.[9] We therefore *recommend* that the court should have power to vary such orders in the future provided that the court order contains a provision enabling the court to do so. Likewise the court should have power when varying settlement of property orders whether by accelerating or extinguishing interests, to order transfer of property or a lump sum. This should in no way affect the principle enshrined in the Children Act that the court may not make more than one property adjustment order of the same type against the same parent in favour of the same child.[10]

Variation of financial provision orders

6.8 At present the court has power to vary a periodical payments order and a secured periodical payments order.[11] In conjunction with this power the court is required to consider whether in all the circumstances it would be appropriate to vary the periodical payments order so that payments continue only for a specified term.[12] Thus the court has power to impose a "clean break" when dealing with a variation application. The length of the period during which payments are to continue should be such period as would enable the payee to adjust without undue hardship to the termination of maintenance.

6.9 When considering the changes in the law relating to financial provision, which were necessary as a result of our recommendations on the ground for divorce, it could not escape our attention that the exercise of the court's power to substitute a "clean break" for a continuing maintenance obligation was unduly hampered by the fact that the court cannot make a property transfer or a lump sum order at that stage.[13] This restriction results in difficulties such as those manifested in *S. v. S.*,[14] where the court was unable directly to order the husband to pay a sufficient lump sum to compensate the wife for loss of future periodical payments, even though he could well have afforded it. Of course, such an arrangement can be brought about by agreement between the parties, but if the payer will not agree the court cannot order it.

6.10 It seems desirable to us that the court should have power to order a transfer of

---

[9] Cf. Sched. 1, para. 1(4) and (5).
[10] Sched. 1, para. 1(5)(b).
[11] MCA, s.31(2)(b) and (c).
[12] s.31(7)(a).
[13] s.31(5).
[14] [1986] 1 F.L.R. 71.

property or a lump sum where this would be appropriate in order to bring about a clean break instead of a continuing periodical payments order. Accordingly, we *recommend* that the courts should have power to make a property adjustment order or lump sum order when discharging or limiting the term of a periodical payments order. This power should in no way derogate from the principle that property adjustment and lump sum orders at, upon, or after, separation and divorce orders should be regarded as once and for all orders. The problem has been that the capital orders made at divorce take into account the continuing maintenance obligations; if that continued obligation is brought to an end, it may well be appropriate for a larger capital settlement to be made.

PART VII

COLLECTED RECOMMENDATIONS

Part III—Divorce

7.1 Irretrievable breakdown of the marriage should remain the sole ground for divorce (para. 3.48; clause 2(1)(a)).

7.2 The ground should be proved by the expiry of a minimum period of one year for consideration of the practical consequences which would result from a divorce and reflection on whether the breakdown in the marital relationship is irreparable (para. 3.48; clauses 2(1), (2)(b), 5(1), (2)).

Part IV—Other matrimonial remedies
Judicial separation

7.3 Judicial separation should remain available as an alternative to divorce (para. 4.11; clause 1(1)(b)).

7.4 Irretrievable breakdown of the marriage should become the ground for judicial separation (para. 4.14; clause 2(1)(a)).

7.5 The ground for judicial separation should be proved in the same way as the ground for divorce, by the expiry of a minimum period of one year for consideration and reflection (para. 4.16; clauses 2(1), (2)(b), 5(1), (2)).

7.6 The procedures for divorce and judicial separation should be integrated into a single system, leaving the choice between the remedies to be made at the end of the period, when the application for an order is made to the court (para. 4.19; clause 2(1)).

7.7 To retain the present position for judicial separation, it should be possible for the period to begin within the first year of marriage and a separation to be granted once it has elapsed. To retain the effect of the present bar on petitioning for divorce within one year of the marriage, however, no divorce should be granted until the parties have been married at least two years (paras. 4.16, 4.19; clauses 2(2), 5(1), (3)).

Financial provision in magistrates' courts

7.8 The grounds for applying for financial provision under section 1 of the Domestic Proceedings and Magistrates' Courts Act 1978 should be limited to failure to maintain the applicant spouse or the children; the present grounds based on behaviour and desertion in section 1(1)(c) and (d) should be repealed (para. 4.28; clause 17(1)).

7.9 The grounds for applying for an order confirming payments made voluntarily during a separation of three months or more should no longer exclude cases where one party has deserted the other (para. 4.28; clause 17(2)).

Part V—The procedures in detail

7.10 The law's terminology should be modified as follows:
 (i) a separation or divorce should be sought by application, rather than "prayed" for by petition (para. 5.3; clause 2(1)(b));
 (ii) the parties should be referred to as "husband" and "wife", rather than "petitioner" and "respondent" (para. 5.3);
 (iii) the title of proceedings should be "In the matter of the marriage of" with the full names of spouses following (para. 5.3);
 (iv) both divorce and separation should be by order rather than decree (para. 5.4; clause 1(1));
 (v) the prefix "judicial" should no longer be applied to a separation order (para. 5.6; clause 1(1)(b));
 (vi) a separation or divorce order should be in neutral form, merely stating that the marriage of named spouses has been dissolved or that the named spouses are separated (para. 5.7).

Initiation of the period of consideration and reflection

7.11 The period should be initiated by a statement that the maker or makers believe that their marital relationship has broken down (para. 5.9; clause 2(2)(a)).

7.12 Where the parties are agreed that their marital relationship has broken down, it should be possible for them to make a joint statement; where they are not so agreed, one party should make the statement and a copy be sent to the other (paras. 5.10–5.11; clause 2(2)(a); see also clause 20(1)(f)).

7.13 Statements of marital breakdown should be made to and lodged at a court (para. 5.14; see clause 20(1)(c)).

7.14 The statements should be made on a prescribed form and sworn before a Commissioner for Oaths or court official (para. 5.17; see clause 20(1)(b)).

7.15 Both parties should also be supplied with a comprehensive information pack dealing with (para. 5.19; see clause 20(1)(e)):

 (i) the purpose of the period, the procedures during it, and the options available at the end of it;
 (ii) the legal effects of divorce and separation;
 (iii) the powers and duties of the court in relation to children, financial provision and property adjustment;
 (iv) the nature and purposes of counselling, reconciliation, conciliation and mediation and the services which are available in the area.

7.16 The Lord Chancellor should have power to make rules requiring each party's legal adviser to state whether information has been given to the client about the nature and purposes of counselling, reconciliation, conciliation and mediation, and the services available in the area, or referrals made to such services (para. 5.20; clause 20(2)).

7.17 Statements of marital breakdown should be accompanied by detailed statements, containing information and proposals relating to the children, home, other property and income resources of the parties (para. 5.21; see clause 20(1)(a), (d)).

7.18 The formalities for making the statement of marital breakdown, lodging it at court, service of documents and the content and distribution of information packs should be prescribed by rules to be made by the Lord Chancellor (para. 5.24; clause 20).

The period of consideration and reflection

7.19 In order clearly to demonstrate that the marital relationship has broken down irretrievably and to give a realistic time for the partners to resolve the practical consequences, the minimum overall period of consideration and reflection should be one year (paras. 5.25–5.27).

7.20 The minimum period between making a statement of marital breakdown and applying for a divorce or separation order should be eleven months (para. 5.27; clause 5(1)(b)).

7.21 The period between making the application and making the order should be one month (para. 5.79; clause 5(2)(b)).

7.22 The Lord Chancellor should have power to vary the periods of eleven months and one month respectively, by order approved by each House of Parliament, but not so as to alter the overall minimum period of one year (para. 5.79; clause 5(6), (7)).

7.23 The period should not automatically be longer where there are relevant children for the purpose of section 41 of the Matrimonial Causes Act 1973 (para. 5.28).

Counselling, conciliation and mediation

7.24 Counselling, conciliation and mediation services are an important element in developing a new and more constructive approach to the problems of marital breakdown and divorce (para. 5.31).

7.25 Undertaking any form of counselling, conciliation or mediation should be purely voluntary (para. 5.35).

7.26 Opportunities and encouragement to resolve matters amicably should be built into the system where appropriate (para. 5.36; clauses 8(2)(a), 9, 10, 20(1)(e), (i), (2)).

7.27 In relation to any proceedings connected with the breakdown of the marriage, the court should have power to direct that the spouses attend a preliminary interview with a specified person or agency in order that they can be given an explanation of the nature and purpose of conciliation or mediation and an opportunity to participate if they agree. That person or agency should be required to report back to the court within a given time limit. This power should be exercisable by the court of its own motion or on application by either spouse (para. 5.38; clause 9(1), (3), (4)).

7.28 The court should have power to adjourn the hearing of any proceedings connected with the breakdown of the marriage to enable the parties to participate in conciliation or mediation or otherwise to seek to resolve their dispute amicably. Such an adjournment should be for a specified period and one or both parties should be required to report back to the court (para. 5.39; clause 9(2), (5), (6)).

Privilege

7.29 A statutory privilege should be conferred on statements made during the course of conciliation or mediation procedures to the effect that no statement made during such procedures should be admissible in any civil or criminal proceedings without the consent of both spouses (paras. 5.44, 5.45; clause 10(1), (2), (3)).

7.30 Statements made during conciliation or mediation which indicate a risk of harm to a child should be privileged but not confidential (para. 5.48).

7.31 Privilege relating to reconciliation procedures and legal professional privilege should continue to be governed by the common law (paras. 5.42, 5.49; clause 10(4)).

Preliminary assessment by the court

7.32 No later than twelve weeks from the date when the statement of marital breakdown is made, the court should hold a preliminary assessment, in order to monitor progress on the arrangements being made and to make any orders or exercise any of its powers which can appropriately be exercised at that time (paras. 5.50, 5.51; clause 8(1)).

7.33 In addition, the court should have the following specific duties (para. 5.51; clause 8(2)):

   (i) to identify any relevant children of the family and to consider whether or not to exercise any of its powers under the Children Act 1989 in respect of them;

  (ii) to identify issues in dispute between the parties and to consider how these might most amicably be resolved, including how best to encourage participation in conciliation or mediation if appropriate;

 (iii) to give directions for the conduct of proceedings relating to those issues which have not yet been resolved;

  (iv) to consider what orders relating to financial provision or property adjustment have already been agreed;

   (v) to consider whether or not to exercise its powers to extend the period on the grounds of incapacity or delay in service; and

  (vi) to consider whether the hardship bar is likely to be raised and on what grounds.

7.34 The court should have power to adjourn and re-convene the assessment within a specified time, and from time to time thereafter, until all matters have been concluded, the proceedings have been withdrawn or have lapsed, or a divorce order has been made (para. 5.51; clause 8(3)).

7.35 The procedures for the preliminary assessment should be prescribed either by rules made by the Lord Chancellor or by rules of court (para. 5.52; clause 20(1)(h), (3)).

7.36 The Lord Chancellor should have power to vary the twelve week requirement by order approved by each House of Parliament (para. 5.52; clause 8(4), (5)).

Orders during the period

7.37 The court should have power, on application or of its own motion, to make orders relating to children, and financial provision and property adjustment orders, at any time during the period of consideration and reflection (para. 5.53; Children Act 1989, s.10(1); clauses 11, 12, 13).

7.38 Financial provision and property adjustment orders should be capable of taking effect during the period, but property adjustment orders should only take effect before separation or divorce where the court is satisfied that there are special circumstances making it appropriate for them to do so (para. 5.54; clauses 11, 12, 13).

7.39 It should be possible, where parties become reconciled, for property and lump sum orders to be set aside upon joint application; where the order has taken effect, setting aside should only be possible if it will not prejudice the interests of children or third parties. Where parties do not make such an application the orders should stand, even if separation or divorce is not proceeded with (para. 5.54; clause 16).

7.40 The court should have power to exercise both its inherent jurisdiction and its powers under the Domestic Violence and Matrimonial Proceedings Act 1976 or any other legislation, to protect parties from violence or molestation, and to determine the occupation of the matrimonial home, at any time during the period of consideration and reflection (para. 5.55; clause 18).

Extending the period

7.41 The court should have power, of its own motion or on application by either party, to extend the period by ordering postponement of divorce or separation on one or more of the following grounds (para. 5.58; clauses 6(1), (2), (5), 7(1)):

(i) that the court is likely to exercise its powers under the Children Act 1989 in relation to any child of the family, but is not yet in a position to do so, and postponement is desirable in the interests of such a child;

(ii) (subject to paragraph 7.43 below) that proper financial arrangements, for either spouse or any child, have not been made and postponement is desirable in order for such arrangements to be made;

(iii) that one party lacks legal capacity and postponement is desirable to enable the necessary steps to be taken to protect his interests;

(iv) that there has been a delay in service of documents, and postponement is desirable in order to prevent prejudice arising from the delay;

(v) that it is desirable, in the circumstances set out in paragraph 7.57 below, for the divorce to be postponed in order for an application for the imposition of a hardship bar to be properly determined.

7.42 When ordering postponement the court should specify the length of the period of postponement and this could be by reference to the taking of specified steps or satisfying the court on specified matters. Orders should be capable of variation or revocation (para. 5.59; clause 7(2), (4), (6)).

7.43 When considering whether or not postponement is desirable in order to enable proper financial arrangements to be made, the court should have regard to whether there are any circumstances making it appropriate for the arrangements to be made before the divorce or separation takes place, the conduct of the parties in relation to making those financial arrangements and any prejudice which either party or any children will suffer if there is a delay (para. 5.60; clause 6(3)).

7.44 Postponement on the grounds (iii) and (iv) should be possible at any time after a statement of marital breakdown has been made; postponement on grounds (i) and (ii) should only be possible after at least six months have elapsed since the statement; postponement on ground (v) should only be possible after a divorce application (para. 5.61; clause 7(5)).

7.45 The Lord Chancellor should have power to alter the six months provision, by order approved by each House of Parliament (para. 5.61; clause 7(7), (8)).

Abridging the period

7.46 The court should not have power to abridge the period of consideration and reflection (para. 5.64).

Reconciliation

7.47 The running of the period of consideration and reflection or of transition (including any period of postponement) should automatically be suspended where both parties jointly notify the court that they wish to attempt a reconciliation. It should be open to either party to start the period running again by notifying the court to this effect (para. 5.66; clauses 5(4), 7(3)).

7.48 Where no notification to this effect is received by the court within eighteen months of the date of suspension, the period which had elapsed before suspension should lapse (para. 5.67; clause 5(5)).

7.49 The Lord Chancellor should have power, by order approved by each House of Parliament, to alter the period of eighteen months (para. 5.67; clause 5(6), (7)).

7.50 It should be possible for the parties jointly to withdraw the statement of marital breakdown in order to stop the period running, should they both wish to do so (para. 5.68; clause 2(5)(a)).

Application for a divorce or separation order

7.51 An order for separation or divorce should not be made unless an application for such an order has been made by one or both spouses and that application has not been withdrawn (para. 5.69; clause 2(1)).

7.52 It should only be possible to apply for a divorce or separation order after at least eleven months have elapsed since the statement of marital breakdown (para. 5.69; clause 5(1)).

7.53 Such application should incorporate a declaration that the maker or makers believe that, having reflected on the breakdown in their marital relationship, the breakdown is irreparable and in consequence ask for either a divorce or separation order (para. 5.70; clause 2(2)(c)).

7.54 It should be possible for either or both parties to apply for an order, irrespective of who made the statement of marital breakdown (para. 5.71; clause 2(4)).

Grave financial or other hardship

7.55 It should be possible for the court to impose a bar on divorce (but not separation) if the dissolution of the marriage would result in grave financial or other grave hardship to one of the parties and it would in all the circumstances be wrong to dissolve the marriage (para. 5.75; clause 4(1)).

7.56 In appropriate cases, consideration should be given at the preliminary assessment to whether or not the hardship bar is likely to be invoked and on what grounds (para. 5.76; clause 8(2)(c)).

7.57 The hardship bar should only be imposed upon the application of one party after the other has made a sole application for a divorce (para. 5.76; clause 4(1)).

7.58 The court should have power to postpone the divorce if it is probable that the applicant for a hardship bar will be able to prove grave financial or other hardship, there are exceptional circumstances making it impracticable to decide the case within the one month period of transition, and postponement is desirable in order that the matter can be properly determined. In deciding whether to postpone the court should have regard to any delay in making relevant matters known to either party (para. 5.76; clause 6(1), (2)(e), (4)).

7.59 The court should have power to revoke an order imposing a bar, upon application by either or both parties, where it is satisfied that the grounds for continuing the bar no longer exist (para. 5.77; clause 4(2)).

7.60 Where the court revokes the order barring divorce, provided that all necessary conditions have been met, the court should have power to make a divorce order after a period of one month, or earlier if appropriate (para. 5.77; clause 4(3), (4)).

Making the divorce or separation order

7.61 Where an application for a separation or divorce order is made, that order should be issued automatically provided that the following conditions are fulfilled (para. 5.78):

(i) an application in the required form, containing the recommended declaration, for divorce or separation has been made by one or both spouses before the time for doing so expired (see paragraph 7.66 below);

(ii) the required period of consideration and reflection had elapsed before the application, taking any suspension or postponement into account;

(iii) the period was initiated in the required manner, by a statement by one or both spouses, of their belief that the marital relationship had broken down and that statement had not been jointly withdrawn;

(iv) the required period of transition (taking into account any suspension or postponement) has elapsed since the application, the application has not been withdrawn (by both if it is a joint application), and no hardship bar has been imposed; and

(v) no stay has been imposed under the Domicile and Matrimonial Proceedings Act 1973.

7.62 A period of transition of one month's duration should elapse between the application for and the issue of an order, making a total minimum overall period of twelve months (para. 5.79; clauses 2(2), 5(1), (2)).

7.63 Where one spouse applies for separation and the other divorce, the court should grant the divorce unless a hardship bar is imposed (para. 5.80; see clause 3(3)).

7.64 There should be no requirement that the parties have ceased to co-habit at the end of the period (para. 5.81).

Position where the parties have not been married for one year

7.65 It should not be possible for either party to apply for a divorce order until they have been married for at least one year and eleven months; the court should not make the order until the one month period of transition has elapsed, making an overall total of two years (para. 5.83; clause 5(3)).

Lapse of proceedings

7.66 Proceedings should lapse automatically if no application is made by either or both spouses for a divorce or separation order within six months of the end of the period of consideration and reflection as extended by any period of suspension or postponement (para. 5.85; clause 2(5)(b)).

7.67 The Lord Chancellor should have power, by order approved by each House of Parliament, to alter the six month time limit (para. 5.85; clause 2(6), (7)).

Conversion of separation to divorce

7.68 Either spouse should be able to apply to the court to convert a separation order into a divorce order at any time after the separation order is made, provided that at the time of application the parties have been married for at least one year and eleven months. The court should automatically convert the separation into a divorce one month after application unless there is a postponement or a hardship bar is imposed (para. 5.87; clause 3(1), (2)).

Part VI—Financial provision and property adjustment orders—further recommendations
Interim financial provision

7.69 The court should have power to make interim financial provision orders during the period if it is not yet in a position to make final orders (para. 6.1; clause 12).

Variation of settlement of property orders

7.70 The court should seek so far as possible to deal with all adjustments of property comprehensively on one occasion (para. 6.2; clause 13).

7.71 The court should have power to vary property settlement orders or variation of marriage settlement orders, which are made in contemplation of, at, or after, the making of a separation or divorce order, at any time thereafter (para. 6.4; clause 15).

7.72 This should only be possible if the original order contains a clause enabling the court so to vary it (para. 6.5; clause 15(1)).

7.73 The court should have power, not only to vary the terms of the settlement, but also to extinguish it. The court should have power at the same time to order transfer of property or a lump sum in substitution for any interests extinguished by the variation, irrespective of whether the court has on a previous occasion made a transfer of property or lump sum order (para. 6.6; clause 15(3)).

7.74 The court should have a similar power under the Children Act 1989, Sched. 1, para. 1(4) and (5) to vary settlement orders made in respect of children, provided that the original order contains a clause giving such a variation power. The power should be the same as in the case of a spouse (para. 6.7; Sched. 2, para. 40(2)).

Variation of financial provision orders

7.75 When dealing with an application for variation or discharge of a periodical payments order, the court should have power to make a property adjustment or lump sum order, where it considers this appropriate in order to enable it to bring about a "clean break" by discharging or limiting the term of the periodical payments order (para. 6.10; Sched. 2, para. 15(4)).

(*Signed*) PETER GIBSON, *Chairman*
TREVOR M. ALDRIDGE
JACK BEATSON
RICHARD BUXTON
BRENDA HOGGETT

MICHAEL COLLON, *Secretary*
21 September 1990.

Draft

Divorce and Separation Bill

ARRANGEMENT OF CLAUSES

Supplemental provisions

DRAFT

OF A

BILL

TO

Make new provision with respect to the circumstances in which orders of divorce and separation may be made in relation to marriages; and to amend the law with respect to connected proceedings in cases of marital breakdown.

BE IT ENACTED by the Queen's most Excellent Majesty, by and with the advice and consent of the Lords Spiritual and Temporal, and Commons, in this present Parliament assembled, and by the authority of the same, as follows:—

Divorce and separation orders

Nature of
divorce and
separation
orders.

1.—(1) The following orders may, in accordance with the provisions of this Act, be made by the court in relation to a marriage, namely—

(a) an order (to be known as an "order of divorce") dissolving the marriage as from the time of the making of the order;

(b) an order (to be known as a "separation order") removing, for so long as it is in force, any obligation of the parties to the marriage to cohabit and having effect as provided in subsection (2) below in relation to any intestacy of a party to the marriage.

(2) Where—

(a) a separation order is in force in relation to a marriage;

(b) the separation of the parties to the marriage is continuing; and

(c) either of the parties to the marriage dies intestate as respects all or any of his real or personal property,

the property as respects which that party to the marriage died intestate shall devolve as if the other party to the marriage had then been dead.

(3) A separation order shall come into force on the making of the order and shall continue in force for so long as the marriage subsists or until it is revoked by the court on the joint application of the parties to the marriage.

EXPLANATORY NOTES

Clause 1

1. This clause deals with the type of orders which the court can make and the nature of those orders. It uses the new terminology recommended in paragraphs 5.1-5.7 of the report.

Subsection (1)
2. This subsection empowers the court to make two types of order:-

(a) an order of divorce which has the effect of dissolving a marriage;

(b) a separation order which has the effect of removing any obligation of the parties to co-habit; this corresponds to the effect of a decree of judicial separation provided for in section 18(2) of the Matrimonial Causes Act 1973 (referred to as the 1973 Act), which is repealed in Schedule 3.

Subsection (2)
3. This subsection provides for the effect of a separation order on the devolution of property should either party to the marriage die intestate. It corresponds to the provision made in respect of decrees of judicial separation by section 18(3) of the 1973 Act, which is repealed in Schedule 3.

Subsection (3)
4. This subsection provides that a separation order will remain in force unless it is subsequently revoked upon joint application by the parties to the marriage, or the marriage ceases to exist, for example if either party dies or there is a subsequent divorce.

Making of orders.

2.—(1) Subject to the following provisions of this Act, where—

(a) a marriage has broken down irretrievably;

(b) an application in relation to the marriage for an order of divorce, or for a separation order, is made by one or both of the parties to the marriage; and

(c) the court has jurisdiction to entertain that application under section 19 below,

it shall be the duty of the court, unless the application is withdrawn, to make that order at the end of the period of transition which, under section 5(2) below, must elapse before the making of an order on that application.

(2) For the purposes of this section a marriage to which an application under this section relates shall be taken to have broken down irretrievably if and only if—

(a) a statement has been made by one or both of the parties to the marriage that the maker of the statement, or each of them, believes that there is a breakdown in the marital relationship and wishes, as a consequence, to make arrangements for the future;

(b) the period for the consideration of future arrangements and for reflection which, under section 5(1) below, must elapse before an application is made by reference to that statement has elapsed; and

(c) the application is accompanied by a declaration by one or both of the parties to the marriage that the maker of the declaration, or each of them, believes that the breakdown is irreparable.

(3) For the purposes of this section and of any other enactment referring to the making of a statement of marital breakdown, such a statement shall be taken to have been made only if the requirements of any rules under section 20 below with respect to the making of the statement and its notification to the court have been complied with; and such a statement shall not be made with respect to a marriage if—

(a) a statement of marital breakdown has previously been made with respect to the marriage and it will become possible, or remains possible, for an application under this section to be made by reference to the previous statement; or

(b) a separation order is in force, or an application under this section is pending, in relation to that marriage.

(4) For the purposes of an application made under this section by reference to a statement of marital breakdown it shall be immaterial that the application and the statement are not both made by the same party or parties.

(5) Where a statement of marital breakdown has been made with respect to a marriage, an application for an order of divorce, or for a separation order, shall not be made by reference to that statement if—

(a) the parties to the marriage have jointly given notice that that statement has been withdrawn; or

EXPLANATORY NOTES

Clause 2

1. This clause deals with the circumstances in which divorce and separation orders are to be made by the court, as set out in paragraph 5.78 of the report.

Subsection (1)

2. This subsection requires the court to make a divorce or separation order where the marriage has broken down irretrievably (as defined in subsection (2)), the court has jurisdiction (as provided in clause 19), and an application for the order has been made by one or both parties to the marriage. The order is to be made after the transition period of one month (prescribed by clause 5(2)) has elapsed, provided that the application has not been withdrawn. This implements the recommendations in paragraphs 3.43 and 4.14 of the report.

Subsection (2)

3. This subsection provides that a marriage has irretrievably broken down if, but only if, the following three requirements have been fulfilled:

(a) a statement of marital breakdown has been made by one or both parties to the marriage;

(b) the period of eleven months (prescribed by clause 5(1)) for consideration of future arrangements and for reflection has elapsed; and

(c) the application is accompanied by a declaration by one or both of the parties to the marriage that he, she or they believe that the breakdown is irreparable.

These matters are discussed, and implement recommendations made, in paragraphs 3.43, 4.16, 5.9, 5.10, 5.11, 5.70 and 5.79 of the report.

Subsection (3)

4. The effect of this subsection is that a statement of marital breakdown shall not be taken to have been "made" for the purposes of this Act, or any other Act, unless the requirements of rules made by the Lord Chancellor under clause 20 as to the formalities for making statements and lodging them with the court have been complied with. It also prevents a second statement of marital breakdown being made in relation to the same marriage whilst a previous statement or application for an order is still "live", i.e. has not been withdrawn or lapsed. It therefore prevents the spouses making separate statements "against" one another or attempting to run two concurrent or overlapping periods. It also prevents a statement being made whilst a separation order is in existence. Where there is such an order, a spouse who wants a divorce should instead apply for the separation order to be converted into a divorce, under clause 3.

Subsection (4)

5. This subsection makes it clear that either or both of the parties may apply for the divorce or separation order, irrespective of which of them made the statement of marital breakdown. This implements the recommendation made in paragraph 5.71 of the report.

(b) more than six months have elapsed since the earliest time when, in accordance with this Act and any directions given for the purposes of section 6 below, an application for an order of divorce could have been made by reference to that statement.

(6) The Lord Chancellor may by order made by statutory instrument amend paragraph (b) of subsection (5) above so as to vary the length of the period for the time being specified in that paragraph.

(7) No order shall be made under subsection (6) above unless a draft of the order has been laid before, and approved by a resolution of, each House of Parliament; and an order under that subsection may contain such transitional provisions as the Lord Chancellor considers appropriate.

EXPLANATORY NOTES

Subsection (5)

6.   This subsection provides that an application for a divorce or separation order cannot be made where (a) the statement of marital breakdown has been jointly withdrawn by the spouses, or (b) the time allowed for making an application has expired. This will happen once six months have elapsed from the earliest time when an application could have been made, taking into account any postponement ordered by the court under clause 6 and any suspension for an attempted reconciliation under clause 5(4). These implement recommendations made in paragraphs 5.68 and 5.85 of the report.

Subsections (6) and (7)

7.   These subsections enable the Lord Chancellor, by order subject to the affirmative resolution procedure, to vary the six month time limit provided for in subsection (5)(b). This implements the recommendation in paragraph 5.85 of the report.

Conversion of separation order into divorce order.

3.—(1) Subject to the following provisions of this Act, where—

(a) a separation order is in force in relation to a marriage; and

(b) an application is made by either or both of the parties to the marriage for an order of divorce in relation to the marriage,

it shall be the duty of the court, unless the application is withdrawn, to make the order of divorce at the end of the period of transition which, under section 5(2) below, must elapse before the making of an order on that application.

(2) Where a separation order is made by reference to a statement of marital breakdown which was made during the first year of a marriage, no application shall be made under this section by reference to that separation order before the earliest time after the making of that statement when, by virtue of section 5(3) below, it would have been possible for an application under section 2 above for an order of divorce to have been made in relation to the marriage.

(3) The making of a separation order at a time when an application for an order of divorce is pending in relation to the same marriage shall not affect either the court's duty to make an order on that application or the time at which the order is to be made.

Cases of grave hardship.

4.—(1) Where an application for an order of divorce in relation to a marriage has been made by one of the parties to the marriage and the court is satisfied, on the application of the other party to the marriage—

(a) that the dissolution of the marriage will result in grave financial or other grave hardship to that other party; and

(b) that it would be wrong, in all the circumstances, for the marriage to be dissolved,

the court may order that the marriage shall not be dissolved while the order is in force, whether on that or on any other application.

(2) Where an order under subsection (1) above has been made in relation to a marriage, the court, on an application made—

(a) by one or both of the parties to the marriage; and

(b) in accordance with such conditions (if any) as may have been imposed by the court when making the order,

shall revoke the order if it is satisfied that the grounds mentioned in that subsection no longer exist.

(3) Where an order under subsection (1) above is revoked, either or both of the parties to the marriage may make an application under this subsection for an order of divorce in relation to the marrriage.

(4) Subject to the following provisions of this Act, where an application is made under subsection (3) above, it shall be the duty of the court, unless the application is withdrawn, to make the order of divorce—

(a) at the end of the period of transition which, under section 5(2) below, must elapse before the making of an order on that application; or

(b) if the court thinks fit, at such earlier time as the court may determine.

EXPLANATORY NOTES

Clause 3

1.   This clause provides for conversion from separation orders to divorce orders.

Subsection (1)
2.   This subsection requires the court, where a separation order is in force, to make a divorce order at the end of the usual period of transition, i.e. one month, where a divorce is applied for by either or both spouses, and that application has not been withdrawn. This implements the recommendation in paragraph 5.87 of the report.

Subsection (2)
3.   This subsection prohibits an application for conversion from separation to divorce being made unless the parties have at the time been married for at least one year and eleven months. The effect of subsections (1) and (2) therefore is that a separation may not be converted into a divorce within the first two years of marriage. This implements the recommendation made in paragraph 5.87 of the report.

Subsection (3)
4.   This subsection provides what is to happen where there is an application for separation, followed within the one month transition period by an application for divorce. The court must make the separation order in the usual way, even though it will then be replaced by a divorce after the one month transition period has elapsed from the divorce application. This is discussed in paragraph 5.80 of the report.

Clause 4

1.   This clause deals with applications to bar divorce on the ground of grave financial or other grave hardship.

Subsection (1)
2.   This subsection gives the court power to refuse a divorce order, once it has been applied for by one party to the marriage, where it is satisfied, on application by the other party, that grave financial or other grave hardship would be caused to that other party by the dissolution of the marriage and that it would be wrong in all the circumstances to dissolve the marriage. Whilst such a bar is in force the court will have no power to make a divorce order upon any application by either or both spouses. This subsection replaces and extends section 5 of the 1973 Act, which has been repealed in Schedule 3, and implements the recommendation made in paragraph 5.75 of the report.

Subsection (2)
3.   This gives the court power to revoke an order barring divorce where revocation is applied for by one or both spouses, provided that the court is satisfied that the ground which gave rise to the bar no longer exists. This implements the recommendation made in paragraph 5.77 of the report.

Subsection (3)
4.   Once the order barring divorce has been revoked, either party, or both, may apply for a divorce, or for conversion from separation to divorce. This implements the recommendation made in paragraph 5.77 of the report.

(5) For the purposes of this section hardship, in relation to the dissolution of a marriage, shall be taken to include the loss of a chance of acquiring any benefit which a party to the marriage might acquire if the marriage were not dissolved.

Periods required to elapse before the making of applications and orders.

5.—(1) In the case of every statement of marital breakdown made with respect to a marriage—

(a) a period for consideration to be given to what (if any) arrangements should be made for the future and for the parties to the marriage to reflect on whether the breakdown is irreparable shall be required to elapse before an application may be made by reference to that statement; and

(b) subject to the following provisions of this section, that period shall be the period of eleven months, beginning with the day after the making of the statement.

(2) In the case of every application made to the court for an order of divorce, or for a separation order—

(a) there shall be a period of transition which shall be required to elapse before an order is made on that application; and

(b) subject to section 4(4)(b) above and the following provisions of this section, that period shall be the period of one month beginning with the day after the making of the application.

(3) For all purposes connected with any application for an order of divorce made by reference to a statement of marital breakdown, the period following that statement for the consideration of future arrangements and for reflection shall, if the statement was made before the first anniversary of the marriage, be treated as extended by a further period equal to the time between the day on which the statement was made and that anniversary.

(4) Where, at any time before the end of the period mentioned in subsection (1) or (2) above, a notice requiring time for an attempt at reconciliation is given jointly by the parties to the marriage in question, time falling—

(a) on or after the day on which the notice is given; and

(b) before the day on which either of the parties to the marriage gives notice that the attempt has been unsuccessful,

shall not count towards the expiry of that period and, accordingly, shall not be treated as included in that period.

(5) Where—

(a) the period mentioned in subsection (1) or (2) above is suspended under subsection (4) above by virtue of a notice requiring time for an attempt at reconciliation by the parties to a marriage; and

(b) the period of that suspension continues for more than eighteen months without either of the parties to the marriage giving notice that the attempt has been unsuccessful,

no order of divorce or separation order, and no application for such an order, shall be made in relation to the marriage except by reference to a statement of marital breakdown made after the end of

EXPLANATORY NOTES

Subsection (4)

5. Once a barring order has been revoked and an application for divorce made, this provides that the court must make the divorce order, after the usual one month transition period, unless it fixes an earlier time. This enables the court, if appropriate, to revoke the bar and make a divorce order, if applied for, on the same occasion. This implements the recommendation in paragraph 5.77 of the report.

Subsection (5)

6. This re-enacts subsection (3) of section 5 of the 1973 Act, which requires the court to take into account loss of contingent benefits, such as widows' pensions, in deciding whether dissolution of the marriage will cause hardship.

Clause 5

1. This clause deals with the periods which must elapse before an application may be made for an order and before the court makes the order applied for.

Subsection (1)

2. This subsection provides that an eleven month period, starting the day after a statement of marital breakdown has been "made" (which, by virtue of clause 2(3), means when it is lodged with the court in accordance with rules made under clause 20), shall elapse before an order may be applied for. The purpose of this period is stated to be consideration of arrangements for the future and reflection on whether the breakdown in the marital relationship is irreparable. The first stated purpose will involve not only the parties making arrangements but also the court considering those arrangements at the preliminary assessment under clause 8. The second purpose, that of reflection, will involve only the parties. It will be for them, or whichever of them makes an application, to declare at that time whether the breakdown is irreparable. This implements the recommendations made in paragraphs 3.43, 4.16, 5.27, 5.69 and 5.79 of the report.

Subsection (2)

3. This subsection provides that a further period, described as a period of transition, of one month's duration, starting the day after an application has been made, must elapse before the court makes a divorce or separation order. This means that after the day on which a statement of marital breakdown has been made, a year and a day must elapse before a divorce or separation order is made. The transition period gives a final opportunity to make applications for the order to be postponed, under clause 6, or for a hardship bar, under clause 4. This implements the recommendations made in paragraphs 3.43, 4.16, 5.27 and 5.79 of the report.

Subsection (3)

4. This subsection produces an effect similar to the ban on petitioning for divorce within one year of the marriage, at present contained in section 3 of the 1973 Act. It allows for the statement of marital breakdown to be made at any time after the marriage, but requires in effect that a period of one year and eleven months must have elapsed from the marriage before an application for divorce can be made. Section 3 of the Act of 1973 is consequently repealed in Schedule 3. The limitation does not apply to separation orders. This implements the recommendation in paragraph 5.83 of the report.

those eighteen months.

(6) The Lord Chancellor may by order made by statutory instrument amend the preceding provisions of this section so as to vary—

(a) the lengths of the periods for the time being specified in subsections (1) and (2) above; or

(b) the length of the period for the time being specified in subsection (5)(b) above;

but no order under this subsection shall be made by virtue of paragraph (a) above unless the effect of the order is that the aggregate of the periods specified in subsections (1) and (2) above continues (subject to subsections (3) and (4) above) to be twelve months.

(7) No order shall be made under subsection (6) above unless a draft of the order has been laid before, and approved by a resolution of, each House of Parliament; and an order under that subsection may contain such transitional provisions as the Lord Chancellor considers appropriate.

EXPLANATORY NOTES

Subsection (4)

5.   This subsection enables the parties to suspend either period, should they both wish to do so, during an attempted reconciliation. It provides that, where they jointly notify the court that they wish to attempt a reconciliation, any time which elapses between the day of this notification and the day of any notification by either party that the reconciliation attempt has failed will not count towards the eleven month period required before an application or, if suspension occurs after an application, towards the one month period required before an order. The period affected will therefore be extended by the amount of time during which the running of that period was suspended. This implements the recommendation made in paragraph 5.66 of the report.

Subsection (5)

6.   This subsection provides that where neither party notifies the court that the reconciliation attempt has failed (thus starting the period running again) within eighteen months of suspension, then the period which is suspended will lapse, so that no application for separation or divorce may be made or no order made on a pending application. A fresh statement of marital breakdown would have to be made, and a new period for consideration and reflection run its course.   This implements the recommendation made in paragraph 5.67 of the report.

Subsections (6) and (7)

7.   These subsections enable the Lord Chancellor, by order subject to the affirmative resolution procedure, to change the balance between the eleven month and one month periods in subsections (1) and (2), but not to change the overall period of twelve months. This implements the recommendation in paragraph 5.79 of the report.

8.   They also allow the Lord Chancellor similarly to vary the period of eighteen months provided in subsection (5).   This implements the recommendation in paragraph 5.67 of the report.

Power of court
to postpone the
making of an
order.

6.—(1) Subject to the following provisions of this section, where—

(a) a statement of marital breakdown has been made with respect to any marriage; or

(b) an application under this Act for an order of divorce, or for a separation order, has been made in relation to any marriage,

the court shall have power, on one or more of the grounds specified in subsection (2) below and in accordance with section 7 below, to require a period of delay before the making of such an order in relation to the marriage.

(2) The grounds on which the court may require a period of delay under this section are—

1989 c. 41.

(a) that, in a case in which the court is likely, but not yet in a position, to exercise any of its powers under the Children Act 1989 with respect to any relevant child of the family, the delay is desirable in the interests of the child;

(b) that, in a case in which—

(i) such financial arrangements as appear to the court to be proper have not yet been made in relation to the parties to the marriage and all the children of the family; and

(ii) it is impracticable, without a delay, for some or all of those arrangements to be made before the time when an order of divorce or separation order would have to be made in relation to the marriage,

the delay is desirable in order to allow time for such arrangements to be made;

(c) that, in a case in which a party to the marriage lacks the legal capacity to act on his or her own behalf, the delay is desirable in order to allow the necessary steps to be taken for protecting the interests of that party;

(d) that, in a case in which a party to the marriage would (if there were no delay) suffer any prejudice by reason of the exceptional length of the period before that party became aware of—

(i) the making of a statement of marital breakdown with respect to the marriage; or

(ii) the making of an application for an order of divorce, or for a separation order, in relation to the marriage,

the delay is desirable in order to prevent that party from suffering that prejudice;

(e) that, in a case in which—

(i) an application for an order under subsection (1) of section 4 above has been made;

(ii) it appears probable that a party to the marriage will be able to establish that there will be such grave hardship as would require the making of an order under that subsection; and

(iii) there are exceptional circumstances making it impracticable, without a delay, for the question whether such an order should be made to be properly determined

EXPLANATORY NOTES

Clause 6

1.   This clause deals with the power of the court, either of its own motion or upon application, to postpone the making of a separation or divorce order.

Subsection (1)
2.   This subsection empowers the court to require a period of delay before a divorce or separation order is made, provided that one or more of the grounds specified in subsection (2) is made out. This implements the recommendations made in paragraph 5.58 of the report.

Subsection (2)
3.   This subsection specifies five grounds on which the court may postpone an order. These are as follows:

(a)   Where the court has decided that it is likely to exercise any of its powers under the Children Act 1989, for example by making a residence or contact order, but is not yet for whatever reason in a position to do so, it may require a delay in the making of a separation or divorce order, provided that this would be desirable in the child's interests. This replaces section 41 of the 1973 Act, as substituted by paragraph 31 of Schedule 12 to the Children Act 1989, in so far as it applies in separation and divorce cases. Section 41 has consequently been amended by paragraph 21 of Schedule 2, so that it will apply only in nullity cases.

(b)   Where financial arrangements, which the court would consider proper, have not been made for the parties or for any child of the family, the court may require a delay where this would be desirable in order to give time for such arrangements to be made before the divorce or separation order.   This provision replaces and extends section 10 of the 1973 Act, which has been repealed in Schedule 3.   It is also subject to subsection (3).

(c)   The court may require a delay where this would be desirable in order to allow steps to be taken to protect the interests of a party who lacks legal capacity to act on his or her own behalf, for example by appointing a guardian ad litem.

(d)   Where a statement of marital breakdown or an application is made by one party only, and there has been exceptional delay in notifying the other spouse of such statement or application, the court may require a delay if this would be desirable in order to avoid that other spouse being prejudiced as a result of the delay in notification.

(e)   Where an application has been made for an order barring divorce on the ground that dissolution of the marriage would result in grave financial or other grave hardship to the applicant, and it is probable that the applicant will be able to prove grave hardship, but exceptionally the whole question cannot be decided within the one month transition period, the court may postpone the divorce if this is desirable in order to enable the application to be properly determined.   This implements the recommendation in paragraph 5.76 of the report.   It is also subject to subsection (4).

Subsection (3)
4.   This subsection requires the court, in exercising its power to postpone on the

before the time when an order of divorce would have to be made in relation to the marriage,

the delay is desirable in order to allow time for that question to be so determined.

(3) In determining for the purposes of paragraph (b) of subsection (2) above whether a delay is desirable in order to allow time for financial arrangements to be made, the court shall have regard, in particular, to—

(a) the extent (if any) to which there are circumstances of the case making it appropriate for financial arrangements to be made before an order of divorce or separation order is made in relation to the marriage;

(b) the extent and nature of any prejudice which will be suffered by either of the parties to the marriage, or any children of the family, if there is a delay; and

(c) the previous conduct of the parties with respect to, or to any proposals for, the making of any such arrangements.

(4) In determining for the purposes of paragraph (e) of subsection (2) above whether a delay is desirable in order to allow time for the question mentioned in that paragraph to be properly determined, the court shall have regard, in particular, to the extent (if any) to which the impracticability of that question being determined without a delay is attributable to the failure of a party to the marriage to make prompt disclosure to the other of—

(a) his intentions with respect to the making of an application for an order under section 4 above; or

(b) any of the matters by reference to which that question falls to be determined.

(5) In this section—

"financial arrangements" means any such arrangements as may be made by an order under Part II of the 1973 Act or by a maintenance agreement within the meaning of section 34 of that Act (validity of maintenance agreements); and

"relevant child of the family" means—

(a) any child of the family who has not reached the age of sixteen at the time when the court is considering whether to require a delay under this section; or

(b) any child of the family who has reached that age but in relation to whom the court has directed that he should be treated as a relevant child of the family for the purposes of this section.

ground of lack of proper financial arrangements, to have regard to any circumstances which make it appropriate that financial arrangements are made before divorce or separation, any prejudice which would result to either party or to the children from the delay and the conduct of the spouses in relation to proposals for, or the making of, those arrangements. This implements the recommendation made in paragraph 5.60 of the report.

Subsection (4)
5.   This subsection requires the court, in exercising its power to postpone where this is desirable in order that an application for a hardship bar can be properly determined, to have regard to any delay in disclosing to the other party an intention to apply for a bar or any matter relevant to deciding upon such a bar.   This implements the recommendation in paragraph 5.76 of the report.

Subsection (5)
6.   This defines "relevant child of the family" for the purposes of postponement on ground (a), and "financial arrangements" for the purposes of postponement on ground (b). The definition of "relevant child of the family" reproduces that contained in section 41(3) of the 1973 Act, as substituted by paragraph 31 of Schedule 12 to the Children Act 1989. It implements the recommendation made in paragraph 5.58 of the report.

Supplemental provision with respect to the court's powers under section 6.

7.—(1) Subject to subsection (5) below, the powers of the court under section 6 above to require a period of delay before the making of an order of divorce or separation order in relation to a marriage shall be exercisable in any proceedings connected with the breakdown of the marriage, whether or not an application for the delay has been made to the court by any person.

(2) Where the court requires a period of delay under section 6 above, it shall do so—

(a) in a case in which a statement of marital breakdown but no application for an order of divorce or for a separation order has been made, by directing that the earliest time for the making of an application by reference to that statement shall be taken to be such time as may be specified in the court's direction; and

(b) where an application for an order of divorce or for a separation order has been made, by directing that the time for the making of an order on that application shall be postponed until such time as may be so specified.

(3) Without prejudice to the court's powers under subsection (6) below, where the court gives a direction under this section for the purposes of section 6 above, subsections (4) and (5) of section 5 above shall have effect in relation to the period ending with the time specified in the direction as they have effect in relation to the periods specified in subsections (1) and (2) of that section 5.

(4) The power for the purposes of subsection (2) above to specify a time shall include power to define that time by reference to such factors (including the fulfilment of certain conditions or the satisfaction of the court as to certain matters) as the court thinks fit.

(5) The powers of the court, where a statement of marital breakdown but no application for an order of divorce or for a separation order has been made, to require a period of delay on either or both of the grounds specified in paragraphs (a) and (b) of section 6(2) above shall not be exercisable until after the end of the first six months of the period for the consideration of future arrangements and for reflection which, under section 5(1) above, must elapse before an application is made by reference to that statement.

(6) Where a period of delay is required under section 6 above, the court, on the application of either or both of the parties to the marriage in question, may revoke that requirement or modify it in such manner as it thinks fit; but the court shall not under this subsection extend a period of delay except on a ground specified in subsection (2) of that section.

(7) The Lord Chancellor may by order made by statutory instrument amend subsection (5) above so as to vary the length of the period for the time being specified in that subsection as that part of the period for the consideration of future arrangements and for reflection which must elapse before the court can require a period of delay on either or both of the grounds referred to in that subsection.

(8) No order shall be made under subsection (7) above unless a draft of the order has been laid before, and approved by a resolution

EXPLANATORY NOTES

Clause 7

1. This clause deals with supplemental provisions relating to the court's power to postpone under clause 6.

Subsection (1)
2. This subsection enables the court to exercise its powers to postpone both upon application and of its own motion. It implements the recommendation made in paragraph 5.58 of the report.

Subsections (2) and (4)
3. Subsection (2) provides that where postponement is ordered before an application for a divorce or separation order, then the court must specify the earliest date upon which an application for an order may be made; where postponement is ordered after an application then the court must specify the date on which the order is to be made. The power to postpone includes a power, not only to delay for a specific period of time, but also to delay until specific steps have been taken, specific conditions have been fulfilled or the court has been satisfied as to specific matters. This implements the recommendation made in paragraph 5.59 of the report.

Subsection (3)
4. This subsection provides that the period of any postponement will be extended by any suspension for an attempted reconciliation under clause 5(4) and that the whole case will lapse if the suspension lasts for 18 months. This implements the recommendation made in paragraph 5.66 of the report.

Subsection (5)
5. This subsection lays down the earliest time at which the power to postpone comes into play. In the case of grounds (a) and (b) (children and finance), the power will not arise until at least six months of the period of consideration and reflection have elapsed; in the case of grounds (c) and (d) (incapacity and delay in notification), the power will arise at any time after the statement of marital breakdown has been made. By its very terms, the power in ground (e) can only be exercised after one party has applied for a divorce and the other has applied to invoke the hardship bar. This implements the recommendation in paragraph 5.61 of the report.

Subsection (6)
6. This subsection gives the court power to revoke or modify any postponement order upon application by either or both spouses; however, the court may not extend the period of postponement unless one of the specified grounds for postponement exists. Modification could include shortening the period of delay, or altering any steps or conditions. This implements the recommendation in paragraph 5.59 of the Report.

Subsections (7) and (8)
7. These subsections enable the Lord Chancellor, by order subject to the affirmative resolution procedure, to vary the length of the period in subsection (5). This implements the recommendation in paragraph 5.61 of the report.

of, each House of Parliament; and an order under that subsection may contain such transitional provisions as the Lord Chancellor considers appropriate.

Preliminary assessments by the court

Preliminary
assessments by
the court.

8.—(1) Subject to section 19 below, it shall be the duty of the court, not more than twelve weeks after a statement of marital breakdown is made with respect to any marriage, to begin an initial consideration of the case (to be known as "a preliminary assessment") for the purpose—

(a) of reviewing progress in the making, in consequence of the breakdown, of arrangements for the future; and

(b) of enabling the court (whether or not any application is made to it) to make such orders and give such directions, in exercise of its powers apart from this section, as it considers appropriate in consequence of the review.

(2) On a preliminary assessment the court's function of reviewing progress in the making of arrangements for the future shall include, in particular, the following duties, that is to say—

(a) a duty to consider how issues which are in dispute between the parties, or may become subject to dispute, can most amicably be resolved and, how, for this purpose, the parties to the marriage might best be encouraged to participate in any conciliation or mediation procedures which the court thinks appropriate in the circumstances;

(b) a duty (subject to its duty by virtue of paragraph (a) above) to consider what directions it should give with respect to the conduct of any proceedings under this Act, under the 1973 Act, under Schedule 1 to the Matrimonial Homes Act 1983 or under the Children Act 1989, for the purpose of—

1983 c. 19.
1989 c. 41.

(i) facilitating the determination of questions arising in those proceedings; and

(ii) ensuring that the proceedings are disposed of without delay;

(c) a duty to consider whether those directions should include a direction to the parties to the marriage to disclose whether an application is likely to be made for an order under section 4 above and the grounds on which such an application would be made;

(d) a duty to consider—

(i) whether there is any child of the family who is, or should be treated as, a relevant child of the family for the purposes of section 6 above; and

(ii) whether (in the light of the arrangements which have been, or are proposed to be, made for the upbringing and welfare of any child who is or should be so treated) the court should exercise any of its powers under the Children Act 1989 in relation to any child of the family;

(e) a duty to ascertain, for the purpose of considering what (if any) provision should be made by orders under Part II of the 1973 Act (financial provision), whether there is any provision the inclusion of which in such an order would be acceptable to each of the parties; and

(f) a duty to consider whether the court should require a period of delay on either or both of the grounds specified in section

EXPLANATORY NOTES

Clause 8

1. This clause deals with preliminary assessments by the court.

Subsection (1)
2. This subsection imposes a duty on the court to arrange an initial consideration of the case, to be known as "a preliminary assessment". The duty will arise where the court has jurisdiction in the case (this is dealt with in clause 19) and the assessment must begin within twelve weeks from when a statement of marital breakdown is made. The function of the court will be to review progress in making arrangements for the future (this will not involve investigating the marital breakdown itself) and to make such orders and give such directions as are appropriate as a result of that review. This implements the recommendation in paragraph 5.50 of the report.

3. The detailed procedural requirements relating to the conduct of the assessment will be the subject of rules to be made by the Lord Chancellor. The power to make such rules is contained in clause 20. These will provide for such matters as attendance by the parties, where and when the assessment is to take place, and power to adjourn the assessment and re-convene from time to time until the court has discharged all its duties.

Subsection (2)
4. This subsection imposes specified duties on the court in the performance of its function under subsection (1). These implement the recommendations made in paragraph 5.51 of the report. They are:-

(a) consideration of how matters in dispute could be resolved other than by conventional litigation and in particular how the parties could be encouraged to participate voluntarily in appropriate procedures, such as conciliation or mediation, in order to bring this about;

(b) subject to the duty in (a) above, consideration of what directions it should give for the conduct of any proceedings under this Act, the 1973 Act, Schedule 1 to the Matrimonial Homes Act 1983, or the Children Act 1989. Proceedings under this Act would include those relating to the hardship bar under clause 4, or to the power to postpone under clause 6, or to the preliminary assessment itself;

(c) consideration of whether the parties should be directed to disclose whether an application for a hardship bar under clause 4 is likely, if a divorce rather than separation is ultimately sought, and if so the grounds for such an application;

(d) consideration of whether there are any relevant children of the family, as defined by clause 6(4), and whether the court should make any orders under the Children Act 1989 in respect of them;

(e) consideration of whether there are any financial and property matters upon which the parties are agreed (so that where appropriate a consent order can be made in respect of them);

(f) consideration of whether to exercise the power to postpone a divorce or separation

6(2)(c) and (d) above.

(3) The powers exercisable from time to time by the court, whether under rules of court or otherwise, for adjourning proceedings on a preliminary assessment in relation to a marriage shall be exercisable so as to continue those proceedings for such period, ending no later than with the making of an order of divorce in relation to the marriage, as the court thinks fit.

(4) The Lord Chancellor may by order made by statutory instrument amend subsection (1) above so as to vary the length of the period for the time being specified in that subsection.

(5) No order shall be made under subsection (4) above unless a draft of the order has been laid before, and approved by a resolution of, each House of Parliament; and an order under that subsection may contain such transitional provisions as the Lord Chancellor considers appropriate.

order under clause 6(2)(c) or (d) on the ground of incapacity or delay in notification.

Subsection (3)

5.　This subsection enables the court to adjourn so as to re-convene and continue the preliminary assessment up to the time when a divorce order is made. This is discussed in paragraph 5.51 of the report.

Subsections (4) and (5)

6.　These subsections enable the Lord Chancellor, by order subject to the affirmative resolution procedure, to vary the length of the period in subsection (1). They implement the recommendation made in paragraph 5.52 of the report.

Conciliation and mediation

Functions of the
court in relation
to conciliation
and mediation.

9.—(1) The court shall have power in any proceedings connected with the breakdown of a marriage to give a direction which—

(a) requires the parties to the marriage to attend an appointment arranged, in accordance with the direction, for the purpose of—

(i) enabling an explanation to be given of the facilities available to them for participation in conciliation or mediation procedures; and

(ii) providing them with an opportunity of agreeing to participate in such procedures;

and

(b) specifies as the person by whom the arrangements for the appointment are to be made such person who has agreed to act for the purposes of the direction as the court thinks appropriate.

(2) Subject to the following provisions of this section, the court's powers to adjourn any proceedings connected with the breakdown of a marriage shall include—

(a) power to adjourn the proceedings for the purpose of allowing the parties to the marriage to comply with a direction under subsection (1) above; and

(b) power to adjourn the proceedings for the purpose of otherwise facilitating the amicable resolution of issues in dispute in the proceedings;

and it shall be the duty of the court, in determining whether to adjourn any such proceedings for either of these purposes, to have regard, in particular, to the need to protect the interests of any child of the family.

(3) Without prejudice to the court's power, with or without an application having been made, to give a direction under subsection (1) above in any proceedings connected with the breakdown of a marriage, an application for such a direction may be made by either party to a marriage at any time after a statement of marital breakdown has been made with respect to the marriage.

(4) Wherever the court gives a direction under subsection (1) above, it shall order the person specified in the direction to produce, at such time as it may direct, a report to the court stating—

(a) whether the parties to the marriage have complied with the direction; and

(b) if they did, whether those parties have agreed to participate in any conciliation or mediation procedure.

(5) Where the court, for the purpose of facilitating the amicable resolution of any dispute, adjourns any proceedings connected with the breakdown of a marriage—

(a) the period of the adjournment shall be a fixed period determined by the court at the time of the adjournment; and

(b) unless the sole purpose of the adjournment is to allow the parties to the marriage to comply with a direction under

Clause 9

1.   This clause deals with the powers of the court in relation to conciliation and mediation procedures during the course of proceedings connected with the breakdown of marriage, defined in clause 21 to include applications for postponement, preliminary assessment, proceedings under the Children Act, and proceedings for financial provision and property adjustment orders under the 1973 Act, as amended.

Subsection (1)
2.   This subsection empowers the court to require the parties to attend an appointment with a specified agency or person in order that the nature and purpose of conciliation or mediation can be explained to them and to provide them with an opportunity of agreeing to participate in conciliation or mediation.   The agency or person specified in the direction must be an agency or person who has made it known, for example by placing their name on a list kept at an appropriate court office, that they are willing to accept such a referral. This implements the recommendation in paragraph 5.38 of the report.

Subsection (2)
3.   This subsection provides that the court may use its powers of adjournment of any connected proceedings, so as to give time to the parties to comply with such a direction or to participate in discussions or procedures which might lead to amicable resolution of matters in issue between them.   In determining whether to adjourn for either purpose, the court must have regard to the need to protect the interests of any child of the family (whether, for example, by facilitating the amicable resolution of the parents' dispute or by avoiding any harmful delay which such an adjournment might cause).   This implements the recommendation in paragraph 5.39 of the report.

Subsection (3)
4.   This subsection provides that the court may give a direction under subsection (1) either of its own motion, or upon application by either party at any time after a statement of marital breakdown has been made.   It implements the recommendation in paragraph 5.38 of the report.

Subsection (4)
5.   This subsection requires a report to be made to the court by the agency or person specified in the direction.   Such report must deal with whether or not the parties attended the arranged appointment and agreed to participate in conciliation or mediation in the future. This implements the recommendation in paragraph 5.38 of the report.

Subsection (5)
6.   This subsection requires the court to specify any period of adjournment under subsection (2)(b), and also gives the court power to require the parties to report back, where the purpose of the adjournment is to facilitate amicable resolution of matters in issue between the parties.   It implements the recommendation in paragraph 5.39 of the report.

Subsection (6)
7.   This subsection provides for the extent of the report which the court may order under subsection (5) above. The report should deal with such matters as whether or not

subsection (1) above, the court shall order one or both of those parties to produce a report under subsection (6) below before the end of that period.

(6) A report under this subsection is a report to the court on—

(a) whether the parties to the marriage have participated, during the adjournment, in any conciliation or mediation procedure;

(b) whether any agreement has been reached between those parties as a result of their participation in any such procedure or otherwise;

(c) the extent to which any issue in dispute between those parties has been resolved in consequence of any agreement which has been so reached; and

(d) the need for, and the prospects for the success of, any further participation by those parties in any conciliation or mediation procedure.

(7) Nothing in this Act with respect to the participation of the parties to a marriage in any conciliation or mediation procedure, or otherwise with respect to the amicable resolution of issues in dispute between the parties to a marriage, shall authorise the court—

(a) to require the giving of a notice for the purposes of section 2(5)(a) or 5(4) above; or

(b) otherwise to require a period of delay before the making of, or of an application for, an order of divorce or separation order in relation to a marriage.

the parties have taken part during the adjournment in any conciliation or mediation procedure and whether as a result any agreement has been reached; whether matters in dispute have been resolved and whether any further future conciliation or mediation is likely to be successful. This implements the recommendation in paragraph 5.39 of the report.

Subsection (7)

8. This subsection makes it clear that the power to give a direction under subsection (1) or to adjourn under subsection (2) is quite distinct from the parties' power to withdraw the statement of marital breakdown, or to suspend the period of reflection and consideration, or the court's power to postpone the making of a divorce or separation order, and cannot be used for any of those purposes.

Privilege for
disclosures
during conci-
liation or
mediation.

10.—(1) Subject to sections 9(4) to (6) above and to subsection (2) below, where—

(a) the parties to a marriage participate in any recognised conciliation or mediation procedure for the purpose of resolving any dispute between them; and

(b) that dispute is one which is or may become the subject of proceedings connected with the breakdown of the marriage,

no statement made at any time in the course of that procedure shall, except with the consent of both those parties, be admissible for any purpose either in those proceedings or in any other civil or criminal proceedings whatever.

(2) Nothing in this section shall prohibit the admission of evidence of any agreement or arrangements made between the parties to a marriage in so far as the evidence is admitted—

(a) for the purpose of enabling the court to exercise any of its powers with respect to the approval, modification or termination of any such agreement or arrangements; or

(b) for the purpose of enabling any person to enforce the agreement or arrangements.

(3) A reference in this section to a recognised conciliation or mediation procedure is a reference to the doing of anything which is done both—

(a) for the purposes of conciliation or mediation; and

(b) in accordance with arrangements made by a person who has given notice that he is available, in cases of disputes between the parties to a marriage, to provide help with conciliation or mediation.

(4) This section shall be without prejudice to any privilege existing apart from this section in respect of statements made in the course of any attempt to effect a reconciliation between the parties to a marriage or of any other procedure in which the parties to a marriage participate for the purpose of securing an amicable resolution to any dispute between them.

Clause 10

1.   This clause deals with privilege in respect of disclosures made during conciliation or mediation.

Subsection (1)
2.   This subsection confers an absolute privilege on any statements made by either party during the course of any "recognized" conciliation or mediation procedure concerning any dispute which is or may become, the subject of proceedings connected with the breakdown in the marital relationship, as defined in clause 21.   This privilege will attach to the parties only, who may jointly waive it, and not to the conciliator or mediator.   This implements the recommendation in paragraph 5.48 of the report.

Subsection (2)
3.   This subsection makes it clear that evidence of any agreement reached or arrangements made, between the parties will be admissable for the purpose of enabling the court to deal with such agreement or arrangement or for the purposes of enforcement by any person.   It implements the recommendation in paragraph 5.48 of the report.

Subsection (3)
4.   This subsection defines a "recognized" conciliator or mediator for the purpose of subsection (1).   If agencies or individuals wish to bring themselves within the definition they will have to give notice to an appropriate court office that they are available to provide such services.   Such lists may then be used by legal advisers whose clients, or parties who themselves, wish to consult such agencies or individuals.   This implements the recommendation in paragraph 5.48 of the report.

Subsection (4)
5.   This subsection preserves the common law privileges which exist in relation to reconciliation and legal professional privilege.   This is discussed in paragraph 5.49 of the report.

Financial arrangements

11. For section 21 of the 1973 Act (definition of financial provision and property adjustment orders) there shall be substituted the following section—

21.—(1) For the purposes of this Act a financial provision order in favour of any person is an order of any of the following kinds, that is to say—

(a) an order ("a periodical payments order") that a party to a marriage shall make in favour of that person such periodical payments, for such term, as may be specified in the order;

(b) an order ("a secured periodical payments order") that a party to a marriage shall, to the satisfaction of the court, secure in favour of that person such periodical payments, for such term, as may be specified in the order;

(c) an order ("an order for the payment of a lump sum") that a party to a marriage shall make a payment in favour of that person of such lump sum or sums as may be specified in the order.

(2) For the purposes of this Act a property adjustment order in relation to a marriage is an order of any of the following kinds, that is to say—

(a) an order that a party to the marriage shall transfer such of his or her property as may be specified in the order in favour of the other party to the marriage or a child of the family;

(b) an order that a settlement of such property of a party to the marriage as may be specified in the order be made to the satisfaction of the court for the benefit of the other party to the marriage and of the children of the family, or either or any of them;

(c) an order varying for the benefit of the parties to the marriage and of the children of the family, or either or any of them, any ante-nuptial or post-nuptial settlement (including such a settlement made by will or codicil) made on the parties to the marriage;

(d) an order extinguishing or reducing the interest of either of the parties to the marriage under any such settlement.

(3) Subject to section 40 below, where an order of the court under this Part of this Act requires a party to a marriage to make or secure a payment in favour of another person or to transfer property in favour of any person, then that payment shall be made or secured or that property transferred—

EXPLANATORY NOTES

FINANCIAL ARRANGEMENTS

Clause 11

1.   This clause is a complete replacement for section 21 of the 1973 Act, which has been repealed in Schedule 3, and describes the different types of orders for financial provision and property adjustment which a court can make. The nature and extent of orders have not been amended. This has been done in order to facilitate the separation (see clauses 12 and 13 and Schedule 2) of the provisions of the 1973 Act relating to nullity cases and those relating to divorce and separation.

(a) if that other person is the other party to the marriage, to that other party; and

(b) if that other person is a child of the family, according to the terms of the order either to the child or for the benefit of that child to such person as may be specified in the order.

(4) References in this section to the property of a party to a marriage are references to any property to which that party is entitled either in possession or in reversion.

(5) Any power of the court under this Part of this Act to make such an order as is mentioned in subsection (2)(b) to (d) above shall be exercisable notwithstanding that there are no children of the family."

Orders for financial provision in divorce and separation cases.

12. Before section 23 of the 1973 Act (which, as amended by this Act, provides for the making of financial provision orders in nullity cases) there shall be inserted the following section—

"Financial provision orders in divorce and separation cases.

22A.—(1) Subject to the restrictions imposed by the following provisions of this Act and to section 19 of the Divorce and Separation Act 1990, the court shall have power—

(a) at any time after a statement of marital breakdown has been made with respect to a marriage and before an application is made by reference to that statement;

(b) at any time when an application made under section 2 of that Act by reference to such a statement is pending in relation to a marriage;

(c) at any time when an application for an order of divorce under section 3(1) or 4(3) of that Act (conversion of separation orders and applications on revocation of grave hardship order) is pending in relation to a marriage; and

(d) at any time after an order of divorce has been made, or while a separation order is in force, in relation to a marriage,

to make one or more financial provision orders in favour of a party to the marriage or any of the children of the family.

(2) The powers of the court under this section in relation to a marriage to make one or more financial provision orders—

(a) shall be exercisable against each party to the marriage either by the making of a combined order on one occasion or, if the court thinks fit, by the making of separate orders on different occasions;

(b) so far as they consist in power to make one or more orders in favour of the children of the family, shall be exercisable differently in favour of different children and from time to time in favour of the same child; and

(c) shall include power, at times when the court would not otherwise be in a position to make a financial provision order in favour of a party to the marriage or child of the family, to make an interim periodical payments order, or a series of such orders, in favour of that party or child.

(3) The court's powers under subsection (1) above shall not include—

(a) any power to make a financial provision order, other than an interim periodical payments

EXPLANATORY NOTES

Clause 12

1.   This clause replaces section 23 of the 1973 Act, by inserting a new section 22A in that Act, as it applied in divorce and separation cases. Section 23 has been amended, in Schedule 2 at paragraph 6, so that it now only applies in nullity cases.   It also implements the recommendations in paragraph 5.54 of the report.   References below are to the subsection of the new section 22A.

Subsection (1)
2.   This subsection gives the court power, subject to certain restrictions in subsection (3), to make financial provision orders, in respect of spouses and children, at any time after a statement of marital breakdown has been made, whether before or after a separation or divorce order has been made, including when an application for conversion from separation to divorce is pending. This power can be exercised by the court of its own motion in proceedings connected with the breakdown, as defined in clause 21, or upon application.

Subsection (2)
3.   This subsection provides that the court may exercise its power to make financial provision orders either by making one order covering all aspects of financial provision for all members of the family, or separate orders for different types of provision in respect of different members of the family on different occasions. It gives power for the court to make interim periodical payments orders for spouses and children where the court is not in a position to make full orders. This, in respect of spouses, will replace maintenance pending suit under section 22 of the 1973 Act which has been repealed in Schedule 3.

Subsection (3)
4.   This subsection limits the court's power to the making of an interim periodical payments order only, during any suspension of the period of consideration and reflection by virtue of a reconciliation notice having been filed. It also provides that the court does not have power to make financial provision orders when the period has lapsed.

Subsection (4)
5.   This subsection provides that the court has power to make orders either upon its own motion or upon application by the parties at any time before the divorce or separation order is made. However, once a separation or divorce order has been made the court will only have power to make a financial provision order upon application, as opposed to of its own motion. Where an application is not filed before the separation or divorce, the parties will have to seek the leave of the court to file such an application.

Subsection (5)
6.   This subsection re-enacts the provisions of section 23 (3), (a) to (c) of the 1973 Act.

Subsection (6)
7.   This subsection re-enacts the provisions of section 23 (6) of the 1973 Act.

order, at any time during the suspension, by virtue of a notice under subsection (4) of section 5 of the Divorce and Separation Act 1990 (reconciliation attempts), of any period which is required to elapse either under that section or under a direction given for the purposes of section 6 of that Act; or

(b) any power, by virtue of the making of a statement of marital breakdown, to make any financial provision order whatever at a time when it has ceased, by virtue of section 2(5) or 5(5) of that Act (lapse of divorce or separation process), to be possible for an application to be made by reference to that statement or for an order to be made on such an application.

(4) The court's powers under this section in relation to a marriage—

(a) shall not be exercisable at any time after an order of divorce has been made, or while a separation order is in force, in relation to the marriage, except—

(i) on an application made for the purpose before the making of the order of divorce or separation order; or

(ii) on a subsequent application made with the leave of the court;

but

(b) so far as they are exercisable at other times, shall be exercisable either on an application made for the purpose or, without an application, in any proceedings under this Act or in any other proceedings which, within the meaning of the Divorce and Separation Act 1990, are connected with the breakdown of the marriage.

(5) Without prejudice to the generality of the power of the court under this section to make an order for the payment of a lump sum or to the provisions of this Part of this Act as to the beginning of the term specified in any periodical payments order or secured periodical payments order—

(a) an order for the payment of a lump sum made in exercise of that power in favour of a party to a marriage may be made for the purpose of allowing that party to meet any liabilities incurred by him or her in maintaining himself or herself or any child of the family at any time before the making of the order;

(b) an order for the payment of a lump sum made in exercise of that power in favour of a party

to a marriage or child of the family may be made for the purpose of enabling any liabilities or expenses reasonably incurred by or for the benefit of such a child at any time before the making of the order; and

(c) any order for the payment of a lump sum made in exercise of that power may provide for the payment of the lump sum by instalments of such amount as may be specified in the order and may require the payment of the instalments to be secured to the satisfaction of the court.

(6) Where the court—

(a) makes an order under this section for the payment of a lump sum; and

(b) directs—

(i) that payment of that sum, or any part of it, shall be deferred; or

(ii) that that sum, or any part of it, shall be paid by instalments,

the court may order that the amount deferred or the instalments shall carry interest at such rate as may be specified in the order from such date, not earlier than the date of the order, as may be so specified until the date when the payment is due."

Property
adjustment
orders in divorce
and separation
cases.

13. Before section 24 of the 1973 Act (which, as amended by this Act, provides for the making of property adjustment orders in nullity cases) there shall be inserted the following section—

"Property
adjustment
orders in divorce
and separation
cases.

23A.—(1) Subject to the restrictions imposed by the following provisions of this Act and to section 19 of the Divorce and Separation Act 1990, the court shall have power, at any such time as is mentioned in relation to a marriage in section 22A(1) above, to make one or more property adjustment orders in relation to the marriage.

(2) Without prejudice to sections 31 and 31A below, the powers of the court under this section to make one or more property adjustment orders in relation to a marriage shall be exercised, so far as practicable, by the making on one occasion of all such provision capable of being made by way of one or more property adjustment orders in relation to the marriage as the court thinks fit.

(3) The court's powers under subsection (1) above shall not include—

(a) any power to make a property adjustment order at a time during the suspension, by virtue of a notice under subsection (4) of section 5 of the Divorce and Separation Act 1990 (reconciliation attempts), of any period which is required to elapse either under that section or under a direction given for the purposes of section 6 of that Act; or

(b) any power, by virtue of the making of a statement of marital breakdown, to make a property adjustment order at a time when it has ceased, by virtue of section 2(5) or 5(5) of that Act (lapse of divorce or separation process), to be posssible for an application to be made by reference to that statement or for an order to be made on such an application.

(4) The court's powers under this section in relation to a marriage—

(a) shall not be exercisable at any time after an order of divorce has been made, or while a separation order is in force, in relation to the marriage, except—

(i) on an application made for the purpose before the making of the order of divorce or separation order; or

(ii) on a subsequent application made with the leave of the court;

but

(b) so far as they are exercisable at other times, shall be exercisable either on an application made for the purpose or, without an appli-

EXPLANATORY NOTES

Clause 13

1. This clause provides for the making of property adjustment orders as defined in clause 11, the replacement section 21 of the 1973 Act. It also provides for when these orders can be made and take effect. It implements recommendations in paragraph 5.54 of the report.

Subsection (1)
2. This subsection gives the court power to make property adjustment orders, provided that it has jurisdiction under clause 19, at such times as are laid down in clause 12, the new section 22A of the 1973 Act, namely at any time after a statement of marital breakdown has been made, whether before or after a separation or divorce order, including when an application for conversion from separation to divorce is pending.

Subsection (2)
3. This subsection provides, subject to the variation powers in section 31 of the 1973 Act and the new section 31A inserted by this Act, that the court should try to deal with all property claims by all members of the same family on the same occasion by the making of one comprehensive property adjustment order.

Subsection (3)
4. This subsection prevents the court making property adjustment orders during the suspension of the period for consideration and reflection or when that period has lapsed.

Subsection (4)
5. This subsection provides that the court has power to make property adjustment orders either of its own motion or upon application at any time before a divorce or separation order is made. However, once a separation or divorce order has been made the court can only make such an order upon application. Where an application is not filed before the separation or divorce, leave to file such an application must be obtained.

Subsection (5)
6. This subsection provides that a property adjustment order, although made, cannot take effect until after separation or divorce unless the court is satsified that there are special circumstances which warrant the order taking effect earlier.

cation, in any proceedings under this Act or in any other proceedings which, within the meaning of the Divorce and Separation Act 1990, are connected with the breakdown of the marriage.

(5) Where—

(a) the court exercises its power under this section to make a property adjustment order in relation to a marriage at a time before an order of divorce or separation order is made in relation to the marriage; and

(b) the court is not satisfied that there are special circumstances making it appropriate for the property adjustment order to take effect at an earlier date,

the court shall provide for the property adjustment order not to take effect until an order of divorce or separation order is made in relation to the marriage."

Period of
secured and
unsecured
payments orders.

14.—(1) In subsection (1) of section 28 of the 1973 Act (duration of a continuing financial provision order in favour of a party to a marriage), for paragraphs (a) and (b) there shall be substituted the following paragraphs—

"(a) a term specified in a periodical payments order or secured periodical payments order, if it is to begin before the making of the order, shall begin no earlier than with—

(i) in the case of an order made under section 22A above by virtue of paragraph (a) or (b) subsection (1) of that section, the beginning of the day on which the statement of marital breakdown in question was made;

(ii) in the case of an order made under that section by virtue of paragraph (c) of that subsection, the date of the making of the application for the order of divorce; or

(iii) in any other case, the date of the making of the application on which the periodical payments order or secured periodical payments order is made;

(b) a term specified in a periodical payments order or secured periodical payments order shall be so defined as not to extend beyond—

(i) in the case of a periodical payments order, the death of the party by whom the payments are to be made; or

(ii) in either case, the death of the party in whose favour the order was made or the remarriage of that party following the making of an order of divorce or decree of nullity."

(2) After subsection (1) of section 29 of that Act (duration of continuing financial provision order in favour of a child of the family) there shall be inserted the following subsection—

"(1A) Subject to the following provisions of this section, the term specified in a periodical payments order or secured periodical payments order made in favour of a child shall be such term as the court thinks fit but, if it is to begin before the making of the order, shall begin no earlier than with—

(a) in the case of an order made under section 22A above by virtue of paragraph (a) or (b) subsection (1) of that section, the beginning of the day on which the statement of marital breakdown in question was made;

(b) in the case of an order made under that section by virtue of paragraph (c) of that subsection, the date of the making of the application for the order of divorce; or

(c) in any other case, the date of the making of the application on which the periodical payments order or secured periodical payments order is made."

Clause 14

1.   This clause amends section 28 of the 1973 Act in respect of the commencement date of secured and unsecured periodical payments orders.

Subsection (1)

2.   This subsection provides that where the court is making a secured or unsecured periodical payments order in favour of a spouse after a statement of marital breakdown, whether before or after an application for separation or divorce has been made, then that order may be back-dated to the date when the statement of marital breakdown was made but no earlier.

3.   Where the court is making such an order pending an application for conversion from separation to divorce or revocation of a hardship bar, then such order may be back-dated to the date of application for conversion or revocation.

4.   Finally, where such an order is being made post separation or divorce, then the order can only be back-dated to the date of the application for that order.

5.   The duration of orders remains the same as in section 28 subsection (1) (a) and (b) of the 1973 Act.

Subsection 2

6.   This subsection applies the same provision in respect of commencement date of periodical payments orders for spouses to such orders for children.

Variation etc. of property adjustment orders where power reserved to the court.

15.—(1) In subsection (2) of section 31 of the 1973 Act, for paragraph (e) (variation of certain property adjustment orders) there shall be substituted the following paragraph—

"(e) any such order for the settlement of property or for the variation of a settlement as—

(i) is mentioned in section 21(2)(b) to (d) above; and

(ii) contains provision reserving power to the court to exercise its power under this section to vary the order (whether generally or in such respects as may be specifed in the order);".

(2) Subsection (4) of that section which restricts the power of the court to vary the property adjustment orders referred to in subsection (2)(e) of that section) shall cease to have effect.

(3) After subsection (6) of that section there shall be inserted the following subsections—

"(6A) The power of the court by virtue of subsection (2)(e) above to vary or discharge a property adjustment order shall be exercisable subject to any restriction contained in the order on the respects in which the power may be exercised and, if the order has taken effect, shall (subject to any such restriction) be a power—

(a) to vary the settlement to which the order relates in any person's favour or to extinguish or reduce any person's interest under that settlement; and

(b) to make such supplemental provision (including a further property adjustment order or an order for the payment of a lump sum) as the court thinks appropriate in consequence of any variation, extinguishment or reduction to be made under paragraph (a) above;

and sections 24A and 30 above shall apply for the purposes of the exercise of the court's powers under this subsection as they apply where the court makes a property adjustment order under section 23A or 24 above.

(6B) The court shall not exercise its power by virtue of subsection (2)(e) above in relation to any property adjustment order unless it appears to the court that the provision to be made in exercise of that power will not prejudice the interests of any person who—

(a) has acquired any right or interest in consequence of that order; and

(b) is not a party to the marriage or child of the family."

Clause 15

1. This clause deals with the power of the court to vary settlement of property orders and the extent of such variation. It implements the recommendation in paragraph 6.4 of the report.

Subsection (1)
2. This subsection amends section 31(2) of the 1973 Act so as to provide for variation of settlement of property orders, or variation of marriage settlement orders, as defined in section 21 (2) (b) to (d) of the 1973 Act as substituted by clause 11.

3. The power to vary will apply where the relevant order reserves either a general power for the court to vary, or a limited power to the extent specified in the order. This implements the recommendation in paragraph 6.5 of the report.

Subsection (2)
4. This subsection repeals subsection (4) of section 31 of the 1973 Act in consequence of the amendment to the power to vary contained in subsection (1) above.

Subsection (3)
5. This subsection inserts new subsections (6A) and (6B) in section 31 of the 1973 Act. It implements the recommendation in paragraph 6.6 of the report. Under subsection (6A), when varying a settlement, or variation of marriage settlement, the court may vary, extinguish or reduce the interest of any person and in consequence of any such variation may make a compensating property adjustment or lump sum order.

6. This subsection confirms that the power to order sale under section 24A of the 1973 Act, and the power to direct settlement of an instrument under section 30 of that Act, shall apply to such compensating orders.

7. Under subsection (6B) the court may not exercise its new powers of variation where such variation would affect the rights of any third party.

Variations etc. following re-conciliations.

16. After section 31 of the 1973 Act (variation of orders) there shall be inserted the following section—

"Variation etc. following re-conciliations.

31A.—(1) Subject to the following provisions of this section, where at a time before the making of an order of divorce in relation to a marriage—

(a) an order for the payment of a lump sum has been made under section 22A above in favour of a party to the marriage;

(b) an order for the payment of a lump sum has been made under that section in favour of a child of the family but the payment has not yet been made; or

(c) a property adjustment order has been made in relation to the marriage under section 23A above,

the court shall have power, on an application made at any such time jointly by the parties to the marriage, to vary or discharge that order.

(2) The power of the court by virtue of this section to vary or discharge an order for the payment of a lump sum in favour of a party to a marriage shall (if the payment has been made) include power to make an order for the re-payment of an amount equal to the whole or any part of that lump sum.

(3) The power of the court by virtue of this section to vary or discharge a property adjustment order shall (if the order has taken effect) be a power—

(a) to order any person to whom property was transferred in pursuance of the original order to transfer the whole or any part of that property, or of any property appearing to the court to represent that property, in favour of a party to the marriage or a child of the family;

(b) to vary any settlement to which the order relates in favour of any person or to extinguish or reduce any person's interest under that settlement; and

(c) to make such supplemental provision (including a further property adjustment order or an order for the payment of a lump sum) as the court thinks appropriate in consequence of any transfer, variation, extinguishment or reduction to be made under paragraph (a) or (b) above.

(4) Sections 24A and 30 above shall apply for the purposes of the exercise of the court's powers under subsection (3) above as they apply where the court makes a property adjustment order under section 23A or 24 above.

EXPLANATORY NOTES

Clause 16

1.   This clause inserts a new section 31A in the 1973 Act, giving power to the court to vary or set aside lump sum and property adjustment orders, on the joint application of parties who have subsequently become reconciled. It implements the recommendation in paragraph 5.54 of the report.   References below are to the subsections of the new section 31A.

Subsections (1) and (2)
2.   These subsections confer power on the court, upon the joint application of the parties, to apply for variation or discharge of lump sum orders made in favour of a child of the family or either party, or any such property adjustment order.

3.   The power to vary or discharge a lump sum in favour of a child only applies where payment under the order has not been made. Variation or discharge in favour of a spouse can be ordered irrespective of whether the order has taken effect; where it has taken effect, repayment of the whole or part of the lump sum can be ordered.

Subsection (3)
4.   This subsection provides that the court may order the transfer-back of property either in whole or part, or property which appears to represent the original property transferred. The court may also vary, extinguish or reduce the interest of any person under a settlement or variation of settlement order, and may make a compensating lump sum or transfer of property order in consequence of such transfer-back or variation.

Subsection (4)
5.   This subsection applies sections 24A and 30 of the 1973 Act to compensating lump sum and property orders made under subsection (3) above.

Subsection (5)
6.   This subsection provides that the court cannot exercise its powers under subsections (2) and (3) above unless there has been a reconciliation between the parties and the exercise of its powers would not prejudice the interest of any third party or a child of the family.

(5) The court shall not exercise its power by virtue of subsection (2) or (3)(a) to (c) above unless it appears to the court—

    (a) that there has been a reconciliation between the parties to the marriage; and

    (b) in the case of any power under subsection (3)(a) to (c) above, that the provision to be made in exercise of that power will not prejudice—

        (i) the interests of any child of the family; or

        (ii) the interests of any person who has acquired any right or interest in consequence of the original property adjustment order and is not a party to the marriage or a child of the family."

Grounds for financial provision orders in magistrates' courts

Grounds for
financial
provision orders
in magistrates'
courts.

17.—(1) In section 1 of the Domestic Proceedings and Magistrates' Courts Act 1978, paragraphs (c) and (d) (behaviour and desertion to be grounds on which an application to a magistrates' court for a financial provision order may be made) shall cease to have effect.

(2) In section 7(1) of that Act (powers of magistrates' court where spouses living apart by agreement), the words "neither party having deserted the other" shall cease to have effect.

Clause 17

1. This clause deals with the grounds for making financial provision orders in magistrates' courts.

Subsection (1)
2. This subsection repeals the grounds of behaviour and desertion as the basis of a periodical payments or lump sum order under section 1 of the Domestic Proceedings and Magistrates' Courts Act 1978. It implements the recommendation in paragraph 4.28 of the report.

Subsection (2)
3. The effect of this repeal is to extend the court's power to make financial provision orders where voluntary payments have been made during a period of separation to all types of separation, whether by consent or desertion or otherwise. It implements the recommendation in paragraph 4.28 of the report.

Exercise of inherent jurisdiction to restrain molestation etc.

Exercise of inherent jurisdiction to restrain molestation etc.

18. The court's jurisdiction, while matrimonial proceedings are pending, to grant relief for the purpose of protecting a party to the marriage or child of the family from molestation or of otherwise affording protection to such a party or child shall also be exercisable at any time when—

> (a) a statement of marital breakdown has been made with respect to the marriage; and
>
> (b) it is or may become possible, as a result of the making of that statement, for any other jurisdiction of the court in proceedings connected with the breakdown of the marriage to be exercised.

Jurisdiction in relation to divorce and separation

Jurisdiction in relation to divorce and separation.

19.—(1) The court shall have jurisdiction in relation to a marriage to entertain an application under section 2 above for an order of divorce, or for a separation order, if and only if—

> (a) the date of the making of the statement of marital breakdown by reference to which the application is made was a date on which at least one of the parties to the marriage was domiciled in England and Wales;
>
> (b) a period of not less than a year throughout which at least one of the parties to the marriage was habitually resident in England and Wales ended with that date; or

1973 c. 45.

> (c) proceedings in respect of which the court has jurisdiction under section 5(3) of the the Domicile and Matrimonial Proceedings Act 1973 (jurisdiction in nullity cases) are pending in relation to that marriage when the application is made.

(2) Any other jurisdiction of the court which (apart from this subsection) is conferred by this Act or any other enactment in consequence of the making of a statement of marital breakdown with respect to a marriage shall be exercisable if and only if—

> (a) the statement was made on such a date as is mentioned in paragraph (a) or (b) of subsection (1) above; or
>
> (b) proceedings such as are mentioned in paragraph (c) of that subsection are pending in relation to that marriage.

(3) Where a separation order is in force or an order under section 4(1) above is revoked, the court—

> (a) shall have jurisdiction in all cases to entertain an application made by reference to the separation order or revocation under section 3(1) or 4(3) above; and
>
> (b) shall be entitled, wherever such an application is made, to exercise any other jurisdiction which is conferred on the court in consequence of the making of such an application.

(4) Schedule 1 to this Act shall have effect for amending Schedule 1 to the Domicile and Matrimonial Proceedings Act 1973 (orders for a stay in respect of concurrent proceedings in other jurisdictions); and the jurisdiction of the court so far as it consists in—

Clause 18

1.   This clause preserves the inherent jurisdiction of the court to protect spouses and children by granting injunctions, so that it can grant them at any time after a statement of marital breakdown has been made.   The court will have jurisdiction until the time when there are no outstanding proceedings connected with the breakdown of the marriage as defined in clause 21(2) and (3).   This implements the recommendation in paragraph 5.55 of the report.

Clause 19

1.   This clause deals with the circumstances in which the courts in England and Wales have jurisdiction to entertain applications for separation or divorce, applications for conversion from separation to divorce, and applications for divorce following revocation of a hardship bar.   Jurisdiction will be based on domicile or one year's habitual residence of either spouse at the time when the statement of marital breakdown is made or alternatively on the basis that nullity proceedings are pending at the date of application and the court had jurisdiction under section 5(3) of the Domicile and Matrimonial Proceedings Act 1973 at the time those proceedings were commenced.   This reproduces the effect of section 5 of the Domicile and Matrimonial Proceedings Act 1973 in relation to divorce and judicial separation and the relevant provisions are therefore repealed in Schedule 3.

(a) jurisdiction to entertain an application for an order of divorce or for a separation order; and

(b) a jurisdiction to which subsection (2) or (3)(b) above applies,

shall be exercisable subject to any order for a stay under Schedule 1 to that Act.

Supplemental provisions

Lord
Chancellor's
rules and rules
of court.

20.—(1) The Lord Chancellor may by rules make provision—

(a) for requiring a party to a marriage, on the making of a statement of marital breakdown with respect to the marriage or subsequently, to make additional statements with respect to, or to that party's proposals for, the arrangements that need to be made in consequence of the breakdown;

(b) for requiring a statement of marital breakdown or any such additional statement to be made in such manner, including by attendance in person at such place, as may be described in or determined under the rules;

(c) for requiring a statement of marital breakdown to be notified to the court in such manner as may be so described or determined;

(d) for requiring either or both of the parties to a marriage with respect to which a statement of marital breakdown has been made to prepare and produce such other documents, and to attend in person at such places and for such purposes, as may be so described or determined;

(e) for requiring the parties to such a marriage to be furnished, in such manner as may be provided for in the rules, with such information and assistance as may be so described or determined;

(f) for requiring the parties to such a marriage to be served, in such manner as may be provided for in the rules, with copies of such statements and with such other documents as may be so described or determined;

(g) for regulating the manner in which, and the persons to whom, any notice is to be given for the purposes of section 2(5)(a), 5(4) or 10(3)(b) above;

(h) for regulating the time and place at which proceedings on a preliminary assessment are to be conducted;

(i) for regulating the conduct, with respect to the production of reports or with respect to the making of any appointment or the giving of any explanation, of persons who—

    (i) are ordered under section 9 above to produce reports; or

    (ii) for the purposes of directions under subsection (1) of that section, make arrangements for appointments or explain the facilities available for participation in conciliation or mediation procedures;

1973 c. 45.

(j) for determining the effect of a stay under Schedule 1 to the Domicile and Matrimonial Proceedings Act 1973 (orders for a stay in respect of concurrent proceedings in other jurisdictions) on the application in relation to any case of any rules made by the Lord Chancellor under this section.

(2) The Lord Chancellor may by rules make provision for requiring the legal adviser of a party to a marriage with respect to which a statement of marital breakdown has been or is proposed to be made, at such time or times as may be specified in or determined under the regulations, to certify—

EXPLANATORY NOTES

Clause 20

1. This clause gives an enabling power to the Lord Chancellor to make rules in respect of the procedural requirements of a number of provisions in this Act.

Subsection (1)
2. This subsection covers rules relating to the statement of marital breakdown, information relating to available counselling, conciliation and mediation facilities, withdrawal of statement of marital breakdown, notification of attempted reconciliation, notice by agencies or individual conciliators or mediators of their availability, preliminary assessments, production of reports by spouses or professionals in respect of use of conciliation or mediation procedures and determination of the effect of stays on the application of rules to any case. These are discussed in or implement the recommendations in paragraphs 5.10, 5.11, 5.14, 5.15, 5.16, 5.19, 5.21 and 5.52 of the report.

Subsection (2)
3. This subsection provides that the Lord Chancellor may by rules require legal advisers to certify the matters specified in paragraphs (a) to (c) in relation to reconciliation, conciliation and mediation. The duty which such rules will impose replaces and extends the duty contained in section 6(1) of the 1973 Act which has been repealed in Schedule 3. This implements the recommendations made in paragraphs 5.20 and 5.36 of the report.

Subsection (3)
4. This subsection saves the power to make rules of court for the purposes of the Bill (see paragraph 24 of Schedule 2).

Subsection (4)
5. This subsection provides that Lord Chancellor's rules may provide that contravention of such rules may be punishable as specified in the subsection.

Subsection (5)
6. This provides that the rules made under this clause shall be subject to a negative resolution by either House of Parliament.

(a) whether the legal adviser and that party have discussed the possibility of a reconciliation, the opportunities for the parties to the marriage to participate in conciliation or mediation procedures or the availability to the parties of any counselling facilities;

(b) which, if any, of those matters they have discussed; and

(c) whether the legal adviser has given that party any names and addresses of persons qualified to help the parties to a marriage to effect a reconciliation, to help them with conciliation or mediation or to help them by means of counselling.

(3) The powers of the Lord Chancellor to make rules under this section shall be without prejudice to any power to make rules of court for the purposes of this Act.

(4) Rules made in exercise of any power of the Lord Chancellor under this section may—

(a) provide for a contravention of, or a failure to comply with, a requirement of the rules to be a summary offence punishable by a fine not exceeding level 5 on the standard scale or for such a requirement to be enforceable by proceedings for contempt of court;

(b) provide for anything falling to be determined under the rules to be determined by such persons, in accordance with such procedure and by reference to such matters, and to the opinion of such persons, as may be specified or described in the rules;

(c) make different provision for different cases; and

(d) contain such supplemental, consequential and transitional provision as the Lord Chancellor considers appropriate.

(5) The powers of the Lord Chancellor to make rules under this section shall be exercisable by statutory instrument subject to annulment in pursuance of a resolution of either House of Parliament.

Interpretation etc.

1973 c. 18.

21.—(1) In this Act—

"the 1973 Act" means the Matrimonial Causes Act 1973;

"child of the family" and "the court" have the same meanings as in the the 1973 Act;

"modifications" includes additions, alterations and omissions;

"statement of marital breakdown" means a statement for the purposes of section 2(2)(a) above.

(2) For the purposes of this Act, proceedings are connected with the breakdown of a marriage if they fall within subsection (3) below and, at the time of the proceedings—

(a) a statement of marital breakdown has been made with respect to the marriage and it is or may become possible for an application for an order of divorce or for a separation order to be made by reference to that statement;

(b) an application in relation to the marriage for an order of divorce, or for a separation order, is pending; or

(c) an order of divorce has been made, or a separation order is in force, in relation to the marriage.

(3) For the purposes of subsection (2) above proceedings fall within this subsection, in relation to a marriage, if they are—

(a) proceedings resulting from any application to the court for, or for the revocation of, an order under section 4(1) above in relation to the marriage;

(b) proceedings resulting from any application to the court for a period of delay to be required under section 6 above before an order is made in relation to the marriage;

(c) proceedings on a preliminary assessment in relation to the marriage;

(d) proceedings resulting from any application for a direction under section 9(1) above in relation to the parties to the marriage;

(e) proceedings resulting from any application for the exercise, in relation to a party to the marriage or child of the family, of any of the court's powers under Part II of the 1973 Act;

1976 c. 50.

(f) proceedings resulting from any application by either party to the marriage for the grant of an injunction under the Domestic Violence and Matrimonial Proceedings Act 1976 or the jurisdiction referred to in section 18 above;

1983 c. 19.

(g) proceedings resulting from an application made by either party to the marriage for an order under section 1 or 9 of the Matrimonial Homes Act 1983 or for an order under Schedule 1 to that Act;

1989 c. 41.

(h) proceedings under the Children Act 1989 with respect to a child of the family; or

(i) without prejudice to the preceding paragraphs, proceedings resulting from any application made to the court with respect to, or otherwise in connection with, any proceedings connected with the breakdown of the marriage.

EXPLANATORY NOTES

Clause 21

1.   This is the interpretation clause and inter alia provides a definition of "proceedings connected with the breakdown of the marriage."

Subsection (1)
2.   This inter alia applies certain definitions from the Matrimonial Causes Act 1973 for the purposes of the Bill.

3.   Section 52(1) of the 1973 Act, as amended by paragraph 33 of Schedule 12 to the Children Act 1989, provides that "child of the family, in relation to the parties to a marriage, means - (a) a child of both of those parties; and (b) any other child, not being a child who is placed with those parties as foster parents by a local authority or voluntary organisation, who has been treated by both of those parties as a child of their family".

4.   Section 52(1) of the 1973 Act, as amended by paragraph 16 of Schedule 1 to the Matrimonial and Family Proceedings Act 1984, provides that "the court (except where the context otherwise requires) means the High Court or, where a county court has jurisdiction by virtue of Part V of the Matrimonial and Family Proceedings Act 1984, a county court".

Subsections (2) and (3)
5.   These define "proceedings connected with the breakdown of the marriage". These cover proceedings between the parties to the marriage, or in relation to a child of the family, for financial provision, property adjustment and related relief under Part II of the 1973 Act; for remedies relating to the occupation of the matrimonial home or transfer of certain tenancies under the Matrimonial Homes Act 1983; for injunctions under the Domestic Violence and Matrimonial Proceedings Act 1976 or under the court's inherent jurisdiction referred to in clause 18; and in relation to the upbringing, maintenance and welfare of the children of the family under the Children Act 1989. They also cover proceedings under the Bill relating to the hardship bar in clause 4, the court's power to require a delay in clause 6, the preliminary assessment under clause 8, and directions to attend an explanatory appointment for conciliation or mediation under clause 9(1). Any proceedings related to proceedings connected with the breakdown of the marriage are also included.

6.   The definition is limited in two ways. First, by subsection (2), the listed proceedings are only included if there has been a statement of marital breakdown which has not lapsed, or there is a pending application for divorce or separation, or a divorce has taken place or a separation order is in force.

7.   Secondly, with the exception of proceedings under the Children Act 1989, where the court has wide powers to intervene for the sake of the children's welfare, "proceedings" only arise when there has been an application to the court or the court has begun the preliminary assessment under clause 8.

125

(4) For the purposes of this Act—

(a) references to the withdrawal of an application for an order of divorce or for a separation order are references, in relation to an application made jointly by both the parties to a marriage, to the withdrawal of that application by a notice of withdrawal given, in accordance with rules of court, either jointly by both parties or separately by each of them; and

(b) where only one party to the marriage gives a notice of withdrawal in relation to such an application, the application shall be treated as if it had been made by the other party alone.

EXPLANATORY NOTES

Subsection (4)

8.   This subsection defines "withdrawal of an application" in relation to a joint application, so that withdrawal by one party means that the application is to be treated as the sole application of the other party. This will enable the divorce order to be made on that application unless the withdrawing party applies to invoke the hardship bar.

Consequential amendments, transitional provisions and repeals.

22.—(1) Subject to the following provisions of this section, the enactments mentioned in Schedule 2 to this Act shall have effect subject to the amendments there specified (being minor and consequential amendments of the 1973 Act and consequential amendments of other enactments).

(2) Subject as aforesaid, the enactments mentioned in Schedule 3 to this Act are hereby repealed to the extent specified in the third column of that Schedule.

(3) The Lord Chancellor may by order make such consequential modifications of any provisions contained in any enactment or subordinate legislation as, by reason of this Act, appear to him necessary or expedient in respect of references (in whatever terms) in that enactment or subordinate legislation—

(a) to a petition for a decree of divorce or for a decree of judicial separation, to the presentation of such a petition or to the petitioner or respondent in proceedings on such a petition;

(b) to proceedings on such a petition or to proceedings in connection with any such proceedings or to any other matrimonial proceedings;

(c) to a decree of divorce (either a decree nisi or a decree which has been made absolute) or to a decree of judicial separation; or

(d) to findings of adultery in any proceedings.

(4) The power to make an order under subsection (3) above—

(a) shall include power to make provision applying generally in relation to enactments and subordinate legislation of a description specified in the order and to modify the effect of subsection (5) below in relation to documents and agreements of a description so specified; and

(b) shall be exercisable by statutory instrument subject to annulment in pursuance of a resolution of either House of Parliament.

(5) Subject to the preceding provisions of this section references (in whatever terms) in any deed, will or other instrument or document, or in any agreement, to the presentation of a petition for a decree of divorce or for a decree of judicial separation or to any such decree shall have effect, in relation to any time after the coming into force of this section—

(a) in the case of a reference to the presentation of either kind of petition, as if that reference included a reference to the making of a statement of marital breakdown;

(b) in the case of a reference to a decree of divorce (whether a decree nisi or a decree which has been made absolute), as if that reference included a reference to an order of divorce; and

(c) in the case of a reference to a decree of judicial separation, as if that reference included a reference to a separation order.

(6) Subject to subsection (7) below, nothing in any provision of this Act shall—

EXPLANATORY NOTES

Clause 22

1.   This clause deals with consequential amendments, transitional provisions and repeals.

Subsections (1) and (2)
2.   These subsections introduce the repeals and minor and consequential amendments affecting the 1973 Act and other enactments set out in Schedules 1, 2 and 3.   All of these repeals and consequential amendments result from the provisions of the Bill implementing the recommendations in the report.   The minor amendments implement recommendations to deal with existing defects in the 1973 Act and are not therefore purely consequential upon repeals and amendments of that Act.

Subsections (3) and (4)
3.   These subsections contain a general power for the Lord Chancellor by Order to make further amendments in any legislation consequent upon the replacement of petitions for divorce and judicial separation, and proceedings relating to them, with the new procedures for and following a statement of marital breakdown, the repeal of adultery as one of the facts proving breakdown, replacement of decree nisi and absolute with one divorce order and decree of judicial separation with separation order.

Subsection (5)
4.   This subsection provides for general modifications to references in deeds, wills, instruments or documents to petitions and decrees of divorce or judicial separation.

Subsection 6
5.   This subsection contains transitional provisions. With the exception of amendments to section 31 of the 1973 Act, no other provisions will affect proceedings started before the commencement of this Act.

(a) apply to or affect any proceedings commenced by petition or otherwise, or any decree granted, before the coming into force of that provision;

(b) affect the operation, in relation to any such proceedings or to any proceedings in connection with any proceedings or decree so commenced or granted, of the 1973 Act, of any other enactment or of any subordinate legislation; or

(c) without prejudice to paragraph (b) above, affect any transitional provision having effect under Schedule 1 to the 1973 Act.

(7) The provisions of section 31 of the 1973 Act (variation and discharge of orders) shall have effect with the amendments made by this Act—

(a) in relation to any order made under Part II of that Act at any time after the coming into force of the amendments, including an order made under that Part as, by virtue of subsection (6) above, it has effect for the purposes of proceedings commenced before the coming into force of the amendments; and

(b) in the case of subsections (7) and (7A) of that section, in relation to any such order and also in relation to any order made under Part II of that Act before the coming into force of the amendments.

(8) In this section "subordinate legislation" has the same meaning as in the Interpretation Act 1978.

1978 c. 30.

Short title, commencement and extent.

23.—(1) This Act may be cited as the Divorce and Separation Act 1990.

(2) This Act shall come into force on such day as the Lord Chancellor may by order made by statutory instrument appoint; and different days may be so appointed for different provisions and for different purposes.

(3) Subject to subsections (4) to (7) below, this Act extends to England and Wales only.

1986 c. 55.

(4) This Act so far as it amends sections 42 and 51 of the Family Law Act 1986 extends to the whole United Kingdom.

(5) This Act so far as it amends section 38 of that Act of 1986 extends to England and Wales and Northern Ireland only.

1926 c. 61.

(6) This Act so far as it amends the Judicial Proceedings (Regulation of Reports) Act 1926 extends to Great Britain only.

1973 c. 45.

(7) This Act so far as it amends Schedule 5 to the Domicile and Matrimonial Proceedings Act 1973 extends to Northern Ireland only.

EXPLANATORY NOTES

Clause 23

1. This clause deals with commencement, short title and extent of this Act.

SCHEDULES

Section 19

SCHEDULE 1

STAY OF PROCESS OF DIVORCE OR SEPARATION OR OF MATRIMONIAL PROCEEDINGS

Introductory

1973 c. 45.

1. Schedule 1 to the Domicile and Matrimonial Proceedings Act 1973 (which relates to the stay of matrimonial proceedings) shall be amended as follows.

Interpretation

2. In paragraph 2 (definition of "matrimonial proceedings"), the words "divorce," and "judicial separation" shall be omitted.

3. After sub-paragraph (2) of paragraph 4 (other definitions) there shall be inserted the following sub-paragraph—

"(3) 'Statement of marital breakdown' has the same meaning as in the Divorce and Separation Act 1990."

Duty to furnish particulars of concurrent proceedings

4.—(1) Paragraph 7 (duty to furnish particulars of concurrent proceedings in another jurisdiction) shall become sub-paragraph (1) of that paragraph; and in that sub-paragraph, for the words from the beginning to "relief" there shall be substituted the words—

"It shall be the duty of any person to whom, in relation to any marriage, this paragraph applies".

(2) After that sub-paragraph there shall be inserted the following sub-paragraph—

"(2) In relation to any marriage, this paragraph applies—

(a) where a statement of marital breakdown has been made with respect to the marriage, to the party or parties to the marriage who made the statement and, in prescribed circumstances where the statement was made by only one party to the marriage, to the other party; and

(b) while matrimonial proceedings are pending in the court in respect of the marriage and the trial or first trial in those proceedings has not begun, to the petitioner and also, if he has included a prayer for relief in his answer, to the respondent".

EXPLANATORY NOTES

THE SCHEDULES

Schedule 1

1. This Schedule makes amendments to Schedule 1 of the Domicile and Matrimonial Proceedings Act 1973 dealing with stay of matrimonial proceedings where the case ought to proceed in another jurisdiction. These amendments are to make it clear when proceedings commence and are continuing for the purposes of the operation of the court's power to stay proceedings here if they ought to take place in another jurisdiction.

Schedule 2

1. Part 1 of this Schedule effects minor and consequential amendments to provisions of the Matrimonial Causes Act 1973 which are not repealed.

2. Paragraph 2 repeals the functions of the Queen's Proctor in divorce and separation cases, while preserving them in petitions for a decree of nullity or presumption of death and dissolution.

3. Other amendments are similarly consequent upon the new procedure and terminology in divorce and separation cases and the resulting distinction between those cases and petitions for nullity or presumption of death and dissolution.

4. Paragraph 15(4) inserts a new subsection (7A) in section 31 of the 1973 Act. This implements the recommendation in paragraph 6.9 of the report that there should be power to order a lump sum or property transfer upon discharging or limiting the term of a periodical payments order in order to achieve a clean break.

5. Part II of this Schedule effects consequential amendments to the provisions of other enactments which are not repealed.

6. Paragraph 40(1) inserts the making of a statement of marital breakdown and proceedings under the Bill in the definition of "family proceedings" for the purpose of making orders relating to children under the Children Act 1989.

7. Paragraph 40(2) makes equivalent provision for the variation of certain property adjustment orders made in favour of children under the 1989 Act as is made for such orders under the 1973 Act by clause 15. This implements the recommendation in paragraph 6.7 of the report.

Schedule 3

1. This Schedule deals with repeals to the Matrimonial Causes Act 1973 and other enactments consequent upon the provisions of the Bill.

2. The major repeals are of sections 1 to 7 of the 1973 Act, which deals with divorce, and sections 17 and 18, which deal with judicial separation.

Obligatory stays

5. In paragraph 8 (obligatory stays in divorce cases), in sub-paragraph (1)—

(a) for the words from the beginning to "the court", in the first place where it occurs, there shall be substituted the words—

> "8.—(1) Where at a time after a statement of marital breakdown has been made with respect to a marriage (including any time while a separation order is in force in relation to the marriage)";

(b) in paragraph (c), for the words "the proceedings in the court were begun" and the words "those proceedings were begun" there shall be substituted the words "that statement was made";

(c) in paragraph (d), for the words "the proceedings in the court were begun" there shall be substituted the words "that statement was made"; and

(d) for the words "order that the proceedings in the court be stayed" there shall be substituted the words "make an order for a stay of the process for divorce in relation to that marriage."

(2) For sub-paragraph (2) of that paragraph there shall be substituted the following sub-paragraph—

> "(2) Where following the making of a statement of marital breakdown with respect to a marriage the court, under sub-paragraph (1) above, makes an order for a stay of the process for divorce in relation to that marriage, that order shall have effect as an order that, for so long as it is in force—
>
> (a) no application for an order of divorce in relation to the marriage shall be made to the court either by reference to that statement or by reference to any subsequent statement of marital breakdown; and
>
> (b) if such an application has been made, no such order of divorce shall be made on that application."

Discretionary stays

6.—(1) For sub-paragraph (1) of paragraph 9 (discretionary stays in any matrimonial proceedings) there shall be substituted the following sub-paragraph—

> "(1) Where at a time after a statement of marital breakdown has been made with respect to a marriage (including any time while a separation order is in force in relation to the marriage) or at any time before the beginning of the trial or first trial in any matrimonial proceedings which are continuing in the court, it appears to the court—
>
> (a) that any proceedings in respect of the marriage in question, or capable of affecting its validity or subsistence, are continuing in another jurisdiction; and
>
> (b) that the balance of fairness (including convenience) as between the parties to the marriage is such that it is

appropriate for proceedings in that jurisdiction to be disposed of before any one or more of the following occurs, that is to say, an order of divorce is made in relation to the marriage, a separation order is so made or further steps are taken in any proceedings in the court so far as they consist in matrimonial proceedings of one or more of the kinds specified in paragraph 2 above,

the court may then make an order for such one or more of the following as it thinks fit, namely, a stay of the process for divorce in relation to the marriage, a stay of the process for separation in relation to the marriage or a stay of any proceedings in the court so far as they consist in matrimonial proceedings of any one or more of those kinds.

(2) In sub-paragraph (2) of that paragraph, for the words "proceedings being stayed or not stayed" there shall be substituted the words "the making or refusal of an order for a stay".

(3) For sub-paragraph (3) of that paragraph there shall be substituted the following sub-paragraph—

"(3) Where an application is pending under paragraph 8 above in relation to any statement of marital breakdown made with respect to a marriage, the court shall not exercise its power under sub-paragraph (1) above to order a stay of the process for divorce in relation to that marriage."

(4) After sub-paragraph (4) of that sub-paragraph there shall be inserted the following sub-paragraph—

"(5) Where following the making of a statement of marital breakdown with respect to a marriage the court, under sub-paragraph (1) above, orders a stay of the process for divorce or a stay of the process for separation in relation to that marriage, that order shall have effect as an order that, for so long as it is in force—

(a) no application for an order of divorce or separation order in relation to the marriage shall be made to the court either by reference to that statement or by reference to any subsequent statement of marital breakdown; and

(b) if such an application has been made, no such order of divorce or separation order shall be made on that application."

Discharge of orders

7.—(1) In sub-paragraph (1) of paragraph 10 (power to discharge orders), for the words "staying any proceedings" there shall be substituted the words "for a stay".

(2) For sub-paragraph (2) of that paragraph there shall be substituted the following sub-paragraphs—

"(1A) Where the court, in relation to a marriage, discharges an order for a stay of the process for divorce or a stay of the

SCH. 1 process for separation, it may direct that the whole or a specified part of any period while the order has been in force—

 (a) shall not count towards any period which is—

  (i) specified for any purpose in sections 2 to 5 of the Divorce and Separation Act 1990; or

  (ii) required to elapse by virtue of a direction given for the purposes of section 6 of that Act;

 or

 (b) shall count only for specified purposes towards any such period.

(2) Where the court discharges any order under paragraph 8 above for a stay of the process for divorce in relation to a marriage, the court shall not again make an order under that paragraph for a stay of the process for divorce in relation to that marriage, except in a case where the obligation to do so arises under that paragraph following a statement of marital breakdown made after the discharge of the order."

Ancillary matters

8.—(1) For sub-paragraph (1) of paragraph 11 (effect of stay on ancillary proceedings) there shall be substituted the following sub-paragraph—

"(1) The provisions of sub-paragraphs (2) and (3) below shall apply (subject to sub-paragraph (4)) where an order for a stay of the process for divorce in relation to a marriage, for a stay of the process for separation in relation to a marriage or for a stay of any proceedings for nullity of marriage is for the time being in force by reason of having been imposed by reference to proceedings in a related jurisdiction for divorce, judicial separation or nullity of marriage; and in this paragraph—

 'lump sum order', in relation to a stay, means either of the following orders so far as it is or (apart from this paragraph) could be made in a case in which a statement of marital breakdown with respect to the marriage in question or an application in relation to that marriage for an order of divorce or separation order under the Divorce and Separation Act 1990 has been made or, as the case may be, in connection with the matrimonial proceedings to which the stay applies, that is to say—

  (a) an order under section 22A or 23, 31 or 31A of the Matrimonial Causes Act 1973 which, within the meaning of Part II of that Act, is an order for the payment of a lump sum; or

  (b) an order made in any equivalent circumstances under Schedule 1 to the Children Act 1989 and of a kind mentioned in paragraph 1(2)(a) or (b) of that Schedule;

 'the other proceedings', in relation to a stay under this Schedule, means the proceedings in another jurisdiction

SCH. 1

by reference to which the stay was imposed;

'relevant order', in relation to a stay, means any of the following orders so far as it is or (apart from this paragraph) could be made in a case in which a statement of marital breakdown with respect to the marriage in question or an application in relation to that marriage for an order of divorce or separation order under the Divorce and Separation Act 1990 has been made or, as the case may be, in connection with the matrimonial proceedings to which the stay applies, that is to say—

(a) any financial provision order (including an interim order), other than a lump sum order;

(b) any order made in equivalent circumstances under Schedule 1 to the Children Act 1989 and of a kind mentioned in paragraph 1(2)(a) or (b) of that Schedule;

(c) any section 8 order under the said Act of 1989; and

(d) except for the purposes of sub-paragraph (3) below, any order restraining a person from removing a child out of England and Wales or out of the care of another person."

(2) In sub-paragraph (2) of that paragraph—

(a) for the words "any proceedings are stayed" there shall be substituted the words "this paragraph applies in relation to a stay";

(b) in paragraph (a) and in paragraph (c), in the first place where they occur, the words "in connection with the stayed proceedings" shall be omitted; and

(c) in paragraph (b) and in paragraph (c), for the words "made in connection with the stayed proceedings" there shall be substituted the words "already made".

(3) In sub-paragraph (3) of that paragraph—

(a) for the words "any proceedings are stayed" there shall be substituted the words "this paragraph applies in relation to a stay";

(b) in paragraph (a), for the words "made in connection with the stayed proceedings" there shall be substituted the words "already made".

(c) in paragraph (b) and in paragraph (c), the words "in connection with the stayed proceedings" shall be omitted.

(4) For sub-paragraph (4) of that paragraph there shall be substituted the following sub-paragraph—

"(4) Nothing in sub-paragraphs (2) and (3) above shall affect any relevant order or lump sum order or any power to make such an order in so far as-

(a) where the stay relates to matrimonial proceedings, the order has been made or the power may be exercised following the making of a statement of marital break-down;

(b) where the stay is of both the process for divorce and the process for separation, the order has been made or the power may be exercised in any matrimonial procee-dings; or

(c) where the stay is of either the process for divorce or of the process for separation but does not apply to the other process, the order has been made or the power may be exercised—

(i) in any matrimonial proceedings; or

(ii) following the making of a statement of marital breakdown in a case in which no application is made for the kind of order to which the stay relates."

(5) In sub-paragraph (5)(c), for the words from "in connection" onwards there shall be substituted the words "where a stay no longer applies".

SCHEDULE 2

MINOR AND CONSEQUENTIAL AMENDMENTS

PART I

AMENDMENTS OF THE MATRIMONIAL CAUSES ACT 1973

Preliminary

1. The 1973 Act shall be amended in accordance with the following provisions of this Part of this Schedule.

Amendment of section 8

2. In section 8 (intervention of Queen's Proctor)—

    (a) in subsection (1), for the words "petition for divorce" there shall be substituted the words "petition for nullity of marriage or of a petition under section 19 below"; and

    (b) in subsection (2) for the words "proceedings for divorce" there shall be substituted the words "proceedings for nullity of marriage or proceedings under section 19 below".

Amendment of section 9

3.—(1) In subsection (1) of section 9 (general powers of court after decree nisi)—

    (a) for the words "decree of divorce has been granted" there shall be substituted the words "decree of nullity of marriage or a decree of presumption of death and dissolution of marriage has been granted under any of the following provisions of this Act"; and

    (b) for the words from "section 1(5)" to "below)" there shall be substituted the words "section 15 or 19(4) below";

(2) In subsection (2) of that section, for the words "decree of divorce has been granted" there shall be substituted the words "decree of nullity of marriage or a decree of presumption of death and dissolution of marriage has been granted under any of the following provisions of this Act".

Substitution of section 15

4. For section 15 (application of provisions relating to divorce to nullity proceedings) there shall be substituted the following section

"Decrees of nullity to be decrees nisi.

15. Every decree of nullity of marriage shall in the first instance be a decree nisi and shall not be made absolute before the end of six months from its grant unless—

    (a) the High Court by general order from time to time fixes a shorter period; or

    (b) in any particular case, the court in which the proceedings are for the time being pending from time to time by special order fixes a shorter period than the period otherwise applicable for the time being by virtue of this section."

Amendment of section 19

5. In section 19 (decrees of presumption of death and dissolution of marriage), for subsection (4) (application of provisions relating to divorce to proceedings under section 19) there shall be substituted the following subsection—

"(4) Every decree under this section shall in the first instance be a decree nisi and shall not be made absolute before the end of six months from its grant unless—

(a) the High Court by general order from time to time fixes a shorter period; or

(b) in any particular case, the court in which the proceedings are for the time being pending from time to time by special order fixes a shorter period than the period otherwise applicable for the time being by virtue of this subsection."

Amendment of section 23

6.—(1) For subsection (1) of section 23 (financial provision orders in certain cases) there shall be substituted the following subsection—

"(1) Subject to the restrictions imposed by the following provisions of this Act, on granting a decree of nullity of marriage or at any time thereafter (whether before or after the decree is made absolute), the court may make one or more financial provision orders in favour of any party to the marriage or child of the family."

(2) For subsection (2) of that section there shall be substituted the following subsection—

"(2) Subject to those restrictions, the court shall also have power—

(a) before granting a decree in any proceedings for nullity of marriage, to make against either or each of the parties to the marriage—

(i) an interim periodical payments order, or series of such orders, in favour of the other party;

(ii) an interim periodical payments order, a series of such orders or any one or more other financial provision orders in favour of each child of the family;

(b) where any such proceedings are dismissed, to make (either forthwith or within a reasonable period after the dismissal) any one or more financial provision orders in favour of each child of the family."

(3) In subsection (3) of that section, for the words "subsection (1)(c) of (f) above" there shall be substituted the words "the power under subsection (1) above to make an order for the payment of a

SCH. 2 lump sum or to the provisions of this Act as to the beginning of the term specified in any periodical payments order or secured periodical payments order".

(4) For subsection (4) of that section, there shall be substituted the following subsections—

"(3A) The powers of the court under this section to make one or more financial provision orders shall be exercisable against each party to the marriage either by the making of a combined order on one occasion or, if the court thinks fit, by the making of separate orders on different occasions.

(4) The powers of the court under this section so far as they consist in power to make one or more orders in favour of the children of the family—

(a) shall be exercisable differently in favour of different children; and

(b) except in the case of the power conferred by virtue of paragraph (b) of subsection (2) above, shall be exercisable from time to time in favour of the same child; and

(c) in the case of the power conferred by that paragraph shall, if it is exercised on the dismissal of the proceedings or within a reasonable period thereafter by the making of a financial provision order of any kind in favour of a child, be taken to include power subsequently from time to time to make further financial provision orders of that or any other kind in favour of that child."

(5) In subsection (5) of that section, for the words from "subsection" to "divorce or" there shall be substituted the words "subsection (1) above in favour of a party to the marriage on or after the granting of a decree of".

Amendment of section 24

7. For subsection (1) of section 24 (property adjustment orders in certain cases) there shall be substituted the following subsections—

"(1) Subject to the restrictions imposed by the following provisions of this Act, on granting a decree of nullity of marriage or at any time thereafter (whether before or after the decree is made absolute), the court may make one or more property adjustment orders in relation to the marriage.

(1A) Without prejudice to section 31 below, the powers of the court under this section to make one or more property adjustment orders in relation to a marriage shall be exercised, so far as practicable, by the making on one occasion of all such provision capable of being made by way of one or more property adjustment orders in relation to the marriage as the court thinks fit."

Amendment of section 24A

8. In section 24A(1) (orders for sale of property), for the words "section 23 or 24 of this Act" there shall be substituted the words "any of sections 22A to 24 above"

Amendment of section 25

9.—(1) In subsection (1) of section 25 (matters to which the court is to have regard in making a financial provision order, a property adjustment order or order for the sale of property), for the words "section 23, 24 or 24A" there shall be substituted the words "any of sections 22A to 24A".

(2) In subsection (2) of that section—

(a) for the words "section 23(1)(a), (b) or (c)" there shall be substituted the words "section 22A or 23 above to make a financial provision order in favour of a party to a marriage or the exercise of its powers under section 23A,"; and

(b) in paragraph (h), the words "in the case of proceedings for divorce or nullity of marriage," shall be omitted.

(3) In subsection (3) of that section, for the words "section 23(1)(d), (e) or (f), (2) or (4)" there shall be substituted the words "section 22A or 23 above to make a financial provision order in favour of a child of the family or the exercise of its powers under section 23A,".

(4) In subsection (4) of that section, for the words "section 23(1)(d), (e) or (f), (2) or (4), 24 or 24A" there shall be substituted the words "any of sections 22A to 24A".

(5) After subsection (4) of that section there shall be inserted the following subsection—

"(5) In relation to any power of the court to make an interim periodical payments order, the preceding provisions of this section, in imposing any obligation on the court with respect to the matters to which it is to have regard, shall not require the court to do anything which would cause such a delay as would, in the opinion of the court, be inappropriate having regard—

(a) to any immediate need for an interim order;

(b) to the matters in relation to which it is practicable for the court to inquire before making an interim order; and

(c) to the ability of the court to have regard to any matter and to make appropriate adjustments when subsequently making a financial provision order which is not interim."

Amendment of section 25A

10.—(1) In subsection (1) of section 25A (requirement to consider need to provide for "a clean break")—

(a) for the words from the beginning to "the marriage" there shall be substituted the words—

"(1) Where the court decides to exercise any of its powers under any of sections 22A to 24A above in favour of a party to a marriage (other than its power to make an interim periodical payments order)";

and

(b) for the words "the decree" there shall be substituted the words "order of divorce or decree of nullity".

(2) For subsection (3) of that section there shall be substituted the following subsection—

"(3) If, at any time when—

(a) the court would have power under section 22A or 23 above to make a financial provision order in favour of a party to a marriage; and

(b) an application for an order of divorce or a petition for a decree of nullity of marriage is outstanding or has been granted in relation to the marriage,

the court considers that no continuing obligation should be imposed on that party to the marriage to make or secure periodical payments in favour of the other, it may direct that that other party to the marriage shall not at any time after the direction takes effect, be entitled to apply to the court for the making against the other party to the marriage of any periodical payments order or secured periodical payments order."

Amendment of section 26

11. In section 26(1) (commencement of proceedings for ancillary relief), for the words from the beginning to "22 above" there shall be substituted the words—

"(1) Where a petition for nullity of marriage has been presented, then, subject to subsection (2) below, proceedings".

Amendment of section 27

12. For subsection (6) of section 27 (orders that may be made on the ground of a failure to provide proper maintenance) there shall be substituted the following subsection—

"(6) Subject to the restrictions imposed by the following provisions of this Act, where on an application under this section the applicant satisfies the court of any ground mentioned in subsection (1) above, the court may make one or more financial provision orders against the respondent in favour of the applicant or a child of the family."

Amendment of section 28

13.—(1) In subsection (1A) of section 28 (duration of continuing financial provision order in favour of a party to a marriage), for the words from the beginning to "nullity of marriage" there shall be substituted the words—

SCH. 2

"(1A) At any time when—

(a) the court exercises, or has exercised, its power under section 22A or 23 above to make a financial provision order in favour of a party to a marriage;

(b) but for having exercised that power, the court would have power under one of those sections to make such an order; and

(c) an application for an order of divorce or petition for a decree of nullity of marriage is outstanding or has been granted in relation to the marriage,".

(2) In subsection (2) of that section, for the words from "on or after" to "nullity of marriage" there shall be substituted the words "at such a time as is mentioned in subsection (1A)(c) above".

(3) In subsection (3) of that section—

(a) for the words "a decree" there shall be substituted the words "an order or decree"; and

(b) for the words "that decree" there shall be substituted the words "that order or decree".

Amendment of section 29

14. In subsection (1) of section 29 (duration of a continuing financial provision order in favour of a child of the family), for the words "under section 24(1)(a)" there shall be substituted the words "such as is mentioned in section 21(2)(a)".

Amendment of section 31

15.—(1) In subsection (2) of section 31 (variation etc. of orders)—

(a) after the words "following orders" there shall be inserted the words "under this Part of this Act"; and

(b) for paragraph (d) there shall be substituted the following paragraph—

"(d) an order for the payment of a lump sum in a case in which the payment is to be by instalments;".

(2) In subsection (5) of that section—

(a) at the beginning there shall be inserted the words "Subject to subsection (7A) below and without prejudice to any power exercisable by virtue of subsection (1)(d) or (e) above or otherwise than by virtue of this section,"; and

(b) for the words "section 23", in each place where they occur, there shall be substituted the words "section 22A or 23".

(3) In subsection (7)(a) of that section—

(a) for the words "on or after" to "consider" there shall be substituted the words "in favour of a party to a marriage, the court shall, where the marriage has been dissolved or annulled, consider"; and

(b) after the word "sufficient" there shall be inserted the words "(in the light of any proposed exercise by the court of its powers under subsection (7A) below)".

(4) After subsection (7) of that section there shall be inserted the following subsection—

"(7A) Where the court discharges a periodical payments or secured periodical payments order made as mentioned in subsection (7)(a) above or varies such an order so that payments under the order are required to be made or secured only for such further period as is determined by the court, the court shall also have power (in addition to any power exercisable by the court apart from this subsection) to make supplemental provision consisting in any of the following, that is to say—

(a) such an order for the payment of a lump sum in favour of a party to the marriage as it thinks appropriate for alleviating hardship which would otherwise result during the period while that party is adjusting to the effects of the discharge or variation;

(b) such one or more property adjustment orders as it thinks so appropriate;

(c) a direction that the person in whose favour the original order was made shall not be entitled to make any further application for a periodical payments or secured periodical payments order or for an extension of the period to which the original order is limited by any variation made by the court;

and sections 24A and 30 above shall apply for the purposes of the exercise of the court's powers under this subsection as they apply where the court makes a property adjustment order under section 23A or 24 above."

Amendment of section 32

16. In subsection (1) of section 32 (payment of certain arrears to be unenforceable), for the words from "an order" to "financial provision order" there shall be substituted the words "any financial provision order under this Part of this Act or any interim order for maintenance".

Amendment of section 33

17. For subsection (2) of section 33 (repayment of sums paid under certain orders) there shall be substituted the following subsection—

"(2) This section applies to the following orders under this Part of this Act, that is to say—

(a) any periodical payments order;

(b) any secured periodical payments order; and

(c) any interim order for maintenance."

Amendment of section 33A

18.—(1) In subsection (1) of section 33A (consent orders), for the words from the beginning to "preceding" there shall be substituted the words—

> "(1) Subject, in the case of an order under section 23A above, to subsection (5) of that section but notwithstanding anything in any of the other".

(2) In subsection (2) of that section, after the word "applies", in the first place where it occurs, there shall be inserted the words "(subject, in the case of the powers of the court under section 31A above, to subsection (5) of that section)".

(3) In subsection (3) of that section, in the definition of "order for financial relief", for the words "an order under any of sections 23, 24, 24A or 27 above" there shall be substituted the words "any of the following orders under this Part of this Act, that is to say, any financial provision order, any property adjustment order, any order for the sale of property or any interim order for maintenance".

Amendment of section 35

19. After subsection (6) of section 35 (alteration of maintenance agreements), there shall be inserted the following subsection—

> "(7) Subject to subsection (5) above, references in this Act to any such order as is mentioned in section 21 above shall not include references to any order under this section."

Amendment of section 37

20. In subsection (1) of section 37 (avoidance of transactions intended to prevent or reduce financial relief), for the words "22, 23, 24, 27, 31 (except subsection (6))" there shall be substituted the words "22A to 24, 27, 31 (except subsection (6)), 31A".

Amendment of section 41

21. In section 41 (restrictions on divorce separation and annulment affecting children)—

(a) in subsection (1), for the words from "divorce" to "separation" there shall be substituted the words "nullity of marriage"; and

(b) in subsection (2), for the words from "divorce" onwards there shall be substituted the words "nullity is not to be made absolute until the court orders otherwise".

Amendment of section 47

22. In subsection (2) of section 47 (relief in cases of polygamous marriages)—

(a) in paragraph (a), after "any" there shall be inserted the words "order of divorce, any separation order under the Divorce and Separation Act 1990 or any"; and

(b) in paragraph (d), after the words "this Act there shall be inserted the words "or that Act of 1990" and for the words "such decree or order" there shall be substituted the words "statement of marital breakdown or any such order or decree".

Repeal of section 49

23. Section 49 (under which a person who is alleged to have committed adultery with a party to a marriage is required to be made a party to certain proceedings) shall cease to have effect.

Amendment of section 50

24. In subsection (1) of section 50 (matrimonial causes rules), after the words "this Act" there shall be inserted the words ", the Divorce and Separation Act 1990".

Amendment of section 52

25.—(1) In subsection (1) of section 52 (interpretation) the following shall be inserted after the definition of "education"—

"'statement of marital breakdown' has the same meaning as in the Divorce and Separation Act 1990."

(2) In subsection (2)(a) of that section, for the words "with section 21 above" there shall be substituted the words "(subject to section 35(7) above) with section 21 above and, in the case of a financial provision order or periodical payments order, as including (except where the context otherwise requires) references to an interim periodical payments order under section 22A or 23 above".

PART II

CONSEQUENTIAL AMENDMENTS OF OTHER ENACTMENTS

The Wills Act 1837 (c. 26)

26. In section 18A(1) of the Wills Act 1837 (effect of dissolution or annulment of marriage on wills), for the words "a decree" there shall be substituted the words "an order or decree".

The Judicial Proceedings (Regulation of Reports) Act 1926 (c. 61)

27. In section 1(1)(b) of the Judicial Proceedings (Regulation of Reports) Act 1926 (restriction on reporting of matrimonial proceedings) after the words "in relation to" there shall be inserted the words "any proceedings under the Divorce and Separation Act 1990 or otherwise in relation to".

28.—(1) For subsection (5) of section 5 of the Domicile and Matrimonial Proceedings Act 1973 there shall be substituted the following subsections—

"(5) Where a statement of marital breakdown (within the meaning of the Divorce and Separation Act 1990) has been made with respect to a marriage, then (notwithstanding that it would not otherwise do so) the court shall, at the following times, have jurisdiction to entertain proceedings in respect of the same marriage for nullity of marriage, that is to say-

(a) if it appears that the court will in due course have jurisdiction by virtue of paragraph (a) or (b) of section 19(1) of that Act to entertain any application made by reference to that statement, any time during the period for the consideration of future arrangements and for reflection which, under section 5(1) of that Act, must elapse before an application is made by reference to that statement; and

(b) any time when the court has jurisdiction by virtue of either of those paragraphs to entertain an application which has been or could be so made, or would have such jurisdiction but for a direction given for the purposes of section 6 of that Act.

(5A) The court shall have jurisdiction to entertain proceedings in respect of a marriage for nullity of marriage at any time when an application in relation to that marriage is pending under section 3(1) or 4(3) of the Divorce and Separation Act 1990."

(2) In Schedule 5 to that Act of 1973 (application of Schedule 1 to Northern Ireland)—

(a) in paragraph 1 after the word "below" there shall be inserted the words "but without the amendments made by Schedule 1 to the Divorce and Separation Act 1990"; and

(b) after paragraph 2 there shall be inserted the following paragraph—

"2A. In paragraph 4(2) at the end there shall be inserted the words '; and, in relation to England and Wales, proceedings for divorce or judicial separation in respect of a marriage and proceedings capable of affecting the subsistence of a marriage shall be taken to be continuing at any time if either—

(a) that time is a time after the making for the purposes of section 2(2)(a) of the Divorce and Separation Act 1990 of a statement of marital breakdown with respect to the marriage when—

(i) it is or may become possible for an application for an order of divorce, or for a separation order, to be made by reference to that statement;

(ii) no order for a stay is in force in England and Wales in relation to the process for divorce or separation; and

(iii) the running of a period which is required to elapse either under subsection (1) of section 5 of that Act or under a direction given for the purposes of section 6 of that Act, is not for the time being suspended by virtue of a notice under subsection (4) of that section 5 (reconciliation attempts);

or

(b) that time is a time while an application under that Act for an order of divorce, or for a separation order, is pending when-

(i) no order for a stay is in force in England and Wales in relation to the process for divorce or separation;

(ii) the running of a period which is required to elapse either under subsection (2) of section 5 of that Act or under a direction given for the purposes of section 6 of that Act is not for the time being suspended by virtue of a notice under subsection (4) of that section 5; and

(iii) in the case of an application for an order of divorce, no order is for the time being in force under section 4(1) of that Act (prohibition on divorce in cases of grave hardship);

and, accordingly, the references in paragraphs 10 and 11 below to any such proceedings being stayed, to a party to any such proceedings, to the prosecution of any such proceedings or to an order in connection with any such proceedings shall have effect with the necessary modifications in relation to the process for divorce or separation in England and Wales.'"

The Inheritance (Provision for Family and Dependants) Act 1975 (c. 63)

29.—(1) In section 1(2)(a) of the Inheritance (Provision for Family and Dependants) Act 1975 (meaning of reasonable financial provision), for the words from "the marriage" to "in force" there shall be substituted the words ", at the date of death, a separation order under the Divorce and Separation Act 1990 was in force in relation to the marriage",

(2) In section 3(2) of that Act of 1975 (matters to which the court is to have regard)—

(a) for the words "decree of judicial separation" there shall be substituted the words "separation order under the Divorce and Separation Act 1990"; and

SCH. 2

(b) for the words "a decree of divorce" there shall be substituted the words "an order of divorce".

(3) In section 14 of that Act of 1975 (provision where no financial relief was granted on divorce)—

(a) in subsection (1), for the words from "a decree" to "granted", in the first place where it occurs, there shall be substituted the words "an order of divorce or separation order has been made under the Divorce and Separation Act 1990 in relation to a marriage or a decree of nullity of marriage has been made absolute";

(b) in paragraph (a) of that subsection, for the words "section 23" and "section 24" there shall be substituted, respectively, the words "section 22A or 23" and the words "section 23A or 24";

(c) in the words after the paragraphing, for the words from "the decree of divorce" onwards there shall be substituted the words ", as the case may be, the order of divorce or separation order had not been made or the decree of nullity had not been made absolute"; and

(d) in subsection (2), for the words "decree of judicial separation" and "the decree" there shall be substituted, respectively, the words "separation order" and the words "the order".

(4) In section 15 of that Act of 1975 (restriction imposed in divorce proceedings on applications under that Act)—

(a) in subsection (1), for the words from the beginning to "thereafter" there shall be substituted the words—

"(1) At any time when the court—

(a) has jurisdiction under section 23A or 24 of the Matrimonial Causes Act 1973 to make a property adjustment order in relation to a marriage; or

(b) would have such jurisdiction if either the jurisdiction had not already been exercised or an application for such an order were made with the leave of the court,";

(b) for subsections (2) to (4) there shall be substituted the following subsections—

"(2) An order made under subsection (1) above with respect to any party to a marriage shall have effect in accordance with subsection (3) below at the following times, namely—

(a) any time after the marriage has been dissolved;

(b) any time after a decree of nullity has been made absolute in relation to the marriage; and

(c) any time while a separation order under the Divorce and Separation Act 1990 is in force in relation to the marriage and the separation is continuing.

152

(3) If at any time when an order made under subsection (1) above with respect to any party to a marriage has effect the other party to the marriage dies, the court shall not entertain any application made by the surviving party to the marriage for an order under section 2 of this Act."

(5) In section 19(2)(b) of that Act of 1975 (effect and duration of certain orders), for the words from "the marriage" to "in force" there shall be substituted the words ", at the date of death, a separation order under the Divorce and Separation Act 1990 was in force in relation to the marriage with the deceased".

(6) In section 25 of that Act of 1975 (interpretation), in the definition of "former wife" and "former husband", for the words "a decree", in the first place where it occurs there shall be substituted the words "an order or decree".

The Domestic Proceedings and Magistrates' Courts Act 1978 (c. 22)

30. In section 28(1) of the Domestic Proceedings and Magistrates' Courts Act 1978 (powers of High Court in respect of orders under Part I)—

(a) after the words "this Act" there shall be inserted the words—

> "(a) a statement of marital breakdown has been made with respect to the marriage for the purposes of section 2(2)(a) of the Divorce and Separation Act 1990 but no application has been made under that Act by reference to that statement; or

> (b)";

and

(b) for the words from "then" to "lump sum" there shall be substituted the words—

> "then, except in the case of an order for the payment of a lump sum, any court to which an application may be made under that Act by reference to that statement or, as the case may be,".

The Civil Jurisdiction and Judgments Act 1982 (c. 27)

31. In section 18(6)(a) of the Civil Jurisdiction and Judgments Act 1982 (decrees of judicial separation), for the words "a decree" there shall be substituted the words "an order or decree".

The Matrimonial Homes Act 1983 (c. 19)

32.—(1) Schedule 1 to the Matrimonial Homes Act 1983 (transfer of certain tenancies on divorce) shall be amended as follows.

(2) In paragraph 1 (general power to make orders), for the words from "then" onwards there shall be substituted the words "then any court which for the time being has power in relation to the marriage to make a property adjustment order under section 23A or 24 of the

SCH. 2 Matrimonial Causes Act 1973 shall have power to make an order under Part II below."

(3) In paragraph 2(3) (entitlement as successor), for the words "in the case of judicial separation" there shall be substituted the words "as the case may be".

(4) In paragraph 7 (remarriage of either spouse)—

(a) for the words "any decree dissolving or" there shall be substituted the words "order of divorce in relation to a marriage or of a decree"; and

(b) for the words "that decree" there shall be substituted the words "that order of divorce or decree of nullity".

The Matrimonial and Family Proceedings Act 1984 (c. 42)

33.—(1) In section 17(1) of the Matrimonial and Family Proceedings Act 1984 (financial relief in the case of overseas divorces etc.), for the words from "of the orders" onwards there shall be substituted the words "orders each of which would, within the meaning of Part II of the Matrimonial Proceedings Act 1973, be a financial provision order in favour of a party to the marriage or child of the family or a property adjustment order in relation to the marriage."

(2) For paragraph (a) of section 21 of that Act of 1984 (provisions of the 1973 Act applied for the purposes of the powers to give relief in the case of overseas divorces etc.) there shall be substituted the following paragraph—

"(a) the provisions contained in sections 22A(5) and 23(3) (provisions about lump sums);".

(3) In section 22 of that Act of 1984 (powers in relation to certain dwelling houses), for the words "a decree of divorce" and "decree of judicial separation in respect of the marriage had been granted" there shall be substituted, respectively, the words "an order of divorce" and the words "separation order under the Divorce and Separation Act 1990 had been made or granted in relation to the marriage".

(4) In section 27 (interpretation) of that Act of 1984—

(a) for the definition of "property adjustment order", there shall be substituted the following definition—

"'property adjustment order' and 'secured periodical payments order' mean any order which would be a property adjustment order or, as the case may be, secured periodical payments order within the meaning of Part II of the Matrimonial Proceedings Act 1973;"

(5) In section 32 of that Act of 1984 (meaning of "family business"), for the definition of "matrimonial cause" there shall be substituted the following definition—

"'matrimonial cause' means an action for nullity of marriage, any application for an order of divorce or for a separation order under the Divorce and Separation Act 1990 or any other application which results in proceedings which, within the meaning of that Act, are connected with the breakdown of a marriage;".

The Housing Act 1985 (c. 68)

34. In each of sections 39(1)(c), 88(2), 89(3), 90(3)(a), 91(3)(b), 101(3)(c), 160(1)(c) and 171B(4)(b)(i) of the Housing Act 1985 (which contain references to section 24 of the 1973 Act), for the words "section 24" there shall be substituted the words "section 23A or 24".

The Housing Associations Act 1985 (c. 69)

35. In paragraph 5(1)(c) of Schedule 2 to the Housing Associations Act 1985 (which contains a reference to section 24 of the 1973 Act), for the words "section 24" there shall be substituted the words "section 23A or 24".

The Agricultural Holdings Act 1986 (c. 5)

36. In paragraph 1(3) of Schedule 6 to the Agricultural Holdings Act 1986 (spouse of close relative not to be treated as such when marriage subject to decree nisi etc.), for the words from "when" onwards there shall be substituted the words "when a separation order under the Divorce and Separation Act 1990 is in force in relation to the relative's marriage or that marriage is the subject of a decree nisi of nullity or of a decree of judicial separation or decree nisi of divorce."

The Family Law Act 1986 (c. 55)

37.—(1) For subsections (1) and (2) of section 2 of the Family Law Act 1986 (jurisdiction to make orders under section 1) there shall be substituted the following subsection—

"(1) A court in England and Wales shall not have jurisdiction to make a section 1(1)(a) order with respect to a child unless either—

(a) the case falls within section 2A of this Act; or

(b) in any other case, the condition in section 3 of this Act is satisfied.

(2) In section 2A of that Act of 1986 (jurisdiction in or in connection with matrimonial proceedings)—

(a) for subsection (1) there shall be substituted the following subsections—

"(1) Subject to subsections (2) to (4) below, a case falls within this section for the purposes of the making of a section 1(1)(a) order if that order is made—

(a) at a time when a statement of marital breakdown has been made for the purposes of section 2(2)(a) of the Divorce and Separation Act 1990 with respect to the marriage of the parents of the child concerned and it is or may become possible for an application for an order of divorce or for a separation order to be made by reference to that statement; or

(b) at a time when an application in relation to that marriage for an order of divorce, or for a separation order under that Act of 1990, is pending; or

(c) in or in connection with any continuing proceedings which are, within the meaning of that Act of 1990, proceedings connected with the breakdown of the marriage and which were begun at such a time as is mentioned in paragraph (a) or (b) above.

(1A) A case also falls within this section for the purposes of the making of a section 1(1)(a) order if that order is made in or in connection with any proceedings for the nullity of the marriage of the parents of the child concerned and either—

(a) those proceedings are continuing; or

(b) the order is made forthwith upon the dismissal, after the beginning of the trial, of the proceedings and is made on an application made before the dismissal.";

(b) in subsection (2), for the words from the beginning to "judicial separation" there shall be substituted the words "A case does not fall within this section where a separation order under the Divorce and Separation Act 1990 is in force in relation to the marriage of the parents of the child concerned if,"

(c) in subsection (3), for the words "in which the other proceedings there referred to" there shall be substituted the words "in Scotland or Northern Ireland in which the proceedings for divorce or nullity"; and

(d) in subsection (4)—

(i) for the words "in or in connection with matrimonial proceedings" there shall be substituted the words "by virtue of the case falling within this section"; and

(ii) for the words "in or in connection with those proceedings" there shall be substituted the words "by virtue of section 2(1)(a) of this Act".

(3) In section 3 of that Act of 1986 (jurisdiction exercisable where child habitually resident or present in England and Wales), for the words "section 2(2)" there shall be substituted the words "section 2(1)(b)".

(4) In section 6 of that Act of 1986 (duration and variation of Part I orders), for subsections (3A) and (3B) there shall be substituted the following subsection—

"(3A) Subsection (3) above shall not apply if the Part I order was made in a case falling within section 2A of this Act."

SCH. 2

(5) In section 38 of that Act of 1986 (automatic restriction on removal of wards of court from the jurisdiction), after subsection (3) there shall be inserted the following subsection—

"(4) The reference in subsection (2) above to a time when proceedings for divorce or judicial separation are continuing in respect of a marriage in another part of the United Kingdom shall include, in relation to any case in which England and Wales would be another part of the United Kingdom, any time when—

(a) a statement of marital breakdown for the purposes of section 2(2)(a) of the Divorce and Separation Act 1990 has been made with respect to that marriage and it is or may become possible for an application for an order of divorce or for a separation order to be made by reference to that statement; or

(b) an application in relation to that marriage for an order of divorce, or for a separation order under that Act of 1990, is pending."

(6) In section 42(2) of that Act of 1986 (times when divorce etc. proceedings are to be treated as continuing for the purposes of certain restrictions on the removal of children from the jurisdiction), for the words from "unless" onwards there shall be substituted the words "be treated as continuing (irrespective of whether a decree or order of divorce, separation or nullity has been made)—

(a) from the time when a statement of marital breakdown for the purposes of section 2(2)(a) of the Divorce and Separation Act 1990 is made in England and Wales with respect to the marriage until such time as the court may designate or, if earlier, until the time when—

(i) the child concerned attains the age of eighteen; or

(ii) it ceases, by virtue of section 2(5) or 5(5) of that Act (lapse of divorce or separation process) to be possible for an application for an order of divorce, or for a separation order, to be made by reference to that statement; and

(b) from the time when a petition for nullity is presented in relation to the marriage in England and Wales or a petition for divorce, judicial separation or nullity is presented in relation to the marriage in Northern Ireland, until the time when—

(i) the child concerned attains the age of eighteen; or

(ii) if earlier, proceedings on the petition are dismissed."

(7) In section 51(4) of that Act of 1986 (definitions for the purposes of provisions about the refusal of recognition), after the definition of "the relevant date" there shall be inserted the following definition—

157

"'judicial separation' includes a separation order under the Divorce and Separation Act 1990;".

The Landlord and Tenant Act 1987 (c. 31)

38. In section 4(2)(c) of the Landlord and Tenant Act 1987 (which contains a reference to section 24 of the 1973 Act), for the words "section 24" there shall be substituted the words "section 23A, 24".

The Housing Act 1988 (c. 50)

39. In paragraph 4(1)(c) of Schedule 11 (which contains a reference to section 24 of the 1973 Act), for the words "section 24" there shall be substituted the words "section 23A or 24".

The Children Act 1989 (c. 41)

40.—(1) In section 8 of the Children Act 1989 (enactments specified for the purpose of the definition of "family proceedings")—

(a) in subsection (3) after the word "means" there shall be inserted the words "(subject to subsection (5))";

(b) in subsection (4), after paragraph (g) there shall be inserted the following paragraph—

"(h) the Divorce and Separation Act 1990."

(c) after subsection (4) there shall be inserted the following subsection-

"(5) For the purposes of any reference in this Act to family proceedings, powers which under this Act are exercisable in family proceedings shall also be exercisable in relation to a child, without any such proceedings having been commenced or any application having been made to the court under this Act, if—

(a) a statement of marital breakdown for the purposes of section 2(2)(a) of the Divorce and Separation Act 1990 has been made with respect to the marriage in relation to which that child is a child of the family; and

(b) it may, in due course, become possible for an application for an order of divorce or for a separation order to be made by reference to that statement."

(2) In Schedule 1 to that Act (financial provision for children)—

(a) in paragraph 1, after sub-paragraph (4) there shall be inserted the following sub-paragraph—

"(4A) Where an order under sub-paragraph (2)(d) above contains provision reserving power to the court to exercise its power under this sub-paragraph to vary the order (whether generally or in such respects as may be specified in the order), then (subject to any restriction contained in the order on the respects in which that power may be exercised) the court shall have power to vary or discharge that order before it takes effect or, at any time after it takes effect—

   (a) to vary the settlement to which the order relates or to extinguish or reduce any person's interest under that settlement; and

   (b) to make such supplemental provision (including a further order under sub-paragraph (2)(d) or an order under sub-paragraph (2)(c) or (e) above) as the court thinks appropriate in consequence of any variation, extinguishment or reduction to be made under paragraph (a) above;

but the court shall not exercise its power by virtue of this subsection in relation to any order unless it appears to the court that the provision to be made in exercise of that power will not prejudice the interests of any person, other than the child, who has acquired any right or interest in consequence of that order."

(b) in paragraph 2(6)(c), for the words "section 23 or 27" there shall be substituted the words "Part II (other than section 35)".

The Housing and Local Government Act 1989 (c. 42)

41. In section 124(3)(c) of the Housing and Local Government Act 1989 (which contains a reference to section 24 of the 1973 Act), for the words "section 24" there shall be substituted the words "section 23A or 24".

SCHEDULE 3

REPEALS

Chapter	Short title	Extent of repeal
1973 c. 18.	The Matrimonial Causes Act 1973.	Sections 1 to 7. Section 10. Sections 17 and 18. Section 20. Section 22. In section 24, subsection (2) and in subsection (3), the words "divorce or". In section 24A(3), the words "divorce or". In section 25(2)(h), the words "in the case of proceedings for divorce or nullity of marriage,". In section 28(1), the words from "in", in the first place where it occurs, to "nullity of marriage". In section 29(2), the words from "may begin" to "but". In section 30, the words "divorce" and "or judicial separation". In section 31, in subsection (2)(a), the words "order for maintenance pending suit and any" and subsection (4). Section 49. In section 52(2)(b), the words "to orders for maintenance pending suit", "respectively" and "section 22 and".
1973 c. 45.	The Domicile and Matrimonial Proceedings Act 1973.	In section 5, in subsection (1)(a), the words "divorce, judicial separation or" and subsection (2). Section 6(3). In Schedule 1, in paragraph 2, the words "divorce," and "judicial separation," and in paragraph 11, in sub-paragraph (2)(a), in sub-paragraph (2)(c), in

SCH. 3

Chapter	Short title	Extent of repeal
1973 c. 45.—*cont.*	The Domicile and Matrimonial Proceedings Act 1973.—*cont.*	the first place where they occur, and in sub-paragraph (3)(b) and (c), the words "in connection with the stayed procee-dings".
1978 c. 22.	The Domestic Proceedings and Magistrates' Courts Act 1978.	In section 1, paragraphs (c) and (d) and the word "or" preceding paragraph (c). In section 7(1), the words "neither party having deserted the other". Section 63(3). In Schedule 2, paragraph 38.
1981 c. 54.	The Supreme Court Act 1981.	Section 26(a).
1983 c. 19.	The Matrimonial Homes Act 1983.	In Schedule 1, in paragraph 6, the words "divorce or". In Schedule 2, the entry relating to section 4(4)(b) of the Matrimonial Causes Act 1973.
1984 c. 42.	The Matrimonial and Family Procee-dings Act 1984.	Section 1. In section 21(f) the words "except subsection (2)(e) and subsection (4)". In section 27, the definition of "secured periodical payments order". In Schedule 1, paragraph 10.
1989 c. 41.	The Children Act 1989.	In Schedule 13, paragraphs 33(1) and 65(1).

APPENDIX B

LIST OF NATIONAL ORGANISATIONS WHO SENT COMMENTS ON
FACING THE FUTURE - A DISCUSSION PAPER
ON THE GROUND FOR DIVORCE

Association of Chief Officers of Probation
Association of County Court and District Registrars
Barnardo's
Bar of Northern Ireland
Board of Deputies of British Jews
Campaign for Justice in Divorce - Scotland
The Catholic Union of Great Britain
The Children's Legal Centre
The Children's Society
Christian Lawyers Action Group
Church of England Board for Social Responsibility
Conservative Family Campaign
Divorce Law Reform Association
Families Need Fathers
Family Charter Campaign
Family Law Bar Association
Family Mediators Association
Family Welfare Association
General Council of the Bar
Gingerbread
International Society for the Rights of Man
Institute of Legal Executives
Jubilee Centre
Justice
The Law Society
League of Jewish Women
Lords and Commons Family and Child Protection Group
Married Women's Association
The Mothers Union
National Board of Catholic Women
National Campaign for the Family
National Children's Bureau
National Council for One Parent Families
The National Council of Women of Great Britain
National Family Conciliation Council
The Official Solicitor
Order of Christian Unity
Relate
The Salvation Army
Society of County Secretaries
Solicitors' Family Law Association
Synod of the Free Presbyterian Church of Scotland
Women's National Commission

LIST OF LOCAL ORGANISATIONS WHO SENT COMMENTS ON FACING THE FUTURE - A DISCUSSION PAPER ON THE GROUND FOR DIVORCE

East Kent Federation of Women's Institutes
East Yorkshire Federation of Women's Institutes
Essex Court Welfare Service
Federation of Essex Women's Institutes
Gloucestershire Federation of Women's Institutes
Holborn Law Society
Hull and North Humberside Family Conciliation Service
Kent Law Society
London Federation of Women's Institutes
Management team and staff of Divorce Section Birmingham County Court
Midlands Probation Service
Newcastle-Upon-Tyne Law Society
Norfolk Federation of Women's Institutes
Poole Mothers Union
The St. Albans Diocesan Board for Social Responsibility
Suffolk Probation Service
Surbiton Christian Response
Wendover Women's Institute

LIST OF INDIVIDUALS WHO RESPONDED TO FACING THE FUTURE - A DISCUSSION PAPER ON THE GROUND FOR DIVORCE

R. Bailey Harris
J. Barron
C. Barton
R. D. Bateman
Canon Bentley
Rabbi Berkovits
P. J. Bishop
E. Board
W. M. G. Bompas
C. Bridge
G. G. Brown
H. Brown
The Rt. Hon. Sir Stephen Brown, President of the Family Division
E. Burgin
M. Churchouse
N. Collins
J. Craven-Griffiths
Professor S. M. Cretney
A. M. Dale
G. Dale
J. Dann
G. Davis
L. Delany

Dr. L. Diwany
G. Douglas
His Honour Judge Dyer
J. Eekelaar
Mr. Registrar Elliot
Professor H. A. Finlay
R. F. Grant
D. Green
J. F. Haderka
J. G. Harniman
Professor D. Hooper
Dr. S. Hopwood
C. Howard
Dr. T. Ingman
T. Jackson
D. D. Jeans
P. J. Jennings
A. Jones
R. Jones
R. F. Land
R. Langton
C. Latham O.B.E., M.A., Stipendiary Magistrate
S. G. Linstead
J. C. Long
Mr. Registrar Lowis
L. Maisey
C. A. Makins Barnett
A. Marlow
F. McManus
J. Mielnik
J. Montgomery
C. Morgan
M. Morgan
C. Moy
J. Mudge
The Rt. Hon. Sir Roger Ormrod
S. and N. Osmond
Lady Oppenheimer
Professor P. Parsloe
A. J. G. Pellman
P. Pettman
A. I. Phillips
S. T. Phillipson
Dr. S. Poulter
M. Prentice
H. A. Prowse
T. S. Rait
S. Reece
N. Rider
J. Richards
J. R. Richardson
R. Richardson

164

R. Ross
D. T. Rymer
E. A. Shimmings
A. K. Smith
G. Smith
W. F. Summers
J. W. Trobridge
B. Wadland
C. Wickham
D. Winton
Professor B. A. Wortley
C. Yates

APPENDIX C

COURT RECORD STUDY

Introduction

1.   The object of the study was to gain more information about how divorce and judicial separation cases progress through the courts.   This analysis is based on an examination of 477 closed files relating to proceedings begun in the years 1980 to 1984 in 18 different county courts in England and Wales and in the Principal Registry of the Family Division.   The courts were chosen to give a wide geographical spread and a balance between those with many cases and those with only a few.   The files were examined in 1988, by which time almost all had been completed or discontinued.   The files were chosen at random by court staff and in general roughly 25 were examined from each court.   Only 43 files from the Principal Registry were analysed for the main study.[1] The object was to obtain, not a statistically representative sample, but a picture of how the law operates in a wide variety of places.   We also held discussions with registrars in some of the courts visited.

2.   Nevertheless, from published statistics for the years in question, we were able to confirm that our sample was very broadly representative of the divorcing population, in such respects as the sex of the petitioner (see below), the facts relied on (see below),the average length of marriage (11 years), and the proportion having children for whom the arrangements had to be considered under section 41 of the Matrimonial Causes Act 1973 (56.4%).[2]

Use of facts

3.   The table on the following page gives the proportions of men and women petitioners and the facts relied upon. It excludes the one nullity petition and one other case where so few details were recorded that it was impossible to classify. It includes six judicial separation petitions and one application for leave to petition within three years of the marriage.

---

1   A pilot study was conducted at the Principal Registry of the Family Division and at another county court in the London area, but only those files from the Principal Registry which were selected in the same way as those for the main study have been included in this analysis.

2   Currently all those under 16; those of 16 but under 18 who are undergoing education or training, even on a day release basis; and any other child of the family directed by the Judge to be included, perhaps because of physical or mental handicap.   Under the Children Act 1989 the comparable duty will be restricted to the under-16s or those whom the Judge directs should be included.

Table 1: Petitions and facts relied on

	Total no. (% of all petitions)	By men (% of petitions on that fact)	By women	
Adultery	140	51	89	
	(29.5%)	(36.4%)	(63.6%)	(100%)
Behaviour	185	16	169	
	(38.9%)	(8.6%)	(91.4%)	(100%)
Desertion	4	1	3	
	(0.8%)	(25%)	(75%)	(100%)
Two years	110	46	64	
	(23.2%)	(41.8%)	(58.2%)	(100%)
Five years	36	21	15	
	(7.6%)	(58.3%)	(41.7%)	(100%)
Totals:	475	135 (28.4%)	340 (71.6%)	
(% of all petitions)	(100%)			

4.   We also made an attempt to assess the use of the different facts according to the petitioner's socio-economic class.[3]   Where the occupation of the petitioner was unknown or described as a housewife, mother or unemployed, the class of the respondent has been used.   The unclassified category includes those where neither petitioner nor respondent was economically active.   We cannot claim that our classification is completely accurate, as the information recorded is sometimes incomplete or ambiguous, nor are the numbers in some sub-groups large.   Nevertheless, Table 2 does show a noticeable bias, particularly in the use of separation.

[3] The Registrar-General's broad classifications are:

I	Professional occupations.
II	Intermediate occupations (including most managerial and senior administrative occupations).
IIIn	Skilled occupations (non-manual).
IIIm	Skilled occupations (manual).
IV	Partly skilled occupations.
V	Unskilled occupations.
Unc.	Residual groups including, for example, armed forces, students, and those whose occupation was inadequately described.

Table 2:   Facts relied on by each social group

| | Total nos. (% of those in that social group) | | | | | | | |
	I	II	IIIn	IIIm	IV	V	Unc.	Total
Adultery	8 (36%)	25 (37%)	37 (30%)	34 (28%)	17 (33%)	8 (33%)	11 (17%)	140 (29.5%)
Behaviour	3 (14%)	18 (26%)	43 (35%)	54 (45%)	25 (48%)	9 (38%)	33 (51%)	185 (38.9%)
Desertion	0 (0%)	0 (0%)	0 (0%)	0 (0%)	1 (2%)	1 (4%)	2 (3%)	4 (0.8%)
Two years	8 (36%)	20 (29%)	38 (31%)	21 (18%)	8 (15%)	4 (17%)	11 (17%)	110 (23.2%)
Five years	3 (14%)	5 (7%)	6 (5%)	11 (9%)	1 (2%)	2 (8%)	8 (12%)	36 (7.6%)
Totals:	22 (100%)	68 (100%)	124 (100%)	120 (100%)	52 (100%)	24 (100%)	65 (100%)	475

5.   We need only comment that this repeats others' findings[4] that the tendency to use separation, and in particular two years' separation, is much more marked among those from the higher socio-economic groups. Five years' separation is in any event relatively rare, but includes several retired couples amongst the unclassified. Adultery is, perhaps unsurprisingly, relatively constant among all groups apart from the unclassified. Behaviour is used noticeably less often by those in the higher groups.

6.   Table 3 shows that there were also differences in the use of each fact, depending on whether or not there were relevant[5] children.

Table 3:   Use of fact by whether there were children

	Total no. using fact: (% of total sample)	No. with children: (% of couples with children)
Adultery	140 (29.5%)	85 (31.7%)
Behaviour	185 (38.9%)	130 (48.5%)
Desertion	4 (0.8%)	3 (1.1%)
Two Years	110 (23.2%)	40 (14.9%)
Five Years	36 (7.6%)	10 (3.7%)
Totals:	475 (100%)	268 (100%)

[4] J. Haskey, "Grounds for Divorce in England and Wales: A Social and Demographic Analysis" (1986) 18 J. Biosoc. Sci. 127; G. Davis and M. Murch, Grounds for Divorce, (1988), pp.78-80.

[5] See n.2 above.

7.   It is not surprising that use of five years' separation was proportionately less amongst couples with children.   But it is noteworthy that petitioners with children were also less likely to use two years' separation and correspondingly more likely to use behaviour rather than adultery.   Indeed, this greater tendency to use fault-based facts amongst petitioners with children seems to have meant that the use of the various facts showed much less difference between the classes in cases where there were children than when there were not.   This emerges from a comparison of Table 2 with Table 4, below.

Table 4:   **Facts relied on by petitioners with children, by social group**

	Total nos. (% of those in that social group)							
	I	II	IIIn	IIIm	IV	V	Unc.	Total
Adultery	5 (62%)	16 (47%)	15 (25%)	24 (34%)	11 (35%)	5 (29%)	9 (20%)	85 (31.7%)
Behaviour	2 (25%)	12 (35%)	30 (49%)	35 (49%)	18 (58%)	7 (41%)	26 (57%)	130 (48.5%)
Desertion	0 (0%)	0 (0%)	0 (0%)	0 (0%)	0 (0%)	1 (6%)	2 (4%)	3 (1.1%)
Two years	0 (0%)	6 (18%)	14 (23%)	10 (14%)	2 (6%)	2 (12%)	6 (13%)	40 (14.9%)
Five years	1 (13%)	0 (0%)	2 (3%)	2 (3%)	0 (0%)	2 (12%)	3 (7%)	10 (3.7%)
Totals:	8 (100%)	34 (100%)	61 (100%)	71 (100%)	31 (100%)	17 (100%)	46 (100%)	268 (100%)

Length of Proceedings

8.   One area of particular interest to us was the length of time taken from filing the petition to the grant of a decree absolute and the factors which affected that time. Table 5 gives the times taken by petitions based on the different facts (excluding desertion because there were so few).   Five year separation petitions took longest overall, but as the number of cases was small too much significance cannot be attached to this; adultery and behaviour petitions slightly exceeded the overall median time; and two year separation with consent petitions were significantly quicker. The time taken has been calculated by reference, not to the average, but to the median, that is the time taken by 50% of cases on each fact to reach decree absolute.   This avoids distortion caused by the few cases taking abnormally long times.

Table 5:   **Length of proceedings by fact relied on**

Adultery	190 days (6 months)
Behaviour	193 days (6 months)
Desertion	*
Two years	148 days (5 months)
Five years	210 days (7 months)
Overall Median	182 days (6 months)

9.   The time taken between decree nisi and decree absolute need only be six weeks (42 days), but the petitioner must apply for the decree absolute to be issued (or if the petitioner does not do so, the respondent may apply after three months from the decree nisi). The median period from decree nisi to decree absolute was less than eight weeks (51 days). Behaviour cases took longest (53 days); two year separation cases were again the quickest (48 days). There were, however, a few couples who waited years before making their decrees absolute.

10.   There was a marked difference between the overall length of proceedings where there were children for whom arrangements had to be considered under section 41 of the 1973 Act.[6] For these cases the median time taken was 192 days, whereas for those with none it was 150 days. The quickest type of case, as might be imagined, was a two year separation case with no children, where the median was 137 days.

11.   There is some reason to think that our cases progressed rather more quickly than may generally happen. Of decrees granted in 1984, for example, 40.2% took less than six months from petition to decree absolute, but only 20.7% did so if there were children under 16. 48.2% of the two-year separation cases took less than six months, but only 34.9% of the behaviour cases did so.[7] The figures for 1988 showed a marked slowing down: 33.7% overall took less than six months, but only 14.5% if there were children; 44.4% of the two year separation cases, but only 28.7% of the behaviour cases.[8] One reason for the difference between these and our own findings may be the under-representation of the Principal Registry and other particularly busy courts in our total sample.

---

[6] See n.2 above.

[7] O.P.C.S., Marriage and Divorce Statistics 1984 (1986), Series FM2 No. 11, Table 4.8.

[8] O.P.C.S., Marriage and Divorce Statistics 1988 (1990), Series FM2 No. 15, Table 4.8.

12. The marked difference between cases with and without children must to some extent be explained by the present requirement in section 41 of the 1973 Act, under which the divorce decree cannot be made absolute until a Judge has certified that the arrangements made for the children are satisfactory.[9] Under the Children Act 1989, the court will still have to consider the arrangements proposed for the children but the decree itself will only be delayed if this is desirable in their interests.[10] It is, of course, impossible to say what effect this will have on the overall duration of proceedings. However, it must also be borne in mind that the use of fault-based facts is more common where there are children and these are also associated with longer durations.

Outcome

13. The original 477 files resulted in one nullity decree, five judicial separation decrees, 433 decrees nisi of divorce and 418 decrees absolute. One decree nisi was later rescinded. Thus 53 cases (11.1% of the total) fell by the wayside at some stage, 28 without any decree at all, and 15 between decree nisi and decree absolute. These included one case (mentioned earlier) where the fact was not recorded. Otherwise, Table 6 shows the facts relied on in the unsuccessful petitions:

Table 6   **Facts relied on in unsuccessful petitions**

	No.	(%)	% of petitions on that fact
Adultery	13	(24.5%)	9.3%
Behaviour	30	(56.6%)	16.2%
Desertion	0	(0%)	0%
Two years	6	(11.3%)	5.4%
Five years	4	(7.5%)	11.1%
Total:	53	(99.9%)	

14. The behaviour cases did tend to run into more difficulty than the others, but it is significant that more than a quarter of these couples were still living at the same address at the date of the petition (see para. 23 below). This in itself was associated with a higher rate of failure to proceed.

15. It was not always possible to deduce the reason why a case had failed to reach decree or decree absolute. It was rarely associated with, let alone attributable to, the intervention of the court. The most common reason appeared to be reconciliation; there were also some who had obtained non-molestation or ouster injunctions but apparently gone no further, some where the proceedings on the file had been superseded by a new petition in that or another court, and some which proceeded no further than notification of an intention to defend.

---

[9] Or the best that can be devised in the circumstances, or that it is impracticable for the party or parties appearing before the court to make any arrangements; s.41(1)(b).

[10] 1989 Act, Sched. 12, para. 31, substituting a new section 41 in the Matrimonial Causes Act 1973.

16.　　　There were at least 21 cases where the respondent had at some stage indicated an intention to defend.　Only three were transferred to the High Court as defended suits.　One of these (referred to in para. 18 below) was eventually dismissed for want of prosecution.　Another proceeded undefended on the prayer in the respondent's answer. The outcome of the third is not known.　In another case, the wife had obtained a judicial separation but was refused legal aid to defend her husband's divorce petition, which was granted.　Of the rest, the petitioner did not proceed in five, and the respondent did not press his objections in the others, where a decree was granted.

17.　　　There were many other cases in which the respondent indicated disagreement with the allegations made, often by resisting a claim for costs on the basis that he was not to blame for the breakdown of the marriage.　There was also a considerable number of respondents who declined to acknowledge service or who had disappeared.　Undefended divorce certainly cannot be equated with divorce by consent.

18.　　　A few petitioners had encountered unusual difficulties.　In one behaviour case, the respondent was in a psychiatric hospital and a guardian ad litem was appointed, but the proceedings were apparently stayed until he was able to manage his own affairs. After the guardian was discharged, a second petition based on two years' separation was filed, but the respondent declined to consent.　A psychiatrist's report lodged with the court explained that the respondent believed that the marriage was still viable and although there had been adultery on his part this had not caused the marriage to break down, as the petitioner maintained.　The case was eventually dismissed for want of prosecution.

Representation

19.　　　It was not always possible to be certain about whether or not the petitioner was legally represented.　Generally, if a petitioner is legally represented for the purposes of the petition, he or she is financing it privately.　Otherwise, legal aid is not available for the presentation of the petition, so that technically the petitioner acts in person at that stage, even though he or she may be in receipt of legal advice and assistance under the Green Form scheme.　Legal aid is, however, available for injunctions and other contentious ancillary relief.　The information recorded could therefore be difficult to interpret.　There were two cases out of the 477 where no information was available.

20.　　　Of the 475 cases remaining, it appeared that 125 (or 26.3%) had a solicitor acting for them, and this was largely borne out by the figures for cases in which there was a "section 6" certificate (see para. 21 below) filed; 275 (or 57.9%) were receiving assistance under the Green Form scheme; and 75 (or 15.8%) were acting in person.　This last does seem rather a high proportion compared with those found elsewhere[11] and it may well be that some who appeared to be acting in person had at some stage had the benefit of legal advice.

Reconciliation certificates

21.　　　A solicitor acting for a petitioner is obliged, under section 6(1) of the 1973

---

[11] E.g. by G. Davis, A. Macleod and M. Murch, in "Special Procedure in Divorce and the Solicitor's Role", (1982) 12 Fam.Law 39.

Act, to file with the petition a certificate stating whether or not he has discussed reconciliation with the client or given the client the names and addresses of persons qualified to assist. There were at least five cases in which certificates were filed apparently unnecessarily because the solicitor was not acting for the purposes of the petition; and four cases where there was no certificate but there should have been. Hence there were certificates in 121 of the 125 cases in which solicitors were acting.

22. Generally, therefore, solicitors were fulfilling their duty to file certificates. More interestingly, perhaps, they gave positive responses in what might be thought a surprisingly high proportion of cases. Thus 85 out of the 125 certificates reported that the solicitor *had* discussed reconciliation with his client, and 29 reported that they had referred the client to other agencies.

Living together

23. Table 7 shows how many couples were still living at the same address at the date of the petition, and the facts which they relied upon.

Table 7:   **Living at same address by fact**

	No.	% of petitions on that fact
Adultery	13	(9.2%)
Behaviour	50	(27.2%)
Desertion	0	(0%)
Two years	2	(1.8%)
Five years	2	(5.6%)
Not known	1	-
Total:	68	(i.e. 14.3% of all divorce and judicial separation petitions)

24. It will be seen that very few of the petitioners relying on separation were still living at the same address as the respondent at the date of the petition. In one of the five year cases, the respondent had a "bedsit" in the matrimonial home, and the registrar expressed disquiet, but the decree was granted. In the other, they were living in "separate apartments", but the petition was abandoned. In one of the two year cases, a decree nisi was granted but a note put on the file that it was not to be made absolute without leave of the court as the couple were still living at the same address. This was apparently common practice on that circuit, whatever the fact relied on. The other case proceeded without question.

25. It is of interest that more than a quarter of behaviour petitioners were still living at the same address at the date of the petition, although in several it was clear that one party had left shortly afterwards. However, 11 of these cases did not result in a divorce, a "failure rate" which is above average. In at least five cases this was because of a reconciliation, but in others it appeared that the petitioner had not gone beyond obtaining an injunction.

Stop notices

26. Unless the case is defended, it will be dealt with under the so-called special

procedure.   This requires the Registrar to scrutinise the petition, supporting affidavit and any other evidence, in order to satisfy himself that the contents of the petition have been proved and that the petitioner is entitled to a decree.   Thus the documents are checked both for their procedural regularity and for their sufficiency in substance to prove the petitioner's case.   If they are found to be lacking in some way, the Registrar may request further information or evidence.   If the Registrar is satisfied, he will issue a certificate that the petitioner is entitled to a decree and the Judge will pronounce it formally in open court.   If the Registrar is not satisfied, he will remove the case from the special procedure list and require that it be heard before the Judge.

27.   One of the major aims of the study was to discover more about the circumstances in which Registrars refused their certificates.   The first difficulty, however, was to define what amounted to a refusal or "stop".   Most circuits use a special procedure checklist detailing everything to which the Registrar should have addressed his mind;   others used their own forms.   It was the duty of court staff to check the documents and draw any errors to the Registrar's attention.   Some Registrars might prefer staff to restrict themselves to administrative errors or inconsistencies, but most were happy for court staff also to draw substantive deficiencies to their attention.

28.   Official "stops" arose where the case did not pass the checklist and a stop would be put on the file, so that it was not included in the automatic directions for trial list.   The petitioner or his solicitor would not necessarily be informed and might have to gather this from the delay and apply to the court for an explanation.   In other cases, the file might reveal that the court had identified a problem and taken it up with the parties.

29.   In addition, many potential problems might be dealt with informally, for example by court staff who would advise petitioners or solicitors over the counter as to what was required.   It is impossible to know how often this happens, but to some extent difficulties (particularly of a substantive nature) which become apparent on the files may be outside the normal run of objections in that particular court, as these would have been picked up earlier by solicitors or by court staff who know what is likely to cause problems with their Registrar.   Thus one of the courts in which there were no stop notices was also one in which the strictest proof of adultery or behaviour was supplied.

30.   As formal "stop notices" are only a proportion of cases in which the court identifies an error or deficiency, we have tried to record all the cases in which there was evidence on the file that the court itself had raised a query.   There was evidence of some sort of "stop" on 104 (21.8%) of the files examined.   The interest lies, however, not so much in how often this occurred but in why it did so.

31.   Procedural or administrative problems fell into the following broad categories: inaccuracies on the face of the documents, for example, names misspelt or inconsistent, sections on standard forms not filled in or filled in incorrectly, documents undated or unsigned;   documents, for example the marriage certificate, not filed or the wrong document, for example an acknowledgment of service relating to the wrong fact, filed; disagreements or problems over costs;   problems with service;   and respondents under a disability for whom a guardian ad litem might have to be appointed.   There were also several cases in which further information about the children was required for the purpose of section 41 of the 1973 Act and one in which the decree absolute was held up because of a continuing access dispute.

32.   Substantive problems arose where the Registrar had questioned the method or sufficiency of proof of the fact asserted in the petition and whether the petitioner was entitled to a decree.   These fell into the following broad categories: insufficient evidence of adultery (14 cases); failure to name the person with whom the adultery was alleged to have been committed (8 cases); and parties still living at the same address (14 cases).   Other examples were a desertion case where the Registrar found it difficult to believe that the petitioner had not agreed to the separation, and the petitioner proceeded on adultery instead; three separation cases where the question was when the petitioner had reached the conclusion that the marriage was at an end; and a behaviour case where the certificate was refused because there was no corroboration.

33.   It is difficult to know why so many queries were raised about whether the parties were still living at the same address.   One related to two years' separation, one to five (these are discussed in para. 24 above), and one to adultery.   The rest were behaviour cases. In at least two cases the reason apparently was that there were children involved and the court considered that it could not be satisfied with the arrangements, as required by section 41 of the 1973 Act, if the parties were still under the same roof. This could lead to the classic "Catch 22" found on at least one file, where the housing department would not rehouse until decree absolute, but the decree absolute could not be obtained while the family remained under one roof. Many of the others resulted from the practice on one circuit of refusing to make a decree absolute if the couple were still living at the same address.   That circuit also provided the one clear example of a case where the Registrar's certificate was refused and a hearing took place before a Judge. This was a behaviour case in which the allegations were not strong, but the trigger seems to have been that the parties were still living at the same address. A decree was eventually granted.   In cases like this, the Registrars may either have taken the view that it could not be unreasonable to expect the petitioner to go on living with the respondent if she was still doing so; or that the marriage had not irretrievably broken down.   Technically, it should be the former, as once a fact has been proved, the court must grant the decree unless satisfied that the marriage has *not* irretrievably broken down.[12]

34.   Procedural problems arose on more files than did substantive problems of this nature, although some files revealed both types.   However, as we have already pointed out, the fact that no query arose on the file does not mean that the court had not had an effect upon how the case was proved.   Local solicitors would already know and accommodate themselves to the court's requirements.   Litigants in person would have received some advice from the court. It is therefore of some interest to note what the files revealed about the way in which, in particular, the adultery and behaviour facts were proved and we discuss this further below.

35.   The great majority of the "stopped" cases proceeded eventually to a decree. Only 10 of them failed to do so and it was not usually possible to conclude that this was the result of the stop.   (One exception was the 2-year separation case referred to in para. 24 above where the decree nisi was not to be made absolute because they were still at the same address.)

---

[12] Matrimonial Causes Act 1973, s.1(3).

36.   Unsurprisingly, the effect of stop notices was to increase the overall length of the proceedings.   As against a median length of 182 days for all proceedings, where there had been stops the median was 200 days, and where there had been no stops the median was 150 days.   This suggests that as a distinct factor in affecting the overall length of proceedings, stop notices have a slightly greater effect (50 days) than the presence of children of the family (43 days).

Adultery

37.   A substantial proportion of problems noted on the files related to proof of adultery.   Generally speaking, some sort of confession or admission from the respondent was required, and this gave scope for considerable technicality, for example as to identifying the respondent's signature or exhibiting the confession to an affidavit.   A good example of the problems was a case in which neither party was represented, where the petition read:

> "The parties separated by mutual consent due to incompatibility. The
> respondent subsequently committed adultery with an unknown woman
> who he now wishes to marry.   I now feel that my marriage is
> seriously prejudicing my chances of forming another lasting
> relationship."

The Registrar objected that "there is not even a hint of a shred of evidence" and required the petitioner to name the other woman if possible and join her as a party.   A letter was received from the respondent who asserted that he did want to marry his new partner but was not prepared to admit to adultery.   The petition was re-presented and the Registrar's certificate refused a second time because "there is still no evidence of adultery."   The case did eventually reach decree absolute (but not until after a further refusal because of a discrepancy over costs).

38.   A formal confession by the respondent, or sometimes by the respondent and the co-respondent, was lodged in approximately half the cases.   It appeared that on one circuit there was a consistent practice of lodging confession statements.   This might reflect the known requirements of Registrars or the established practice of the profession or a combination of the two.   Otherwise, reliance might be placed on an admission in the acknowledgment of service or some other evidence.   In one case a love letter was exhibited by the petitioner.   In another, however, a birth certificate naming the respondent as the father of a child born to the co-respondent during the marriage was not considered sufficient.

39.   Generally, therefore, there had to be something more than the petitioner's assertion that adultery had taken place.   This, of course, distinguishes adultery from the general run of behaviour cases.   It can also make them more expensive, if a formal confession has to be obtained (usually through a private inquiry agent) rather than a simple admission.

40.   A further technicality with adultery cases relates to naming the person with whom it is alleged that the adultery has been committed.   The Matrimonial Causes Rules 1977[13] require this to be done, if the person is known to the petitioner, unless the requirement is dispensed with.   Section 49 of the 1973 Act requires that if the person is

---

[13]   Rule 13(1).

named then he or she should normally be made a party to the suit so that he or she can defend. Reluctance to do this had led to a practice of glossing over the name, or pretending that this was unknown; but this was disapproved in *Bradley* v. *Bradley*[14] which held that the person should be named if possible.

41. There was evidence on the files, which related to cases begun before *Bradley* v. *Bradley* was decided, of considerable inconsistency in practice. Some Registrars were uneasy with cases where the allegation was of adultery with "a person unknown to the petitioner", or with "a person known only to me as June", feeling that this left the door wide open to perjury. Others were content to accept these. Practice may, of course, have become more consistent recently; but even then, the need to name the other person was a considerable source of difficulty between courts and petitioners.

42. In 32 (25%) of the adultery cases which reached decree absolute a co-respondent was not named. In eight of these the Registrar issued a stop notice in order that a co-respondent might be joined. However three of these were allowed to continue even though the name was not forthcoming. In the other five the co-respondent was eventually named. There was also evidence on the files that the papers had been amended to include a co-respondent's name even though the proceedings had not been officially halted.

43. Where adultery is being used as evidence that the marriage has irretrievably broken down, it is necessary not only to prove that the respondent has committed adultery but also that the petitioner finds it intolerable to live with the respondent. However, the adultery need not be the reason why the petitioner finds life with the respondent intolerable nor need the petitioner's attitude be reasonable provided that it is genuinely held. It is perhaps unsurprising, therefore, that not one case examined in the study gave details of intolerability.

Behaviour

44. It might have been thought that assessing behaviour cases would also cause some problems. Registrars might have been unpersuaded, either that the behaviour complained of had in fact taken place or had the effect alleged, or that however accurately described it was such that it was unreasonable to expect the petitioner to live with the respondent. The files examined did not reveal evidence of this, apart from the problems arising where the couple were still living at the same address (see para. 33 above). The behaviour itself was generally proved by the assertions made in the petition and subsequently confirmed in the petitioner's affidavit.

45. However, there was one case in which a certificate was refused because there was no corroborative evidence. Further inquiry revealed that it was the practice on the circuit in question to require an affidavit from a witness to the behaviour or a medical report if violence was alleged. Of the 18 behaviour cases on that circuit, 15 included corroborative evidence from a friend, colleague, relative or doctor. Another did not proceed beyond lodging the petition. Surprise was expressed by court staff that this was not the practice on other circuits.

---

[14] [1986] 1 F.L.R. 128.

46.   There was also a definite impression that the quality of behaviour pleaded in some places, including the circuit in question, was much worse than in others. In some courts virtually all of the cases involved violence, whereas in others hardly any did so. Whatever this says about standards of "conjugal kindness" in different parts of the country, it probably says much more about the expectations of petitioners, their solicitors and the courts. This is not to say that the same petition filed in, say, Epsom would not succeed in, say, Durham. The files could not tell us this, but they did reveal that the general character of petitions in the two places was quite different.

47.   Table 8 below gives an indication of the types of conduct complained of in petitions alleging that the respondent has behaved in such a way that the petitioner cannot reasonably be expected to live with him. Some petitions were longer or more detailed than others. Thus, some may have mentioned all the above in order to satisfy the Registrar, whereas others may only have mentioned one for a decree to be granted.

Table 8   **Factors Alleged in Behaviour Petitions**

Behaviour	Number of Cases	% of Cases Mentioning such Behaviour
Violence to Petitioner	96	64%
Personality Clashes	85	56%
No Interest in Home	72	48%
Unreasonable Habits	64	42%
Financial Problems	58	38%
Abusive Language	46	30%
Alcohol Abuse	43	28%
Violence to Children	31	21%
Improper Associations	31	21%
Sexual Problems	30	20%
Violence to Property	16	11%

48.   What the files do reveal is that, unlike adultery, there are few technicalities, other than continued cohabitation, for the court to pick out in a behaviour case. It can single out those when the parties are still living under the same roof, but there could be mutual reasons for doing so (see para. 33 above); it can, as happened in one case, question why the couple remained under the same roof for more than six months after the last act of behaviour complained of;[15] or it can express a general suspicion about the petitioner's truthfulness as also happened in one case.

---

[15] Under Matrimonial Causes Act 1973, s.2(3), cohabitation of less than six months after the last act complained of is to be ignored in deciding whether or not the petitioner can reasonably be expected to live with the respondent; thereafter, it is a matter of judgment.

49.   It does, however, appear to be extremely rare for the Registrar to refuse a certificate simply because the allegations, even if true, seem insufficient to make it unreasonable to suspect the petitioner to go on living with the respondent. The only possible example, amongst all the files examined, was the case referred to in para. 33 where the parties were still living under the same roof. Although behaviour petitions certainly encounter more difficulties than most, these appear generally to be of the parties' rather than the courts' making.

Separation

50.   Separation, as we have seen, was relatively straightforward. It encountered fewer objections (including procedural or administrative problems) from the courts. There were only four cases where the couple were still at the same address and the court raised a query in two of them (see para. 24). There were three cases in which the court raised a query about when and in what circumstances a petitioner had reached the conclusion that the marriage was at an end. This reflects the decision in *Santos* v. *Santos*[16] that "living apart" involves a mental as well as a physical element. In all of these cases the matter was resolved and a decree granted, although one of them may have involved a hearing before a Judge. The petitioner had dated her conclusion that the marriage was at an end less than two years before the date of the petition; there was also confusion about when they had ceased living in the same household. There was also a case in which the court queried the signature on the acknowledgment of service in which consent is given. However, there was no separation case in which corroborative evidence appears to have been required. Generally, separation cases progressed more quickly and fewer failed to reach a decree.

Conclusion

51.   It is certainly difficult to conclude from the files which we studied that the intervention of the courts, considerable though this may be, has a noticeable impact upon the outcome of cases. Of the cases which failed to proceed, far more did so because of the decisions of the parties themselves than because of the problems of proving the ground. Of the cases where there had been such problems, the great majority eventually reached a decree.

---

[16] [1972] Fam. 247.

APPENDIX D

THE PUBLIC OPINION SURVEY

Public Attitude Surveys Ltd (PAS) were commissioned to conduct a survey of adults living in England and Wales in order to obtain their views on the present ground for divorce and possible models for reform. A representative sample of 1001 individuals was recruited from 99 different locations to quota controls on sex, age and social class. Face-to-face interviews were conducted in December 1988 and January 1989. Respondents were each given an introductory letter from Professor Hoggett at the Law Commission, which in the view of PAS "contributed to the careful attention paid by them to the questions asked". The interview also contained questions on the law on intestacy, which has already been reported.[1] The questionnaire was developed in consultation with the Law Commission and amended in the light of 25 pilot interviews which took place in November 1988. We reproduce below the text of the PAS report on the ground for divorce together with the relevant tables. Further information may be available on application to the Law Commission.

THE PAS REPORT

THE GROUND FOR DIVORCE

1. THE CURRENT LAW

Opinions on the current law

1.1   As an introduction respondents were told:-

"What we would like your opinions about is the ground for divorce, that is the basis upon which people can apply to the courts to get a divorce. This is quite separate from the rules about their property, or financial support, or custody of their children".

They were then shown a card setting out the present law on the ground for divorce. This read:-

"At present, the only ground for divorce is that the marriage has broken down irretrievably, but this has to be proved in one of five ways. These are:-

(i)   adultery
(ii)   intolerable behaviour
(iii)   desertion for two years
(iv)   two years' separation plus the other party's consent
(v)   five years' separation (no consent needed)

---

[1] Family Law: Distribution on Intestacy, (1989) Law Com. No. 187.

* 99% of all divorces are undefended
* Over 70% of decrees are based on adultery or intolerable behaviour
* Older couples are more likely to use the fact that they have been separated for five years
* Those with dependent children are more likely to use adultery and behaviour facts to prove that their marriage has irretrievably broken down."

1.2   After being given time to study this card, respondents were presented with a number of comments identified as being made by "other people about the present law". For each comment, respondents were asked whether they agreed, disagreed, or were undecided.

1.3   Full results are shown on Tables 15 and 16, and summarised below.

1.4   There was widespread agreement (and little disagreement) that two strengths of the present law were its capacity for allowing an immediate start of proceedings in the case of adultery or intolerable behaviour and, in different circumstances, for allowing blame free proceedings (see below).

The present law is good because one person can start proceedings at once if the other one has committed adultery or behaved intolerably:

Agree - 84% Disagree - 9%

The present law is good because couples who do not want to put the blame on either of them do not have to do so:

Agree - 83% Disagree - 11%

1.5   On certain other aspects of the law there was overall agreement but with a sizeable minority disagreeing. Thus the majority agreed that the present law was good in that it would ultimately grant a divorce to anyone who wanted one, but there was criticism of the five year separation period as being too long; of the potential for one partner to refuse consent as a bargaining counter; and of the possibility of the spirit of the law being abused by individuals lying in order to get a quick divorce (see below).

The present law is good because anybody who wants a divorce can get one sooner or later:

Agree - 72% Disagree - 19%

The present five year separation period is too long:

Agree - 71% Disagree - 24%

The present law is bad because, when a couple is separated, one person can refuse to consent to a divorce in order to obtain a better bargaining position:

Agree - 63% Disagree - 22%

The present law is bad because it may encourage couples to tell lies to get a quick divorce - e.g. they could pretend that one of them had behaved intolerably, or claim to have been separated when this was untrue:

Agree - 61% Disagree - 27%

Base: All Respondents (1001).

1.6   A further criticism of the present law which provoked a broad division of opinion was its potential for forcing a person who wanted a divorce quickly to accuse the other party of adultery or intolerable behaviour - *54% agreed [this was bad], 31% disagreed.*

1.7   Finally on two other aspects, the majority disagreed: people did *not* think the present two year separation period too long; and they did *not* think it was an advantage of the present law that an unwilling party could delay the divorce for a long time (see below).

The present two year separation period is too long:

Agree - 32% Disagree - 61%

The present law is good because anyone who does not want a divorce can delay it for a long time:

Agree - 30% Disagree - 58%

Base: All Respondents (1001)

1.8   Table 15 shows that respondents who were divorced, or had remarried, generally were of the same mind as the total sample. Divorced people, however, were more likely to feel that the present two year separation period was too long, and remarried respondents to consider that the five year separation period was too long. These variations hardly suggest fundamental differences in attitudes. Similarly, while there are isolated differences in the opinions of respondents of differing age, sex and religious affiliation, no clear pattern is discernible.

Acceptability of Current Law as Compared to Alternatives

1.9   Respondents were asked to say whether they found each of a number of possible bases for divorce - including the present law - acceptable or unacceptable.

1.10   Four of the alternatives were not only thought widely acceptable, but were viewed more favourably than the present law. Divorce on demand was, on balance, unacceptable; however a substantial minority of one in three found it acceptable (see Table 17 and overleaf).

Proportions finding each base for divorce "acceptable"

Divorce after a period of separation	– 91%
Divorce by mutual consent, i.e. provided both parties wish to get divorced, they should be able to start proceedings right away	– 90%
Divorce after a fixed period of time to allow for a process of reflection and for arrangements to be made about children, money and property	– 87%
Divorce for fault, i.e. where one party can show adultery/intolerable behaviour/desertion by the other	– 84%
Divorce under the present law	– 67%
Divorce on demand – i.e. if either party wishes to get divorced, he or she should be able to start proceedings right away	– 33%

Base: Total Respondents (1001)

1.11   The opinions of those respondents who were divorced differ from those of the population as a whole in that:-

*   they are much more likely to find divorce on demand acceptable;
*   they are also more likely to find divorce by mutual consent, and divorce for fault, acceptable;
*   they are slightly less likely to find divorce after a process acceptable.

There is a little difference in the opinions of people of different ages and religious affiliations (Table 18).

Summary

1.12   When their attention was focused on the present law on ground for divorce, respondents found it, like the curate's egg, to be good in parts. Its beneficial aspects were that: it offered an immediate prospect to individuals who had been wronged; it could operate without blame having to be apportioned and it would, ultimately, produce a divorce for those who wanted one. On the other hand, a wait of five years was too long; and the need for a divorce might prompt couples to lie, or for one partner to behave in a way which was bound to aggrieve the other.

1.13   Not suprisingly, first reactions to a number of alternatives suggested that, with the one exception of divorce on demand, all were more acceptable than the present law. The next section of the report is concerned with two of these alternatives.

2.   ATTITUDES TO TWO POSSIBLE CHANGES IN THE LAW ON DIVORCE

Divorce after a period of separation

2.1   One suggestion was that "the sole ground for divorce would be a fixed period of separation".

2.2   Respondents were given details about the implications of such a change as follows:-

" a)   Couples would not have to blame each other
  b)   Divorce might not be available so quickly in cases where there was adultery or intolerable behaviour
  c)   Couples would learn what it was like to live apart before beginning divorce proceedings
  d)   Some people, especially young mothers with children, would find it difficult to separate because of problems with money and accommodation
  e)   At the end of the period, one of the couple would be able to get the divorce even if the other did not want it
  f)   The law would be simple and clear and the same for everyone. "

2.3   Among the total sample 52% approved, 28% disapproved and 20% were undecided. Respondents who were divorced were more likely than the population as a whole to disapprove (Table 19A).

2.4   When asked to nominate the appropriate duration for the period of separation, responses were spread over a considerable period of time, from 6 months to more than 2 years (see below).

Appropriate Period of Time

6 months or less	17%
9 months	3%
1 year	32%
2 years	26%
More than 2 years	13%
Other	3%
Don't know	7%

Base: Total Respondents (1001)

Divorce after a process

2.5   The other suggestion was that "the sole ground for divorce would be a fixed period of time to allow for a process of reflection and for arrangements to be made about children, money and property".

2.6   The implications were set out as follows:-

" a)   Couples would not have to blame one another or live apart for a period
  b)   The divorce process would take longer than it can do under the present law
  c)   Couples would have to agree, or have decided for them, all the practical consequences before their divorce was made final
  d)   During the process they would have time to reflect and consider whether this is what they really wanted
  e)   At the end of the period, one of the couple would be able to get the divorce even if the other did not want it

184

f) The law would be simple and clear and the same for everyone. "

67% of all respondents approved of this suggestion, 15% disapproved and 18% were undecided. Again respondents who were divorced tended to be less approving (Table 20A).

2.7 As with the other suggestion, opinions as to the appropriate duration of the period of time were variable (see below).

Appropriate Period of Time

6 months or less	16%
9 months	4%
1 year	35%
2 years	24%
More than 2 years	11%
Other	2%
Don't know	9%

Base: Total Respondents (1001)

Preference Between Two Suggestions

2.8 As would be expected from the results given above, divorce after a process was preferred by more people than divorce after a period of separation. However a substantial proportion of the total sample declared themselves as having no preference, and 5% were "Don't knows".

Preference

Divorce after process of reflection	37%
Divorce after a period of separation	29%
No preference	28%
Don't know	5%

Base: Total Respondents (1001)

2.9 Among those who were divorced the margin in favour of a process was slightly higher, as was the proportion with no preference or not knowing (Table 21). Among those who wanted the present law changed 43% favoured divorce after a process, 29% favoured divorce after a period of separation.

Opinions about Desirability of Changing the Law

2.10 When asked directly whether, "taking everything into consideration", the present law on the ground for divorce should be changed, or remain as at present, respondents were about evenly divided between the two options, with one in ten not knowing (see below).

Opinions on Desirability of Changing the Law

Law should be changed	45%
Law should remain as at present	43%
Don't know	11%

Base: Total Respondents (1001)

2.11   Those with experience of divorce were slightly more likely to say that the law should be changed (49%); respondents from the oldest age group more likely to say that it should remain as at present (49%) (Table 22).

2.12   The attitudes underlying these options can be illustrated in two ways;

(i)   by looking at the reasons given by respondents wanting a change;

(ii)   comparing opinions on the present law and alternatives given by the two groups.

2.13   Asked to say in their own words why they thought the law should be changed, respondents frequently answered in terms of recommending, on the one hand, quicker, easier divorce (57%) on the other, harder, more difficult divorce (32%). Younger people (18-44 years) and those who preferred the separation suggestion were more likely to justify their desire for change in terms of easier divorce (Table 24).

2.14   Individual comments subsumed under the heading Easier, Quicker Divorce related to shorter waiting times, a simpler procedure, and divorce on demand. Those who wanted Harder and More Difficult Divorce stressed the relevance of counselling in promoting reconciliation and thought waiting times should be extended.

2.15   Other comments made justifying change related to the interests of any children being paramount, and the need for the financial circumstances of the parties being taken into account (Table 23).

2.16   As is evident from the above commentary some respondents, once given the chance of replying in their own words, enlarged the scope of the question beyond the ground for divorce to the broader social aspects. There is no such tendency present in the second analysis of attitudes.

2.17   Table 25 shows opinions on the present law held, on the one hand by those who felt it should be changed, (henceforward called reformers), and on the other by those who felt it should remain as at present (henceforward called conservatives).

2.18   Reformers are much more likely than conservatives to agree that the present law is bad because, in order to get a quick divorce, individuals may have to lie, or to make wounding accusations. They also repudiate the idea that one virtue of the present law is that it allows an unwilling party the power to delay the divorce for a long time.

2.19   Conservatives are much more likely than reformers to praise the present law for allowing anyone who wants a divorce to achieve this "sooner or later". They also agree that a further virtue of the present law is that it allows for blame free proceedings.

2.20   When it came to opinions about the desirability of "some possible bases" for divorce, there is little difference between the two groups on the acceptability of the majority of the suggestions, including divorce after separation, and divorce after a process. On divorce under the present law, there is the expected divergence of opinion; however it is worth noting that there is no evidence of wholesale rejection of the present law among reformers (see below and computer table 15/3).

Divorce under the Present Law

	Reformers %	Conservatives %
Acceptable	51	85
Unacceptable	33	5
Don't know	16	10

Bases: Various (see Computer Table 15/3)

Summary

2.21   Both divorce after a fixed period of separation, and divorce after a process are approved by a majority of the population: about eight out of ten when prompted by summary descriptive statements; by lower proportions (67% for divorce after a process, 52% for divorce after a period of separation) when each was identified as the sole ground for divorce and a number of implications set before the respondents.

2.22   While the above findings are not only supported by the evidence but are also relatively unambiguous, nevertheless there are ample indications of doubt, indecision, and disagreement regarding the ground for divorce. Thus there is no unanimity over the appropriate length of the fixed period: one in five respondents say less than a year, one in three a year, one in four two years and one in seven more than two years. Moreover, substantial minorities of the population admitted to being "Don't knows"; for example one in five did not know whether they approved or disapproved of the two suggestions for changes in the law; and one in ten did not know whether a change was desirable or not.

2.23   Other findings indicate that this level of indecisive opinion exists alongside responses associated with a complex set of preconceptions, attitudes and opinions. The population was about equally divided in wanting a change in the law, and feeling it should remain as it is. Some of those favouring a change wanted easier, quicker divorce; others wanted divorce to be made more difficult. Those who felt the law should remain as at present thought its virtues were that it allowed blame free proceedings, and that, sooner or later, anyone who wanted a divorce could have one. However, the detailed findings make plain that the words "on balance" could well have been added to the question on the desirability of change: those wanting a change can nevertheless see some virtue in the present law; those wanting it to remain the same nevertheless saw scope for improvement.

Table 15 PROMPTED OPINIONS ON PRESENT LAW ON GROUND FOR DIVORCE—BY MARITAL STATUS

	Total		Married	Single	Co-habit	Re-married	Widowed	Divorced
					Marital Status			
Base: All Respondents	1001		633	109	48	42	96	59
	%		%	%	%	%	%	%
The present law is good because anybody who wants a divorce can get one sooner or later								
Agree	72		73	64	69	81	68	80
Disagree	19		18	23	25	14	18	19
Undecided	9		8	13	4	5	15	1
The present law is good because couples who do not want to put the blame on either of them do not have to do so								
Agree	83		84	77	88	90	77	85
Disagree	11		10	12	12	5	10	12
Undecided	6		5	11	0	5	13	2
The present two year separation period is too long								
Agree	32		29	37	46	31	23	46
Disagree	61		62	53	54	64	69	49
Undecided	7		8	10	0	5	8	5
The present five year separation period is too long								
Agree	71		69	68	77	90	67	75
Disagree	24		26	20	21	7	25	22
Undecided	5		4	12	2	2	8	3
The present law is good because anyone who does not want a divorce can delay it for a long time								
Agree	30		30	28	21	26	39	31
Disagree	58		59	57	73	67	40	61
Undecided	12		11	16	6	7	21	7
The present law is bad because it forces a person who wants a divorce quickly to accuse the other one of adultery or intolerable behaviour								
Agree	54		55	56	73	50	46	53
Disagree	31		32	28	19	36	32	32
Undecided	14		14	16	8	14	21	15

188

Table 15 *(continued)*

Base: All Respondents	Total	Marital Status					
		Married	Single	Co-habit	Re-married	Widowed	Divorced
	1001	633	109	48	42	96	59
	%	%	%	%	%	%	%
The present law is good because one person can start proceedings at once if the other one has committed adultery or behaved intolerably							
Agree	84	84	86	90	83	80	83
Disagree	9	9	6	8	14	6	12
Undecided	7	7	8	2	2	14	5
The present law is bad because it may encourage couples to tell lies to get a quick divorce—e.g. they could pretend that one of them had behaved intolerably, or claim to have been separated when this was untrue							
Agree	61	61	57	65	52	61	63
Disagree	27	26	30	25	38	21	29
Undecided	12	12	13	10	10	18	8
The present law is bad because when a couple is separated, one person can refuse to consent to a divorce in order to obtain a better bargaining position							
Agree	63	64	64	75	69	49	69
Disagree	22	23	19	13	21	23	20
Undecided	15	14	17	13	10	20	10

Table 16 PROMPTED OPINIONS ON PRESENT LAW ON GROUND FOR DIVORCE—BY AGE, SEX, AND RELIGION

	Total	Age					Sex		Religion		
		18–30	31–44	45–59	60+		Men	Women	RC	Other Christian	Other
Base: All Respondents	1001	213	251	269	268		482	519	107	768	41
	%	%	%	%	%		%	%	%	%	%
The present law is good because anybody who wants a divorce can get one sooner or later											
Agree	72	69	76	72	72		74	71	66	73	71
Disagree	19	22	15	21	17		18	19	24	18	10
Undecided	9	9	9	7	11		8	10	9	8	20
The present law is good because couples who do not want to put the blame on either of them do not have to do so											
Agree	83	85	84	85	79		81	85	77	84	80
Disagree	11	11	12	9	12		13	9	13	11	15
Undecided	6	5	4	5	9		6	5	9	5	5
The present two year separation period is too long											
Agree	32	40	32	30	26		36	28	31	31	37
Disagree	61	54	59	62	66		57	64	61	61	56
Undecided	7	6	9	7	7		7	8	7	7	7
The present five year separation period is too long											
Agree	71	72	75	69	68		73	69	67	71	66
Disagree	24	21	22	26	27		22	26	26	24	29
Undecided	5	7	3	5	6		5	5	6	5	5
The present law is good because anyone who does not want a divorce can delay it for a long time											
Agree	30	30	29	29	32		27	38	33	31	37
Disagree	58	61	63	54	54		67	49	55	58	56
Undecided	12	9	7	17	13		11	13	12	11	17
The present law is bad because it forces a person who wants a divorce quickly to accuse the other one of adultery or intolerable behaviour											
Agree	54	61	55	54	49		59	51	60	53	59
Disagree	31	27	34	28	35		30	32	33	32	27
Undecided	14	13	11	18	16		12	17	7	15	15

Table 16 *(continued)*

Base: All Respondents	Total 1001 %	Age				Sex		Religion		
		18–30 213 %	31–44 251 %	45–59 269 %	60+ 268 %	Men 482 %	Women 519 %	RC 107 %	Other Christian 768 %	Other 41 %
The present law is good because one person can start proceedings at once if the other one has committed adultery or behaved intolerably										
Agree	84	90	85	81	82	85	84	73	85	83
Disagree	9	6	10	10	8	8	9	17	8	7
Undecided	7	4	5	8	9	7	7	9	7	10
The present law is bad because it may encourage couples to tell lies to get a quick divorce—e.g. they could pretend that one of them had behaved intolerably, or claim to have been separated when this was untrue										
Agree	61	64	58	57	63	62	59	63	60	59
Disagree	27	25	30	30	22	26	27	25	27	37
Undecided	12	11	12	12	15	11	13	11	13	5
The present law is bad because when a couple is separated, one person can refuse to consent to a divorce in order to obtain a better bargaining position										
Agree	63	65	66	62	60	69	58	64	62	61
Disagree	22	19	24	23	21	20	24	21	23	22
Undecided	15	16	10	15	19	12	18	14	16	17

Table 17 PROMPTED OPINIONS ON ACCEPTABILITY OF SOME POSSIBLE BASES FOR DIVORCE—BY MARITAL STATUS AND PRESENCE OF CHILDREN

Base: All Respondents	Total	Marital Status							Children		
		Married	Single	Co-habit	Re-married	Widowed	Divorced		0–17	18+	None
	1001	633	109	48	42	96	59		394	469	213
	%	%	%	%	%	%	%		%	%	%
Divorce on demand—i.e. if either party wishes to get divorced, he or she should be able to start proceedings right away											
Acceptable	33	32	37	38	40	26	46		35	31	38
Unacceptable	57	61	52	42	50	58	42		56	60	52
Undecided	9	7	11	21	10	16	12		9	9	10
Divorce by mutual consent, i.e. provided both parties wish to get divorced, they should be able to start proceedings straight-away											
Acceptable	90	88	91	98	90	91	97		89	90	90
Unacceptable	8	11	6	2	7	4	2		9	9	8
Undecided	2	1	4	0	2	5	0		1	1	2
Divorce after a fixed period of time to allow for a process of reflection and for arrangements to be made about children, money and property											
Acceptable	87	88	88	85	93	90	78		88	86	88
Unacceptable	8	8	6	6	5	4	12		8	8	5
Undecided	5	4	6	8	2	6	7		3	3	7
Divorce for fault, i.e. where one party can show adultery/intolerable behaviour/desertion by the other											
Acceptable	84	84	83	79	90	78	93		86	83	83
Unacceptable	8	8	7	13	7	7	0		7	8	9
Undecided	8	8	10	8	2	14	7		7	10	8
Divorce after a period of separation											
Acceptable	91	91	93	94	100	89	92		92	90	92
Unacceptable	5	6	5	2	0	3	5		6	6	4
Undecided	4	3	3	4	0	8	3		3	4	4
Divorce under the present laws											
Acceptable	67	67	67	56	60	69	73		65	69	66
Unacceptable	18	18	20	21	29	13	20		21	15	20
Undecided	15	15	13	23	12	19	7		14	16	14

Table 18 PROMPTED OPINIONS ON ACCEPTABILITY OF SOME POSSIBLE BASES FOR DIVORCE—BY AGE, SEX AND RELIGION

Base: All Respondents	Total	Age				Sex		Religion		
		18–30	31–44	45–59	60+	Men	Women	RC	Other Christian	Other
	1001	213	251	269	268	482	519	107	768	41
	%	%	%	%	%	%	%	%	%	%
Divorce on demand—i.e. if either party wishes to get divorced, he or she should be able to start proceedings right away										
Acceptable	33	42	32	32	29	37	30	36	32	37
Unacceptable	57	45	59	62	60	55	59	51	59	56
Undecided	9	13	8	7	11	8	11	12	9	7
Divorce by mutual consent, i.e. provided both parties wish to get divorced, they should be able to start proceedings straight-away										
Acceptable	90	93	89	90	87	90	90	84	90	93
Unacceptable	8	6	9	9	9	9	8	12	8	5
Undecided	2	1	2	n	3	1	2	4	1	2
Divorce after a fixed period of time to allow for a process of reflection and for arrangements to be made about children, money and property										
Acceptable	87	85	92	84	88	86	88	88	87	88
Unacceptable	8	9	6	9	6	9	7	6	8	2
Undecided	5	6	2	6	6	5	5	6	5	10
Divorce for fault, i.e. where one party can show adultery/intolerable behaviour/desertion by the other										
Acceptable	84	85	86	84	81	84	84	83	84	80
Unacceptable	8	8	6	8	8	9	6	7	8	10
Undecided	8	7	8	9	10	7	9	9	8	10
Divorce after a period of separation										
Acceptable	91	93	92	92	88	92	90	91	92	83
Unacceptable	5	5	6	5	6	5	6	6	5	10
Undecided	4	2	2	3	7	3	4	4	3	7
Divorce under the present laws										
Acceptable	67	67	63	67	70	67	66	62	68	63
Unacceptable	18	18	23	17	16	21	16	21	18	22
Undecided	15	15	14	15	14	11	18	17	14	15

Table 19A ATTITUDES TO FIXED PERIOD OF SEPARATION BEING THE SOLE GROUND FOR DIVORCE—BY MARITAL STATUS AND PRESENCE OF CHILDREN

	Total	Marital Status						Children		
		Married	Single	Co-habit	Re-married	Widowed	Divorced	0–17	18+	None
Base: All Respondents	1001 %	633 %	109 %	48 %	42 %	96 %	59 %	394 %	469 %	213 %
Attitude										
Approve	52	53	40	60	57	54	44	51	57	48
Disapprove	28	27	31	25	29	22	41	32	25	27
Undecided	20	19	28	15	14	24	15	17	18	25
Appropriate Period of Time										
Less than 6 months	1	1	2	2	0	2	0	0	1	2
6 months	16	12	22	23	33	10	27	15	13	21
9 months	3	3	6	2	0	3	2	4	3	3
1 year	32	33	32	44	33	25	29	35	30	33
1–2 years	1	n	1	0	0	2	0	1	1	1
2 years	26	27	18	19	29	28	24	26	29	19
More than 2 years	13	14	10	10	2	14	8	11	14	12
Other	2	2	2	0	0	4	0	2	2	2
Don't Know	6	6	6	0	2	11	10	7	6	6

Table 19B ATTITUDES TO FIXED PERIOD OF SEPARATION BEING THE SOLE GROUND FOR DIVORCE—BY AGE, SEX AND RELIGION

	Total	Age				Sex		Religion		
		18–30	31–44	45–59	60+	Men	Women	RC	Other Christian	Other
Base: All Respondents	1001 %	213 %	251 %	269 %	268 %	482 %	519 %	107 %	768 %	41 %
Attitude										
Approve	52	45	54	55	53	51	53	50	55	34
Disapprove	28	33	31	25	24	30	26	28	26	46
Undecided	20	22	15	20	23	19	20	22	20	20
Appropriate Period of Time										
Less than 6 months	1	1	1	1	1	2	n	1	1	0
6 months	16	23	16	13	13	16	15	10	16	22
9 months	3	4	4	2	3	5	2	3	4	0
1 year	32	36	36	30	27	32	32	36	32	32
1–2 years	1	n	1	n	1	n	1	0	1	0
2 years	26	19	23	34	26	23	28	23	27	24
More than 2 years	13	8	13	13	16	14	11	17	13	5
Other	2	1	2	1	4	5	8	4	2	2
Don't Know	6	8	5	5	8	n	n	7	5	15

Table 20A ATTITUDES TO DIVORCE AFTER A PROCESS BEING THE SOLE GROUND FOR DIVORCE—BY MARITAL STATUS AND PRESENCE OF CHILDREN

	Total	Marital Status						Children		
		Married	Single	Co-habit	Re-married	Widowed	Divorced	0–17	18+	None
Base: All Respondents	1001 %	633 %	109 %	48 %	42 %	96 %	59 %	394 %	469 %	213 %
Attitude										
Approve	67	68	61	67	69	68	59	65	71	62
Disapprove	15	14	16	21	12	10	24	17	12	17
Undecided	8	17	23	13	19	22	17	18	17	21
Appropriate Period of Time										
Less than 6 months	1	n	2	0	0	2	2	0	1	1
6 months	15	11	21	27	33	13	27	14	13	20
9 months	4	4	6	2	0	3	3	5	3	4
1 year	35	37	36	42	31	23	27	39	32	33
1–2 years	n	n	1	n	0	1	0	n	n	1
2 years	24	26	17	17	21	24	24	24	27	19
More than 2 years	11	11	9	4	5	16	8	8	12	12
Other	2	2	1	4	0	3	0	1	2	2
Don't Know	9	8	7	4	10	15	8	8	9	7

Table 20B ATTITUDES TO DIVORCE AFTER A PROCESS BEING THE SOLE GROUND FOR DIVORCE—BY AGE, SEX AND RELIGION

	Total	Age				Sex		Religion		
		18–30	31–44	45–59	60+	Men	Women	RC	Other Christian	Other
Base: All Respondents	1001 %	213 %	251 %	269 %	268 %	482 %	519 %	107 %	768 %	41 %
Attitude										
Approve	67	61	62	71	71	67	66	64	67	56
Disapprove	15	20	18	13	11	16	14	20	14	29
Undecided	18	20	20	16	18	17	19	16	19	15
Appropriate Period of Time										
Less than 6 months	1	1	0	1	1	1	n	1	1	2
6 months	15	21	16	12	12	16	14	14	15	17
9 months	4	7	4	3	3	4	4	4	4	0
1 year	35	38	39	31	31	33	36	36	34	44
1–2 years	n	n	0	n	n	n	n	0	n	0
2 years	24	16	22	32	24	22	25	23	25	20
More than 2 years	11	7	10	11	14	11	10	11	11	2
Other	2	1	1	2	3	2	2	2	2	5
Don't Know	9	8	8	8	10	7	10	9	8	10

Table 21 PREFERENCE BETWEEN TWO POSSIBLE CHANGES IN THE GROUND FOR DIVORCE—BY MARITAL STATUS AND DESIRE FOR CHANGE

| | Total | Marital Status | | | | | | Change of Law | |
		Married	Single	Co-habit	Re-married	Widowed	Divorced	Should be	Should not be
Base: All Respondents	1001 %	633 %	109 %	48 %	42 %	96 %	59 %	454 %	435 %
Preferred									
Divorce after separation	29	28	27	33	36	34	22	29	30
Divorce after process	37	40	38	31	38	27	36	43	33
No preference	28	27	32	33	21	28	34	25	31
Don't Know	5	4	4	2	5	9	8	3	5

Table 22 OPINIONS ON THE DESIRABILITY OF CHANGING THE PRESENT LAW ON THE GROUND FOR DIVORCE—BY AGE, SEX AND EXPERIENCE OF DIVORCE

| | Total | Age | | | | Sex | | Exp. of Divorce | |
		18–30	31–44	45–59	60+	Men	Women	Some	None
Base: All Respondents	1001 %	213 %	251 %	269 %	268 %	482 %	519 %	618 %	380 %
Law should be changed	45	46	53	46	36	47	44	49	39
Law should remain as at present	43	42	40	42	49	43	44	42	47
Don't Know	11	11	7	12	15	10	12	9	14

Table 23   REASONS FOR THINKING LAW SHOULD BE CHANGED

Base: All Respondents thinking law should be changed

	Total Sample 454 %
Easier/Quicker Divorce	57
Should be shorter waiting time/separation period (general)	29
Should be shorter waiting time/separation period if both consent	11
Should be shorter waiting time/separation period if abuse/intolerable behaviour	7
Law/divorce procedure should be simplified	4
Should be made a less traumatic experience/cause less bitterness	4
Should be available on request/demand if both parties want this	3
Should be available on request/demand if one party want this	3
Should be less expensive	1
Should be available on request (general)	1
Harder/More Difficult Divorce	32
Should be more attempts at reconciliation/counselling	13
Divorce should be made harder/more difficult to get	10
Waiting times/separation periods should be extended (general)	9
Waiting times/separation periods should be extended when only one party wants divorce	2
Other Comments	27
Interest of children paramount	10
Financial status to be taken into account	8
Should be no bias/favouritism towards women/mothers	6
Should be more thought before marriage	2
Should be a bias towards women/mothers	1
Interests of innocent party must be protected	1
Other comments	9

197

Table 24   REASONS FOR THINKING LAW SHOULD BE CHANGED—SUMMARY—BY SUB GROUPS

	Total	Age				Sex		Exp. of Divorce	
		18–30	31–44	45–59	60+	Men	Women	Some	None
Base: Respondents thinking law should be changed	454 %	99 %	133 %	125 %	97 %	127 %	130 %	304 %	108 %
Easier/Quicker Divorce	57	63	64	53	45	56	57	60	51
Harder/More Difficult Divorce	32	28	26	37	36	29	35	29	38

	Marital Status						Preference	
	Married (295) %	Single (44) %	Co-habit (27)	Re-married (21)	Widowed (31) %	Divorced (29) %	Separation (131) %	Process (194) %
Easier/Quicker Divorce	54	68	*	*	45	62	64	54
Harder/More Difficult Divorce	34	23			42	24	27	38

Table 25 OPINIONS ON THE PRESENT LAW, AND ITS ACCEPTABILITY AS COMPARED TO ALTERNATIVES ANALYSED BY THOSE WITH DIFFERING OPINIONS AS TO WHETHER A CHANGE IS DESIRABLE

Base: All Respondents	Law should be changed 454 %	Law should remain as at present 435 %
OPINIONS ON PRESENT LAW—NEW AGREEMENT		
The present law is good because anybody who wants a divorce can get one sooner or later	33	76 (43)
The present law is good because couples who do not want to put the blame on either of them do not have to do so	65	81 (16)
The present law is good because a person who does not want a divorce can delay it for a long time	−45	−13 (32)
The present law is good because one person can start proceedings at once if the other one has committed adultery or behaved intolerably	70	81 (11)
The present two year separation period is too long	−13	−43 (30)
The present five year separation period is too long	52	43 (9)
The present law is bad because it forces a person who needs a divorce quickly to accuse the other one of adultery or intolerable behaviour	32	16 (16)
The present law is bad because it may encourage couples to tell lies in order to get a quick divorce	45	19 (26)
The present law is bad because, when a couple is separated, one person can refuse to consent to a divorce in order to obtain a better bargaining position	47	37 (10)
OPINIONS ON ALTERNATIVES—NET ACCEPTABILITY		
Divorce on demand	−27	−21 (6)
Divorce by mutual consent	78	85 (7)
Divorce after process	76	84 (8)
Divorce for fault	75	82 (7)
Divorce after separation	83	89 (6)
Divorce under present law	18	80 (62)

Note: Figures in brackets represent the quotient—33 minus 76 etc.

199

Table 15/3   THE GROUND FOR DIVORCE IN ENGLAND AND WALES—SURVEY OF PUBLIC ATTITUDES—PAS 12096

Q.16 PROMPTED OPINIONS ON ACCEPTABILITY OF SOME POSSIBLE BASES FOR DIVORCE

Base: All respondents

	Total	Experience of Divorce		Religion			Preference		Law on Divorce	
		Exp. Divorce	Have not	R.Cath.	Other Christian	Other	Separation	Process	Should be changed	Should not
	1001	618	380	107	768	41	292	375	454	435
Divorce after a period of separation										
Acceptable	911	579	329	97	706	34	278	331	410	404
	91%	94%	87%	91%	92%	83%	95%	88%	90%	93%
Unacceptable	53	26	27	6	37	4	9	26	30	16
	5%	4%	7%	6%	5%	10%	3%	7%	7%	4%
Undecided	37	13	24	4	25	3	5	18	14	15
	4%	2%	6%	4%	3%	7%	2%	5%	3%	3%
Divorce under the present law										
Acceptable	668	422	246	66	520	26	205	236	233	369
	67%	68%	65%	62%	68%	63%	70%	63%	51%	85%
Unacceptable	185	110	73	22	137	9	52	86	150	22
	18%	18%	19%	21%	18%	22%	18%	23%	33%	5%
Undecided	146	86	59	18	111	6	35	52	71	42
	15%	14%	16%	17%	14%	15%	12%	14%	16%	10%

Printed in the United Kingdom for HMSO
Dd 0505755 C10 11/90 ON 127758